ECONOMY AND DEMOCRACY

ECONOMY AND DEMOCRACY

Edited by

R. C. O. Matthews

St. Martin's Press   New York

© The British Association for the Advancement of Science 1985

All rights reserved. For information, write:
St. Martin's Press, Inc., 175 Fifth Avenue, New York, NY 10010
Printed in Great Britain
Published in the United Kingdom by The Macmillan Press Ltd.
First published in the United States of America in 1985

ISBN 0–312–23679–4

Library of Congress Cataloging in Publication Data
British Association for the Advancement of Science.
Section F (Economics)
Economy and democracy.
Includes index.
Contents: Competition in economy and polity / R. C. O. Matthews—The interaction between policy and political performance / Vani Borooah—Prisoners' dilemma and Coase's theorem / Michael Lipton—[etc.]
1. Economic policy—Political aspects—Addresses, essays, lectures.   I. Matthews, R. C. O. (Robert Charles Oliver), 1927–   .
HD87.B73   1985   338.9   85-11869
ISBN 0–312–23679–4

Contents

Notes on the Contributors   vii

    Introduction   R. C. O. Matthews   ix

1 Competition in Economy and Polity   R. C. O. Matthews   1

2 The Interaction between Economic Policy and Political Performance   Vani Borooah   20

3 The Prisoners' Dilemma and Coase's Theorem: A Case for Democracy in Less Developed Countries?   Michael Lipton   49

4 The Political Process: Market Place or Battleground?   William Rodgers   110

5 The Relationship between Economics, Politics and the Law in the Formation of Public Policy   Charles Rowley   127

6 Legislation, the Courts and the Demand for Compensation   Anthony Ogus   151

7 Economy, Democracy and Bureaucracy   Peter Jackson   168

8 Industrial Democracy at Enterprise Level: Problems and Prospects   John Eldridge   204

9 Can Democracy be Tamed?   Ralph Harris   219

10 Economic Obstacles to Democracy   Keith Cowling   235

Index   255

Notes on the Contributors

Vani Borooah is Senior Research Officer at the Department of Applied Economics, University of Cambridge, and also a Fellow of Queen's College, Cambridge. He was elected by the British Association to the Lister Lectureship for 1984. He is the co-author of *Political Aspects of the Economy* and the author of several papers in the fields of political economics, consumer economics and housing economics.

Keith Cowling is Professor of Economics at the University of Warwick. His most recent book is *Monopoly Capitalism*. He is currently editor of the *International Journal of Industrial Organisation*.

John Eldridge is Professor of Sociology at the University of Glasgow. He is the author of a number of books, including *Max Weber* (1982) and (with A. D. Crombie) *Sociology of Organizations* (1974).

Ralph Harris has been General Director of the Institute of Economic Affairs since 1957. He was educated at Tottenham Grammar School and Queen's College, Cambridge, and lectured in political economy at St Andrews University from 1949 to 1956. He has lectured and written extensively on the failure of successive governments to achieve their declared economic objectives. In 1979 Ralph Harris was created a life peer.

Peter Jackson is Professor of Economics and Director of the Public Sector Economics Research Centre, University of Leicester. His publications include *The Political Economy of Bureaucracy* (1982).

Michael Lipton is Professorial Fellow of the Institute of Development Studies at the University of Sussex, and a Fellow of All Souls College, Oxford. He works mainly on the economics of tropical agriculture and rural development in South Asia and Africa. His work includes *Why Poor People Stay Poor: Urban Bias in World Development* (1977).

Currently he is working on aid-evaluation and on the characteristics of poverty groups.

Robin Matthews is Professor of Political Economy and Master of Clare College, Cambridge. He was previously Drummond Professor of Political Economy in Oxford and is currently President of the Royal Economic Society. He is the author of many books and articles, particularly on the history and theory of growth and fluctuations and, more recently, on the psychological and institutional underpinnings of competitive economic systems. In 1972–5 he served as Chairman of the Social Science Research Council.

Anthony Ogus is Professor of Law at the University of Newcastle-upon-Tyne. He is the editor (with C. G. Veljanovski) of *Readings in the Economics of Law and Regulation* (1984) and has written widely on topics including law and economics and the law of social security.

William Rodgers is Vice-President of the Social Democratic Party. He was Member of Parliament for Stockton-on-Tees from 1962 to 1983 and served as a Minister in both the 1964–70 and 1974–9 governments, latterly in the Cabinet. He was one of the 'Gang of Four' who founded the SDP in 1981. He is the author of *The Politics of Change* (1982).

Charles Rowley graduated from the University of Nottingham with first-class honours in 1960 and a PhD in 1964. He has been a Lecturer at the Universities of Nottingham and Kent and a Senior Lecturer at Kent. He has also been a Reader at the University of York. From 1972 to 1984 he was David Dale Professor of Economics at the University of Newcastle-upon-Tyne. Professor Rowley has published in the fields of welfare economics, public economics, public choice, law and economics and industrial economics. He is now Professor of Economics at George Mason University.

Introduction

R. C. O. MATTHEWS

This book is about economy and democracy. It is therefore about public choice and competition; for in a political democracy with a market economy we expect to exercise our vote with respect to our leaders and our parties as well as our beavers and our deer. Our choices in the political market are particularly significant in a country such as Britain where the State plays so active a role in economic and social life.

Because this book is about economy and democracy, it is about markets and competition. Competition serves as some safeguard against inefficiency and exploitation; and in my own paper I distinguish two types. Most familiar in economics is competition-in-transactions, where buyers compete with buyers and sellers with sellers. More familiar in politics (though not confined to politics) is competition-for-authority, where there are rival aspirants to authority within an organisation (such as the State). Neither type of competition works perfectly. The peculiarity of competition-for-authority, for example, is that it is all-or-none: the winner typically takes all, which can cause his policies then to diverge considerably from the wishes of the electorate (to say nothing of minorities, which remain unprotected). Business competition can lead to monopoly; unrestrained political competition can enable the winner to rig or cancel subsequent elections (the phenomenon of one man one vote – once); but correctives do exist (international trade in the case of economic competition, consensus and moderation in the case of political competition), and moreover *some* competition is better than *no* competition at all.

The parallels and interaction between political and economic behaviour are explored further in the paper by Vani Borooah, who supports his theories with empirical evidence relating to the British experience in the period 1955–9. Borooah initially analyses the proposition that a government's economic policies and performance significantly influence its electoral popularity. He finds some empirical support for this hypothesis, but notes that there is some debate among investigators about the nature of the economic factors that concern the electorate (not least because different voters of different class and social backgrounds are vulnerable to different aspects of the economy and hence have different economic interests) and about the stability over time of the popularity/performance relationship. Dr Borooah also examines the possibility of governments' manipulating policy in order to seek electoral advantage. After reviewing theories of politically-motivated economic policy-making, he concludes that these theories are not relevant for an understanding of the British experience in the last two decades.

Borooah's conclusion – that there is economic and political life beyond self-interest narrowly understood – is reassuring in the light of the conflicts to which Michael Lipton draws attention in his contribution. Lipton points out that in many real-life situations (and not exclusively in the Third World countries with which his paper is explicitly concerned) if each person acts in his own best interests, the result will be fairly bad for all persons taken together: the sea will be over-fished, taxes will be under-paid, the towns will be over-crowded. If each party acts *as if* all were prepared to cooperate, then there is an acceptable outcome for all. For each, however, self-interest narrowly understood dictates that the best result is to get away with greed (via over-grazing or tax evasion, for example) while the others exercise restraint. There are two 'parables' describing how such conflicts might be resolved – Coase's Theorem and the Prisoners' Dilemma – and Lipton, after examining these parables, reaches the following conclusion: democratic political systems are likely to represent the most promising (and least costly) way of achieving general agreement on the moderate degree of altruism and internalised values necessary to avoid conflicts of interest associated with the problem of free riders.

Bill Rodgers, approaching the topic of this book from the standpoint of a practical politician, welcomes such a defence of democracy. His own paper, indeed, indicates a belief in the increasing efficiency of the political market in Great Britain. Voters, he says, now show sophistication and rationality (as opposed to tradition and knee-jerk loyalty) in judging the alternatives offered to them by political parties. Again, voters now look beyond immediate self-interest and have a growing understanding of the external factors that constrain a government's freedom for manoeuvre. And members of Parliament, he reports, cannot realistically be regarded either as selfish careerists or as doctrinal zealots: public service and a sense of moral imperatives play their part. As with any market, however, the political market is subject to change and process; and his views on the case both for the supplying of a new product (to satisfy the potential demand on the middle ground) and for a new mode of payment (proportional representation) are stimulating and at the same time controversial.

Not all of our leaders and decision-makers are, of course, elected. Some are appointed; and it is with the interface between law and economics that the papers by Charles Rowley and Anthony Ogus are concerned. Rowley, welcoming the multiple bridges now being built between the law and economics and the public choice schools, draws attention to the impact on economic affairs of the decrees and not only of politicians but of judges as well. He refers to the extensive legal immunities in tort and in contract that have been conferred in the United Kingdom on trades unions and their leaders and speaks with obvious reservations of the manner in which such rent-seeking behaviour has been validated in the court-room. Anthony Ogus, continuing the theme of law and economics (with particular reference, in his case, to the demand for compensation), argues that theorists have seriously exaggerated the differences between judicial and legislative processes. Judicial rules, he says, are not necessarily (economically) efficient, and statute law (despite the well-known argument that legislation is primarily a response to the demand by influential pressure-groups for benefits) is not necessarily inefficient. Judges respond to moral ideals and distributional objectives as well as to considerations of allocative efficiency; legislators (while seeking perhaps to preserve power through the granting of rights to compensation to those with electoral power to pay for them) create rights which affect distribution and efficiency as well; and too radical a divorce should therefore not be posited between the work of the British courts and the British Parliament.

There is, apart from judges, another group of non-elected decision-makers who exercise an influence on economic affairs, and that is bureaucrats. Peter Jackson, in his paper, examines the possible goals of bureaucrats (ranging from job-satisfaction to maximisation of the size of the bureau and its budget) and asks the fundamental question about the accountability of the organisation-man. He finds no single solution to the undeniable problem (especially in highly centralised systems) of bureaucratic inefficiencies; but he warns that privatisation does not necessarily discipline the man on a fixed income, and indicates the need for greater scrutiny and greater freedom of information. His model, as it happens, is the usual Weberian one of hierarchy; and, as John Eldridge reminds us, an alternative model of men in organisations is one of which the centrepiece would be consultation, cooperation and participatory decision-making. Eldridge would accept that employee involvement is not a solution to the problem of accountability but would stress that trust and improved morale can make a considerable contribution to the internal efficiency of a bureaucratised organisation. His essay is particularly interesting in the context of *Economy and Democracy* because of its concern with democracy *within* economy.

The final two chapters of this book – those by Ralph Harris and Keith Cowling – look to the future and make recommendations for reform. It would be fair to say that these two authors are not always in complete accord. They cannot both be right. Is either? Ralph Harris, on the one hand, argues that government should be tamed. Since the war, he says, governments of all parties have expanded the scope of government far beyond its essential functions of supplying public services and of topping up low incomes so as to enable all to satisfy their needs in the market-place. The net result, he asserts, is a system detrimental to adaptation, allocative efficiency, growth, individual freedom and personal responsibility – a system which should therefore be replaced by one which relies more extensively on the market. Keith Cowling, on the other hand, argues that full democracy implies equal participation for all in *all* aspects of society, and that capitalism must deny such equality within the economic arena. A fundamental antagonism therefore exists, in his view, between capitalism and democracy, an antagonism which is obscured but not eliminated by the existence of universal suffrage. While accepting the importance of universal suffrage and even the possibility of further gains within the present system, the paper suggests none the less that further democratic advance will ultimately require a transformation in the capitalist economy itself.

The no-man's-land between economics and politics was long regarded as barren and unfruitful and was left uncultivated. The truth is that political economy *matters* and that the no-man's-land has the potential to become a productive field for research and debate. It is hoped that the present volume will make a genuine contribution to such investigation and speculation.

1 Competition in Economy and Polity[1]

R. C. O. MATTHEWS

1. TWO OBJECTIVES AND TWO TYPES OF COMPETITION

I propose to define competition as a situation in which two or more people or groups of people are vying for the favours of some person or groups of persons, who thus act as arbiters between them. From the point of view of the arbiters, the existence of competition means the existence of choice between people – a particular case of choice between options. In a competitive market, characterised by voluntary exchange, the arbiters are typically the other parties to the exchange: the buyers are arbiters between the competing sellers and *vice versa*. In political elections, the arbiters are the voters. Competition is a particular kind of contestation. It is not the only kind. Anything in the nature of a two-person game is excluded, as not being contestation for the favours of a third party. Thus a fight or a race, real or ritualised, does not rank as competition on the present definition. Nor does bargaining, as such, though bargains, particularly bargains about the formation of alliances, may be an important tactic in competition.[2]

The antithesis of economic competition is monopoly or monopsony. The antithesis of political competition is autocracy. Political competition is not, however, identical to democracy. Political competition is compatible with a very restricted franchise, and, on the other hand, democracy may take the form of direct voting on issues rather than of choice between people. In practice, the scope for direct democracy in political affairs is extremely limited, so competition is a necessary condition for democracy, though not a sufficient one.

There are two purposes for which the existence of competition is commonly regarded as desirable: to prevent inefficiency and to prevent exploitation. Inefficiency is about being off the contract curve, being in a situation where potentially everyone is worse off than he might be. Exploitation, as normally understood, is about distribution. A monopolist or a political autocrat is in a position to enforce a distribution of the gains from production and exchange, or the gains from the exercise of government power, that is unduly favourable to himself or his friends. I propose to use the term exploitation in an extended sense to include also the imposition of an unwelcome ideology; I will be saying more about that later. Inefficiency and exploitation may go together, as in the cases of the textbook monopolist and the corrupt official, who carry out exploitation by means that involve allocative inefficiency. Conceptually, however, inefficiency and exploitation are separate. Inefficiency of the X-efficiency type may be disadvantageous even to its practitioners. Exploitation may be practised without X-inefficiency and without allocative inefficiency (as by the perfectly discriminating monopolist).

Neither inefficiency nor exploitation is an unambiguous concept. In a general way, however, it is easy to see that both represent something that may be objected to and that the danger of both is present in both economics and politics, though not necessarily to the same degree.[3] The way in which competition may cause the dangers to be less than they would be in its absence is also obvious. If you are inefficient, competition will reduce the sphere of your operations or cause you to be displaced altogether. Before that stage is reached, moreover, competition provides a source of information: loss of ground to a competitor warns you that your performance leaves room for improvement and it may also signal to you where improvement is needed. As regards exploitation, competition provides an alternative person to deal with if the present one seeks to arrogate too much advantage to himself.

These are the *prima facie* arguments in favour of competition. Of course, competition cannot do everything. In the first place, competition is a supplement to rational optimisation, including bargaining, not a substitute for it. Indeed, one of the purposes of competition is to give greater weight in the system to people who have more than average skill in exercising rational optimisation. In the second place, competition may be compatible with inequalities that many people would regard as exploitative and with manifold inefficiencies. In addition, competition does have costs, and these may sometimes make competition undesirable or even impossible. To quote examples: no one (or hardly anyone) advocates competition within society in the use of armed force; competition would lead to waste of resources if economies of scale create natural monopolies; monopoly may be better than competition if the other side of a class of transactions is going to be monopolised anyway (countervailing power). Finally, competition may be destructive of mutual trust. This is an argument that we view with suspicion when it is advanced as a pretext for the establishment of a one-party state, but we have more sympathy for it as a justification for tenure in academe and in marriage. In cases where competition has these or other costs, its advantages have to be weighed against its disadvantages. The question is not whether competition works perfectly, which it never does, but whether it works better than the absence of competition, which it will do in some cases and not in others.

Competition may be more or less severe. Moreover, it can take various forms and they will not all have the same effects. For example, it may or may not be oligopolistic. The distinction between types of competition that will be central in this address is the following. Competition of the kind that is most familiar to economists is competition between rival individuals or organisations in their transactions with third parties – competition, say, between firms for labour or for customers. The favours competed for are the opportunity to do business with the arbiter. I shall call this *competition-in-transactions* (CT). The private sector of the economy is the most characteristic stamping-ground of CT, but it also affects the state: only in the most totalitarian states does the government use its powers to exempt itself from all CT – most governments are content to hire labour and buy supplies in competition with other economic agents. CT may be contrasted with *competition-for-authority* (CA), which is competition between rival claimants for the right to wield authority within an organisation. CA is characteristic of political competition. However it is not confined to competition for control over the ship of state. CA takes place in innumerable private organisations – not only in political parties, where it is a crucial part of political competition, but also in joint-stock companies, in trade unions, in charities and other non-profit bodies, in fact in all institutions that rank as clubs in the sense of Buchanan. Hence the distinction between CT and CA is not the same as the distinction between competition in the private sector and in politics. However, the state in the exercise of its most distinctive domestic functions is not subject to CT, so if competition is to be a safeguard against the twin dangers of state inefficiency and state exploitation, it is CA that must be mainly relied on.

CA can take a great variety of forms. Indeed, one of the most striking features of competition for political authority as it actually exists is its extreme complexity and diversity, even within democratic countries. One was brought up to regard the Westminster model as a paradigm, but in fact only in New Zealand (the most British of overseas Commonwealth countries) are the arrangements at all closely similar to our own. Likewise in reading the public choice literature, mostly of American origin, one is continually struck by how much of it is inapplicable without considerable modification to countries other than the United States, which is even less typical than our own. There exists in democratic countries an endless variety of relations between the executive and the legislature and the electorate, of voting systems, of party structures and so on. Similar variety exists in the forms of CA in private bodies, in the amount of authority conferred and in the relations laid down between the various persons and sub-bodies involved. CT, by contrast, is a good deal more similar everywhere, at least in formal arrangements.

One naturally thinks of voting as the means by which CA is conducted, but it is not the only one. CA may be carried out by market means, as in takeover situations. However, overt use of the price mechanism in CA is exceptional, apart from takeovers. We do not observe what would be the most direct form of price-CA, namely offers to do the job for less pay. Price does not equate supply and demand for authority. Access to authority is always quantity-constrained. On the other hand, a bargain with an effect similar to price-cutting occurs in the quite frequent case where candidates try to broaden their support by offering a share of office or influence to some other individual or group, thereby diluting their own return from success in the competition. Contests for authority may also, of course, be conducted by means that are not competition in the sense of being determined by arbiters' preferences. Bargaining between management and unions over the right to control work practices is a case in point. Civil war is another.

CA implies, by definition, the existence of *organisations*. If all decisions were made by atomistic individuals, the question of authority would not arise. The characteristic of organisations is that they have a machinery for making collective decisions. An organisation without such a machinery would be a contradiction in terms. There is endless scope for variation in the composition of the body that exercises the collective authority and in the scope of that authority, but at the least there must be agreement by members, enforced by threat of some form of sanction, to abide by the decisions that fall within its purview. To that extent the existence of authority in organisations is inherent; and in any but the very smallest organisations (such as the family) the authority is bound to have a hierarchical character.

A large part of this address will be concerned with comparisons between these two forms of competition, CT and CA, characteristic, though not exclusively so, of economics and politics respectively. I should note that the line between CT and CA is not always perfectly sharp. Grey areas include, for example, competition for promotion within hierarchies and competition between organisations for members.[4]

As far as inefficiency is concerned, the safeguards afforded by CT and CA are those already mentioned as resulting from competition generally. The main role of CA in this regard is to assist towards effective optimisation, given that rationality is bounded: it helps to ensure that those entrusted with the difficult tasks of decision-making are suitable to do so and are not incompetent or indolent or dishonest or too old (gerontocracy is a common failing of autocracies, both public and private). The position regarding exploitation is rather different. How far CA provides a safeguard against exploitation depends on how broadly representative the competitors and the arbiters are of all those who are members of an organisation or are affected by its operations. Active CA among a very restricted group in an organisation may, besides checking inefficiency, prevent members of that group from exploiting one another. However, it will not have any tendency to prevent the group as a whole from exploiting everyone else. Thus, in the case of the state, democracy is more of a safeguard against exploitation than oligarchy is, even though both involve CA.

In private organisations the authority that people compete for is not absolute. It is confined to the affairs of the organisation, for a start. Moreoever, while it is convenient, and indeed essential, for the members of an organisation to entrust many decisions to the management, it is customary to reserve some classes of decision for direct voting by members of the organisation – for example, alterations in a company's Articles of Association. As far as those decisions are concerned, the members prefer to collectively carry out their own optimisation rather than to proceed indirectly by competitive choice of delegates with discretionary authority.

As this example shows, not all voting ranks as CA, or indeed as competition at all in the sense of choice between people. Likewise in a committee where the members are agreed on objectives and confer together in order to share information and decide the best course of action in face of uncertainty, voting less resembles competition than it resembles the weighing up of alternatives that goes on in the mind of a rational individual, i.e. optimisation. This is still the case if the source of disagreement between the members lies in divergence of interest rather than divergence of opinion, so that their debate has the character of bargaining. The comparison with the rational individual still holds up to a point, since the individuaal too has to weigh up his own conflicting interests (e.g. between consumption now and consumption in his retirement). Grey areas between competition and optimisation arise when the options voted on are closely identified with the views of individuals or factions who vie for the support of uncommitted voters.

Reverting to the extent of authority, restrictions on the scope of what is competed for are less clear-cut in the case of the state. It is difficult to say what belongs within the realm of the government and what does not. Moreover, although the powers of individual organs of government may be restricted, on the principle of checks and balances, reservation of classes of issue for decision by a referendum of all voters are exceptional in democratic countries. This applies even to changes in the national equivalent of Articles of Association, namely a country's written constitution.[5] The potentially unlimited scope of political authority, conferred by most countries' constitutions and supported, in all countries, by the government's access to physical force, is one of the reasons why competition for it can be more crucial than CA in private organisations. How to prevent rulers from becoming tyrants has been designated the First Problem of Politics.[6]

CA can vary not only in its scope but also in its frequency. Authority can range from permanent, as in the case of a hereditary monarchy or a self-perpetuating Board of Directors, to only a few years, as with democratically elected governments. Correspondingly, the arbiters get a look in infrequently or frequently. Much the same is true of CT: it will be relatively infrequent in cases where contracts, or implicit contracts, are agreed that have substantial duration, as sometimes in the labour market and in relations with suppliers or distributors; at the other extreme CT may be virtually continuous, as in the foreign exchange market or on the stock exchange. During the tenure of the authority or the contract, competition is supended and to that extent made less severe overall, though participants may doubtless be influenced in their conduct by consideration of the next round (the 'reputation' factor). The duration of the time for which authority is conferred never approaches zero, unlike that of a transaction, because that would be inconsistent with the nature of authority itself. However, though there are never daily elections, there can exist continuous verbal opposition to the incumbent authority from an organised opposition party. This serves, up to a point, to prevent the suspension of competition from being absolute. It thereby intensifies competition in the regime generally. Such continuous verbal competition is a characteristic of politics but not, on the whole, of non-political bodies. It is true that chronic divisions and disputes do quite often occur within private organisations, sometimes on explicitly party-political lines and sometimes not, as in the Yorkshire Cricket Club and the RSPCA and of course in takeover contests. But the permanent existence of an opposition party in a private body is usually regarded as abnormal and a sign of something amiss. Why is this? Why does ICI not have a shadow Board to keep the actual Board on its toes? A large part of the explanation is surely that the organisation is thought of as a team, subject to CT with other organisations. Chronic opposition to the management from within would distract energies from the common task and be disloyal. The organisation may be thought to be less comparable to a government than to a family, with its need for mutual trust and support. In just the same way, in politics, even in democratic countries, opposition to the government is regarded as disloyal in times of war, when, exceptionally, competition with an outside opponent is the main business of the day (it is well-known that wars are attractive to dictators on this account). In the case of businesses, the lack of continuous CA, or even the lack of much CA at any time, matters less from the social point of view for the very reason that the firm is subject to the discipline of external CT. The existence of CT thus both makes CA less important and discourages it, at least unless CT becomes so severe as to threaten the survival of the organisation and makes a change in the management seem imperative. Conversely, the *absence* of CT in politics in peace-time creates the need for CA. The two forms of competition are thus to a large extent substitutes for each other, from both the positive and the normative points of view.

2. THE WORKING OF COMPETITION-FOR-AUTHORITY

How may CA be expected to work out? In particular, to what extent is CA an adequate substitute in the political arena for the CT that is not available there, for the twin purposes of avoiding inefficiency and exploitation?

Authority is a public good in the Samuelsonian sense. Whoever is successful in CA in a polity or organisation wields authority over all its members, not just over his own supporters. The winner takes all. This is one of the fundamental respects in which CA differs from CT. CT in fully private goods enables everyone to deal with the partner he prefers, even though his preference may be a minority one.

Closely related to this is the tendency for CA to be oligopolistic. The win or lose nature of voting creates large economies of scale in the form of a premium on alliances. There is room for only very few political parties. The extent of the economies of scale, as is well known, is affected by the voting system in use: it is greatest in first-past-the-post systems, where more than two parties are unlikely to be able to survive indefinitely, at least in a single constituency, because the smallest party suffers not only from being small but also from being thought to be small and hence being disadvantaged by tactical voting. Under any voting systems, however, the feasible number of parties is likely to be small. Likewise new entry is much more difficult than in business, where a new entrant can carve out a small niche for himself; small niches are little use in national politics (though a regionally concentrated niche may be effective in local affairs). Tendencies to oligopoly are familiar enough in CT in economics but a reduction in the number of competitors to two is unusual, at least in the case of tradable goods, because of the presence of foreign competition – a safeguard absent in the political sphere in normal times. CA in private bodies can also be oligopolistic, but less regularly so than in politics because party alignments are less common, for the reasons I have mentioned.

CA is competition between people. The winner will be called upon to exercise discretion. Otherwise there would be no point in having authority at all, and all questions could be decided directly by the full membership of the organisation. At the same time candidates to a greater or less extent do commit themselves by espousing policies. The efficacy of CA thus turns in part, though only in part, on whether it results in success for candidates who espouse and adopt policies that avoid inefficiency and exploitation and therefore conform with public wishes.

Insofar as CA consists in this way of indirect social choice between policies, assessment of its performance is bedevilled by the well-known difficulty in the theory of social choice of defining uniquely what the wishes of the public are and hence what should rank as inefficiency or exploitation. There is no ideal system of expressing social choice. The theorems here are remarkably strong. It has been shown that, where there are many issues at stake, there will almost always exist for any policy package some alternative policy package that would defeat it in a vote.[7] Likewise, any proposal, however atrocious, would be preferred to *some* alternative. The outcome is likely to depend on the choice of which packages are to be put to the vote, in what order, and with what procedure for bringing voting to a conclusion. Whereas in general equilibrium theory of CT the possibility of multiple equilibrium can usually not be ruled out, in social choice it is the rule rather than the exception. The resolution is achieved by the voting rules and by control of the agenda.

The difficulty is compounded by the malleability of preference. The implementation of policies may alter people's preferences, in just the same way as consumers' preferences are altered by the habits and aversions created by past purchases. If a given policy is unwelcome both before and after it is implemented, deliberate adoption of it by the authority is clearly exploitative. But the situation is less clear if it was unwelcomed beforehand but welcomed in retrospect, or welcomed beforehand but regretted in retrospect. A further difficulty arises from lack of information. The ordinary voter, even if he has the capacity to study public policy issues thoroughly, lacks the inducement to do so because his single vote counts for so little – a well-known theme in public choice theory. So there are 'don't knows' as well as yesses and noes. Governments can affect preferences by words, as well as by deeds, just as advertisers can. Neither this nor the disregard of alterable preferences is necessarily sinister. In some areas the public may be glad for governments to show 'leadership', indeed expect it of them. The difficulty is where to draw the line between leadership and brainwashing. At any rate, a condition of effective CA is that the public should have a choice as to *who* is to wash their brains.

I make no claim to resolve these philosophical dilemmas. In what follows I shall cut the knot, in a negative sense, by assuming that, notwithstanding the philosophical difficulties, there exist *some* policies that are sufficiently unpopular to be classed as exploitative or inefficient or both. Whether CA serves to prevent such policies from being adopted then remains a meaningful question.

At the same time, many of the problems about political CA in a representative democracy do reflect the underlying social choice problem. Under any form of social choice, someone has to decide what options are put on the agenda and in an oligopolistic party system it is the parties. One cannot say that this is as such undemocratic, it is just one form of democracy, subject to defects as other forms would be. Even such apparent abuses as paying disproportionate regard to special interest groups or voters in marginal constituencies could have their counterpart, through log-rolling, in direct democracy. Much the same is true of the problem of oligopolistic indeterminacy: the choice of vote-maximising package by each party depends on the package that is put forward or is expected to be put forward by the other, and a tendency to an indefinite cycle is possible, a tendency which has its counterpart in direct voting on options.

What does follow, however, is that it is not a matter of indifference as to what motivates politicians, and in particular whether they are selfish careerists or ideological zealots. The optimistic belief sometimes held that it *is* a matter of indifference is based on the idea that voters will vote for the candidates espousing the policies the voters like, whether those policies have been designed simply to please them and win their votes or whether they have been dictated by the candidates' ideologies. This is not valid under oligopoly, because the voter's choice is confined to a very short menu and the politicians are in charge of the kitchen where the dishes are prepared. This problem arises even where there is only one political issue, say Left-Right, and the options can be arranged in one dimension, as in Hotelling's original model of spatial competition.[8] It is even more prominent where there are several issues, and policies relating to them are offered to the voter under conditions of joint supply.[9] This does not relate only to elements in an ideological package: voters may find that they have to choose between the party or candidate with the ideology they prefer and the one they think is more efficient. In that case they are bound to regard the outcome as either inefficient or exploitative, if not both.

The question of how to model politicians' motivations has been much discussed since Downs published his famous book.[10] His suggestion was that, as a first approximation, we could disregard ideology. Politicians want office, just as businessmen want profits. Sausage-makers supply sausages, politicians supply political services, why suppose that one is more ideologically motivated than the other? Self-interest is what matters – tempered, presumably, in all occupations to a greater or less extent by some regard to general moral considerations about honesty and such like.

Downs's hypothesis has had a useful astringent effect. I daresay that if there were nothing else to choose from it would be preferable to the hypothesis at the opposite extreme, that politicians are would-be philosopher kings, motivated solely by concern for the public interest as they see it. But it goes too far.[11] Most people have some views about how public affairs should be conducted and it is reasonable to suppose that people who enter politics for a career have stronger views than most.[12] The same is perhaps even more true of party activists who do not seek office themselves but devote unpaid time to party work. Downs's down-grading of ideology seemed more plausible when his book was published in 1957 than it does in the more polarised political environment of the present time. Doubtless the balance between ideology and the pursuit of self-interest will differ between individual politicians and between societies. It will be affected by the financial rewards of a political career compared with alternatives (conspicuously low in this country; probably higher as a rule in less developed countries than in advanced countries). It will also be affected by the consequences of losing office once you have it (a Life Peerage or the firing squad). It will doubtless vary in the course of an individual's lifetime, with self-interest typically gaining ground as he gets older. But none of this means that ideology is not frequently important. It can always be argued, of course, that ideological considerations are in some deeper sense a cloak for self-interest. That may be true. But it is irrelevant if politicians behave *as if* their motivation was ideological. This applies both to the policy position chosen on a given issue and to the choice of what to make an issue of.

The working of an oligopolistic party system gives great importance to the decisions made within parties. The process of decision-making within parties differs profoundly from the process of electoral choice. Decisions are transferred from the general public to party activists, so that the franchise is greatly reduced. One result is to reduce the transaction costs of repeated voting or of more informal bargaining to accommodate the divergent wishes of party members. However, as the views of party activists are likely to have a larger and possibly more extreme ideological content than those of the general public, a further result is to create a chronic tension: should policy be nearer to that of the median party activist, as being the line preferred within the party, or should it be nearer to that of the median voter in the electorate, so as to maximise the chances of winning the election? It is not surprising that the outcome has gone sometimes one way, sometimes the other. Everyone in the party wants it to win, but they differ in the ideological price they are prepared to pay. The ideological zealots can support their case by pointing to the uncertainty that exists anyway about what the vote-maximising policies would be. They can argue, reasonably enough, that policies may not make all that difference to electoral support anyway, particularly the policies of non-incumbent parties. If the party's electoral prospects are bad, they may say that a sell-out would not do any good and would merely prejudice their position for the next time. If the electoral prospects are good, they may advocate vote-satisficing (trying to make sure that you get enough votes to win) rather than vote-maximising. A curious consequence of vote-satisficing is that it may cause a party to respond to a change in its opponent's policies in the opposite direction from what it would do under vote-maximising. Under vote-maximising, a move by the Left party further to the Left induces the Right party to move further to the Left too, so as to capture voters in the vacated middle ground. Under vote-satisficing, a leftward move by the Left party may cause the Right party to move further to the Right, if this is the underlying preference of the median party member. By so doing, the Right party will lose some votes, but it may now be less concerned about that because of the extra votes that have been conferred on it by its opponent's more extreme stance. Call the difference between the position of the median party member and the position actually adopted the ideological gap. The ideological gap can be regarded as the ideological price paid for support by voters. An outward move in the position of the opposing party has a substitution effect, increasing the number of votes that can be bought by increasing the ideological gap. Under vote-satisficing, however, the opponent's move also has the equivalent of an income effect, tending to reduce the ideological gap by reducing the party's need for extra votes. Recent British experience seems to conform more to the satisficing model (greater polarisation), recent American experience more to the maximising model (both parties move to the Right) – though of course this may reflect differences between the two countries in trends in public opinion rather than differences in party strategies.

The existence of disciplined parties carries a degree further the winner-take-all principle. Within a polity whose legitimacy is not in dispute, everyone agrees to abide by the authority established by the votes of the majority; there is loyalty to the social contract. Likewise within a party all members agree to abide loyally by the decision of the majority of party members, whether it be on the choice of the party leadership, CA, or on the choice of policies, optimisation by voting. This can lead to the phenomenon of pyramiding, the 26 per cent phenomenon. Given party discipline, a choice may be made that has the support of 51 per cent of the members of the party that itself has the support of 51 per cent of the electorate – even though the outcome is opposed by all but 26 per cent of the electorate. This is not, of course, an inevitable result; the outcome may be supported by some of the minority party. Equally, however, matters can be even worse. The 26 per cent arithmetic ignores the distinction between electorate and activists; when that is taken into account the figure could be reduced considerably below 26 per cent, as it could also if there existed a disciplined faction within a disciplined party. Pyramiding is plainly a potential source of exploitation in the sense of leading to ideological policies that are contrary to most people's preferences. It is restrained to some extent by the ill effect of the policy on the party's electoral standing; but this cannot be relied on, especially when voting between parties is dictated by many issues.

All this relates to CA as a form of choice between policies. But of course CA is also a choice about who should exercise discretion in areas outside stated policies. Indeed for the candidates themselves it is an important matter how far they should commit themselves to stated policies. Insofar as they seek an open mandate, the voters are having to choose between personalities, on the basis of such information as they have. This is the most usual situation in CA in private bodies, where there is a reasonable chance of the voters' having first-hand information about the candidates. In politics, where the numbers are too large for this, voters are liable to be influenced, *faute de mieux*, by irrelevant considerations, such as physical appearance, and they are very exposed to propaganda, for or against, which they are not in a position to check. The request for an open mandate sounds agreeably unideological, but it gives the voter very little to go on.[13]

All this sounds rather depressing. Largely because of its oligopolistic character, CA cannot be relied on to avoid either inefficiency or exploitation. Thinking about these inevitable deficiencies of political CA, with its winner-take-all characteristics, enables one to see the force of Hayek's contention that the larger the scope of CT and the less the scope of the authority for which politicians are able to compete, the better. But of course this begs the question of how effectively CT avoids inefficiency and exploitation. Perhaps one should not take *too* tragic a view. Not only are the wishes of the public ill-defined anyway, but also the worst abuses do contain some tendencies to correct themselves so long as CA persists. CA is certainly better than the absence of *any* form of competition, since then there are no corrective tendencies at all.

At the same time one is left a little uneasy about the possible malfunctions. There is also the even more fundamental problem that arises from the winner-take-all character of CA (and of other forms of social choice), namely the oppression of minorities.[14] Is anti-Semitism all right if supported by the majority of the population? Obviously not. What about the oppression of non-racial minorities, like the rich or the unemployed? This is more debatable ground. Constitutional law does not usually provide against the oppression of minorities as such (though it may protect particular minorities, e.g. religious or racial ones). Company law does; and more generally, it is often the practice in committees to dispense with voting and instead leave the chairman to state the 'sense of the meeting', it being understood that in so doing he may, if he thinks fit, give special weight to strongly held minority views. Perhaps the open mandate in politics can be interpreted in a similar sense, as a means of allowing the government to take the sense of the national meeting. This depends on the government, of course, so it is not a reliable safeguard. An entrenched constitution is a safeguard against certain types of oppression. But entrenched constitutional protection that will serve all necessary purposes is difficult to devise and constitutions can usually be amended anyway. The only ultimate safeguard is an ideological one, a consensus about the extent to which the majority can reasonably use its powers. An ideological consensus among politicians may actually be desirable for this purpose, even if it runs against the wishes of the majority of the public.

3. THE STABILITY OF COMPETITION

Analysis of the consequences of a given set of social arrangements is incomplete if the consequences include changes in the arrangements themselves. If the existence of competition is held to be desirable, competition must be deemed to have functioned faultily if it leads to its own disappearance. Let me refer to three possible sources of this kind of 'contradiction': economies of scale, collusion, and loss of legitimacy. Each of these is applicable to both CT and to CA, and in the case of CA both to the state and to private bodies.

(i) Economies of scale

CT in the presence of scale economies can lead to monopoly. In fact, as Schumpeter taught us, the establishment of *some* sort of monopoly is typically part of the purpose of the firm in a competitive system. In practice the attainment of a world-wide monopoly over an important product as a result of scale economies does not often seem to have happened in the case of goods where there is international competition, but of course it does happen locally in the case of industries of the public utility type. The equivalent in CA is more drastic and has often been observed, both in politics and in private bodies. Scale economies here are of the essence. Under a constitution where there is no effective separation of powers, the party that gets the majority of the votes does not just get most of the power, it gets all of it. If it is sufficiently ruthless, it can use that power to perpetuate its hold of office, by gerrymandering subsequent elections or, in the extreme case, abolishing them altogether. Democracy then takes the degenerate form that has been described as One Man One Vote Once. In private bodies the ill-effects of this are limited by the presence of CT and by the possibility of exit, though those may take some time to work. In the case of the state, they can be avoided only if the parties exercise some moderation in their pursuit of power: while wanting to win, they must also want their adversary – or at least some adversary – to live to fight another day.

(ii) Collusion

Again, the economic form is familiar. Permanently effective market-sharing collusion has usually been dependent on support or connivance by the government, because of its vulnerability to free riders. Collusion to avoid CA or severely restrict it happens all the time in private bodies, but again the ill-effects are limited by the existence of CT and the scope for exit. The political equivalent would come about if all the parties were to form a 'grand coalition' to share office. This does not seem to happen very often, presumably because it would render the parties too vulnerable to a new entrant. Parties do, of course, collude on particular issues. Moreover in a many-party system a sufficient number of parties may collude to keep the remaining onces permanently in opposition so long as public opinion does not shift too much. CA is then reduced but not abolished.

(iii) Loss of legitimacy

If people become sufficiently impatient with the perceived failures of the working of competition they may take steps to abolish it. In the case of economic competition, the steps will typically be pressure for government action; in the case of political competition the only means are a coup or a revolution (including a coup by the incumbent party). Loss of legitimacy may be occasioned by perceived failure in either the avoidance of inefficiency or the avoidance of exploitation. I emphasise *perceived* failure, because the saliency of a visibly bad outcome may be what matters rather than a considered assessment of the relative merits of competition and non-competition. Loss of legitimacy may arise if the problems are very bad and none of the politicians seem to have the answers, despite their mutual wrangling. Political competition does have visible costs. The greater the divisions between the parties, the greater will these costs tend to be, in the form of discontinuity on policy and suspicion by the incumbent party that the opposition is not wholly loyal to the underlying social contract. With regard to exploitation, similarly, loss of legitimacy is most liable to arise if the parties are irreconcilably divided from each other. This may result from the predominance of ideology among politicians, supported by pyramiding. It may also result if society itself is deeply divided. Experience suggests that this is most likely if the groups are divided on racial or religious lines, lines that are sharp and discontinuous, rather than on economic lines, where, *pace* Marx, there is much more of a continuum. However, as Sam Brittan argued some years ago,[15] the same effect of irreconcilability may be created if occupational groups severally have economic aspirations that add up to more than the total of what is available.

In case I seem unduly disposed to exaggerate the instability of competition, let me refer to one danger which I think has been overstated. This is Hayek's idea that the enlargement of the economic activities of the state in a democracy not only reduces CT, which it obviously may do, but also threatens the survival of democracy itself. One can see reasons why this might be so, but the idea seems to lack empirical backing. There have been plenty of historical examples of democracies becoming autocracies, but not many cases come to mind where this was brought about by an enlargement of the domain of the state. It is true and important that political autocracy, if it exists, is more all-pervasive and hence possibly more stable if there is central control of economic activity. But that is a different point.

4. CONCLUDING REMARKS

In a world of organisations, CA may serve as a substitute for CT or they may coexist. In the case of the state, CA is the only form of competition there is, and that is why in democratic countries CA is particularly keen. Both forms of competition serve up to a point as safeguards against inefficiency and exploitation, but neither is perfect.

Of the two, CA is probably subject to more limitations and is perhaps also more liable to prove unstable. However, the disappearance of CA, insofar as it relates to the political sphere, has the more far-reaching effects.

There are circumstances when competition is not a feasible form of social organisation: the costs would be too great in relation to the benefits. This may be for a welcome reason, that the organisation gets on perfectly well without it and might do worse with it. For example, there are innumerable non-profit-making bodies (like the British Association) that by their nature are not subject to much CT and operate with little complaint of inefficiency or exploitation, without there being any very active CA. As is well known, too, there are many primitive societies in which the spirit of competition is almost entirely lacking, yet the societies are at least internally stable.

CA may also be ruled out for darker reasons. The divisions within society may be too deep – whether these divisions have purely social causes or whether they have been created or fostered in the past by political or religious zealots among their leaders, who should have been resisted at that stage but were not. Political CA depends on the existence of some underlying consensus between the competitors. The need for consensus is less inherent in CT because the winner does not necessarily take all. In the absence of consensus, autocrats may argue, with some plausibility, that active CA would be too destructive and would fan flames of discord which in its absence would do no more than smoulder. The avoidance of inefficiency then depends on the ability of the non-democratic rulers, and the avoidance of exploitation depends on their public-spiritedness. How far these are likely to prove reliable is a matter of the theory of autocracy, which lies beyond the scope of this address.

NOTES

1. In revising this address for publication I have been helped by remarks made during the discussion at the meeting and also by comments from Samuel Brittan and James Cornford. The responsibility for the opinions expressed and for remaining errors is my own.
2. The distinction between modes of contestation is appropriately reflected in the language of Marxism, which speaks of class *war* but *competition* between capitalists.
3. It might be argued that the exploitative aspect of private monopolies need not be a matter for social concern at all, inasmuch as it affects only the

distribution of the gains on particular transactions, whereas social concern about distribution should relate to the distribution of income as a whole. Do we mind about poor monopolists, provided that they are not a source of inefficiency? As against this, it may be held that public policy should concern itself also with the *ways* in which people should be allowed to enrich themselves: we disapprove of slave-traders and blackmailers regardless of whether they are rich or poor.

4. This form of competition features prominently in Albert O. Hirschman, *Exit Voice and Loyalty* (Harvard UP, 1970). Hirschman's 'exit' includes both CT and competition between organisations for members. The *interaction* between the different forms of competition, which I shall be discussing relatively little, is one of the central themes of Hirschman's book.
5. Only 5 of the 22 democratic countries studied by A. Lijphart, *Democracies* (Yale UP, 1984), had mandatory provision for referendums on constitutional change (p. 202).
6. R. E. Dahl and C. E. Lindblom, *Politics, Economics and Welfare* (New York: Harper, 1953), p. 273.
7. K. A. Shepsle and B. R. Weingast, 'Institutionalizing Majority Rule: A Social Choice Theory with Policy Implications', *American Economic Review*, May 1982, pp. 367–71 and references there cited.
8. H. Hotelling, 'Stability in Competition', *Economic Journal*, March 1929, pp. 41–57.
9. Suppose there are two major issues, Left–Right and Catholic–Protestant. The candidate who offers himself as, say, a Left Catholic is unlikely to get much more than a quarter of the votes. Candidates will do better to form themselves into parties associated with the issue regarded by voters as the more important, say religion. The Left–Right issue will then fall to be resolved within the Catholic and Protestant parties, not by voting between the parties.
10. A. Downs, *An Economic Theory of Democracy* (New York: Harper & Row, 1957).
11. For some *a priori* and empirical objections to it, see J. P. Kalt and M. A. Zupan, 'Capture and Ideology in the Economic Theory of Politics', *American Economic Review*, June 1984, pp. 279–300.
12. Not *necessarily* more extreme ones: it is possible to be an ideologist of the centre. Hirschman made the interesting suggestion that ideologues who stand towards the extremist end of the party are likely to make the greatest effort to influence its policies because they do not have the option of defecting (*Exit Voice and Loyalty*, p. 70). This applies particularly under first-past-the-post voting systems. It is less valid under voting systems that give small independent extremist parties some chance of representation, as in Israel and in some continental European countries.
13. Thus the account of true Tory philosophy given by Mr Francis Pym in his recent book (*The Politics of Consent*, Hamish Hamilton, 1984, pp. 113–15), attractively open-minded though it sounds, leaves the reader wondering what sort of person other than a hard-line communist would *not* find himself at home in the Conservative Party, if only its affairs were properly conducted.
14. This was the basis of Wicksell's advocacy of a unanimity rule instead of a

majority rule in voting on public goods (see Dennis C. Mueller, *Public Choice*, Cambridge, 1979, chapter 11). This idea is not as absurd as it sounds. However, it is not theoretically valid unless transaction costs are sufficiently low to allow a long series of alternative proposals to be devised and put to the vote. Moreover, unless it has always been in force, it is open to the charge of inconsistency, in treating as sacrosanct the initial distribution of welfare, notwithstanding that the distribution may itself have owed much to past non-unanimous decisions.

15. S. Brittan, 'The Economic Contradictions of Democracy', *British Journal of Political Science*, April 1975, pp. 129–59.

2 The Interaction between Economic Policy and Political Performance

VANI BOROOAH

1. INTRODUCTION

My theme is political economy and I use the term in its most literal sense to mean the complexity of interaction between political and economic behaviour. It is a truism that in societies characterised by democratic political systems, governments have periodically to submit themselves to the judgement of their electorates. All those who participate in democratic political processes have therefore an interest, first in identifying the factors that exert a significant influence on the electorate's judgement and second in manipulating these factors so as to elicit, for themselves, a favourable verdict from the electorate. These two aspects – the identification and manipulation of electorally significant factors – form the theme of this chapter.

In discussing these, I would like to confine myself to economic factors and I would prefer not to stray into a discussion of non-economic events, the electoral impact of which I am even less competent to judge. In doing so I shall be guided by Harold Wilson's often quoted statement that 'all political history shows that the standing of a Government and its ability to hold the confidence of the electorate at a General Election, depends upon the success of its economic policy', though I remain conscious that such a statement must appear of doubtful validity to those of you who believe that events in far-off places, like the Falklands or Oman, are of far more importance in determining electoral outcomes in Britain.

In the face of such scepticism, I can only say that there is a great deal of evidence that, over the past two decades, the British voter has been greatly preoccupied by economic matters. At the time of the 1959 General Election, when the Tories were re-elected under Macmillan, the British voter perceived the twin problems of international affairs and of armaments and defence as constituting the major problems facing the country. Economic affairs came a poor second with pensions and services for old people an also ran. Over the years, as the sun set with increasing rapidity on the Empire, there was a dramatic shift in the British electorate's perception of the relative importance of issues, to the extent that by September 1963, 26 per cent of Gallup respondents were prepared to assign the highest priority to economic affairs and only 18 per cent to the combined issues of international affairs and defence. By March 1966, 48 per cent of Gallup respondents put economic affairs as 'the most urgent problem facing Britain today', though there was a brief assertion of national pride when 40 per cent of respondents felt that the government should resign if Britain had to devalue her currency. Needless to say the government did not oblige and life continued as usual.

To demonstrate that preoccupation with economic matters was not solely the consequence of life in 'socialist' Britain, the Tories, under Edward Heath, failed to divert people's attentions from problems of labour relations and cost of living increases; to make matters worse for them 52 per cent of Gallup respondents sympathised with the miners in their pay dispute and almost the same number thought the three-day week to be unnecessary. The predominance of economic affairs in the minds of the electorate continued to increase over the seventies and by October 1977, 70 per cent of respondents felt that unemployment, inflation and labour relations were problems of the greatest urgency facing Britain. The evidence for the early eighties only confirms this pattern with the British public consistently regarding the state of the economy as being the most important problem facing the country.

On the above evidence therefore, there would appear to be a strong case for investigating the relationship between changes in the economic environment and the reactions of the electorate. This I shall attempt to do in the first part, where I shall try to identify the economic factors of consequence to the electorate and to articulate the manner in which they affect the electorate's judgement. In particular, in this part, I shall be concerned with two issues: whether the nature of the influence of economic issues on political popularity is stable over time and whether, at a point in time, the nature of this influence is the same across the electorate. In the second part I shall consider the obverse question – can and do governments manipulate economic policy to their electoral advantage? In this part I shall begin by briefly reviewing some of the theoretical approaches to this question and then proceed to consider whether such theories are relevant for an understanding of British economic policy over the past twenty years.

2. ECONOMIC PERFORMANCE AND POLITICAL POPULARITY

The hypothesis that there is a causal connection between a government's economic performance and its political popularity has attracted the attention of both political scientists and economists. Two aspects of this relationship deserve attention. The first is the logic of the voter. Why do (or do not) voters respond to economic issues? Do voters respond to certain issues but not to others? Do different voters respond differently to particular issues and if so why? These are some of the questions to which the theory of voting addresses itself. The second aspect is empirical. What are the issues with which voters are concerned? Is it inflation, unemployment, incomes? What is the relative strength of their concern with these issues and does this vary across time and across voters?

Perhaps the most celebrated work on the theory of voting is due to Downs (1957) and coincidentally, since it is a view that accords most closely with standard economic theory, it has been used by economists as a framework for much of the applied work in this area. In a Downsian world of two parties (though the analysis could be modified for a multi-party system) a voter is rational in the sense that he casts his votes for the party he believes will provide him with more benefits than any other. These benefits, which may be many and various, are reduced to a common denominator, which Downs refers to as the *utility income* of government activity. To discover which party he would vote for, the voter compares the utility incomes he would receive over the coming election period from each of the parties and votes for the party from which he expects the highest utility income. The analysis recognises that, since no party can do – or will wish to do – everything it promises, party manifestoes are a poor basis for forming expectations about future utilities. Instead the voter must form some judgement about what the parties would actually do should they come to power. For the incumbent party, its performance in the current period, assuming its policies have some continuity, offers a reliable guide to its future deeds;

for the party in opposition, however, no such guide exists. The model then assumes that the rational voter constructs in his mind such a hypothetical guide, that is, how the opposition party would have performed had it been in power in the current period, and then uses the present utility incomes, the one actual and the other hypothetical, to form expectations about the post-election period. It is recognised however that collecting information for an evaluation of the different utility income streams is a costly process and for this reason no voter would attempt a comprehensive evaluation. Instead each voter will base his evaluation upon those areas where the differences between parties are sufficient to impress him. Thus the voter remains indifferent as to which party is in power until the difference in utility flows is large enough, that is until his party differential threshold has been crossed.

Within the framework of the Downsian world, one can distinguish between 'valence' issues on which there is essentially one body of opinion and 'position' issues on which there may be rival bodies of opinion (cf. Butler and Stokes, 1974). Thus, for example, a government's views on nationalisation or labour relations may be regarded as 'position' issues. On the other hand a reduction in unemployment or growth in real incomes could be regarded as valence issues. As will be discussed below, most empirical work in this area has regarded the economy as a valence issue, that is, one which has been based on a view of voter behaviour in which the government has been electorally rewarded or punished for the attainment or non-attainment of certain universally desired goals.

While it is true that several economic issues command a near unanimity of opinion as to their desirability or otherwise, and as such are valence issues, 'position' models of voting behaviour are important because they highlight the differences between the different voters and the different parties, differences which are undeniably important to understanding electoral outcomes. Two examples will suffice to illustrate this point. One position model is that of Converse (1958), who begins by noting that the view that different status groups in society have different interests and that these different interests are expressed in differential voting behaviour, is fairly widely accepted. Thus, for example, 'over the last 25 years, high status persons in the United States have favoured the Republican party while the less fortunately placed have subscribed instead to the Democratic party' (Converse, 1958, p. 388). The status-vote relationship is termed 'status polarisation' and Converse takes as his purpose to study the factors that may account for variations over time in status polarisation. The hypothesis put forward is that 'polarisation would increase in terms of depression and decrease in periods of prosperity' (p. 396). Thus on this view the consequence of hard times is not a general reduction in the support for the ruling party but an increase of support for each party in the class whose interests it represents and a decline in the support for each party in the class whose interests it does not represent. Another 'position' hypothesis, that of Butler and Stokes (1974), is that voters might view one party as expansionist and the other not. Thus the consequences of an economic downturn might increase rather than decrease the popularity of the government if it was formed by the expansionist party. As a historical example they quote the American experience during the 1930s when economic distress did not diminish support for the Democrats who, under Roosevelt, were seen as more expansionary than the Republicans under Hoover.

Turning to the empirical results in this area I shall for reasons of economy confine myself to the United Kingdom. The earliest study for the UK investigating the link between economic performance and political popularity was that of Goodhart and Bhansali (1970). Using Gallup poll data the first question that they asked was whether political popularity was affected significantly by economic developments, when the level of unemployment and the rate of inflation were chosen as the variables of greatest concern to the electorate.

The strongest relation between unemployment and government popularity was found between popularity and the lagged level of unemployment and the most successful lag structure was a simple six-months lag. The inflation rate also had a significant immediate effect on popularity. The results also suggested that the response of the electorate to economic events was more marked and volatile in the years since 1959 than in earlier years. At the same time there was statistical evidence for certain regular movements in the popularity of the government of the day between elections. These suggested that immediately after an election there was a sizeable increase in the support for a newly-elected government. Then there followed a period of slow but steady decline in popularity, but this unpopularity was reversed in the final few months preceding the next elections. The significance, strength and regularity of such movements ('the electoral cycle') were measured using dummy variables.

The Goodhart and Bhansali conclusions were questioned by Miller and Mackie (1973) whose objective was to test the economic influence model against an electoral cycle model that is, a model which explained variations in popularity purely in terms of cyclical variables.

Two major conclusions emerged from the Miller and Mackie study. First, the link between economic performance and popularity was not so strong as had been thought. The cyclical pattern of government popularity continued over the sample period although it was not always accompanied by a similar cyclical movement in the economic variables. An alternative explanation suggested for the observed cycles in government popularity was that the nature of the response altered as time passed. When a general election was near, the nature of the response was likely to involve comparisons between the government and the opposition parties. On the other hand, away from a general election, the response was likely to be non-comparative and hence, as a consequence, the incumbent party would emerge more unpopular in mid term than nearer elections.

The second conclusion was that, even if economic affairs did exert an influence, the relevant determinants of popularity that should be used are the voters' perceptions of economic performance. Yet most studies employed as explanatory variable time series published by the government statistical service. Thus a major area for research was the link between objective events and their reporting by the media and between this and the electorate's perceptions and thence its evaluation of the government.

One study which was based on individual perceptions was that of Butler and Stokes (1974). Their major conclusion, based on survey data, was that the influence of the economy on the electorate's mood had two channels. First, there was the link between perceptions of direct changes in individual well-being and changes in party support and, second, there was the link between perceptions – derived from the media – of the general state of the economy and party support, irrespective of whether such a state impinged directly on the well-being of the individual.

An examination of perceptions of individual well-being revealed unmistakably that 'reactions to changes of economic condition followed the lines of a "valence" model, with the Government of the day, whichever party was in power, being rewarded for good times and disapproved of for bad times' (Butler and Stokes, 1974, p. 384).

As regards perceptions of the state of the economy, the link between such perceptions and party support depended on the extent to which the electorate held the different parties responsible for current economic conditions. Here the ability of the government of the day to unload responsibility for the current economic state on to its predecessor could be important in determining the electorate's attitude. Also the particular features of the economy that were of current electoral importance depended on the economic debate between the parties and such features were therefore capable of change over time.

The Butler and Stokes (1974) study based on individual perceptions represented a departure from the mainstream tradition of econometric work based on data from officially published sources. This tradition was continued by Pissarides (1980) who re-examined the relation between voting intentions and economic performance with a view to investigating the extent to which 'it is possible to model the relation between voting intentions and a few macroeconomic indicators in a stable and systematic fashion' (Pissarides, 1980, p. 569). Pissarides argued that if a government's popularity was indeed stable and systematically affected by its economic performance then popularity functions would contain useful information on how to manage the economy to ensure re-election. On the other hand if a stable, systematic relationship did not exist then such functions would not influence the policy-making process.

To investigate the relationship, Pissarides employed as his explanatory variables the percentage growth in consumption, the change in the rate of inflation, the percentage rate of unemployment, the change in the exchange rate and the ratio of GDP taken in by the government in direct and indirect taxes. In addition modified versions of the Miller and Mackie (1973) type of electoral variables were used in conjunction with the lagged value of the dependent variable which was the lead of the government over the main opposition party in the voting intentions figures.

The main conclusion of the study was that, though there was evidence of a systematic relation between economic performance and government popularity over the sample period 1955–77, taking account of this relation in making out-of-sample forecasts reduced forecasting errors only marginally. Thus an excessive preoccupation by a government about the effect of its policies on its popularity would not appear to be justified. At the same time the popularity function estimated appeared to be stable on conventional statistical criteria. Economic conditions that favoured a faster growth in consumption, a 'stronger' pound, lower inflation and lower unemployment, all had a favourable effect on lead, though quantitatively inflation and unemployment appeared to be the least important of the economic influences.

This selective list of four studies highlights some of the empirical work done in this area for the United Kingdom. The basic technique employed by these studies (except Butler and Stokes (1974)) is regression analysis in which movements in certain economic variables are correlated against movements in voting intentions – in the jargon they estimate 'popularity functions' – and the majority opinion of investigators in this area is that movements in economic variables do influence voting intentions, though of course the list of relevant variables differs between investigators. However, all work in this area, is characterised by two fundamental (and restrictive) assumptions. These are first, that the reactions of respondents do not change over time and second, that all respondents are alike in the sense of having identical reactions to changes in the economic environment. I now consider briefly the consequences of relaxing these assumptions.

3. THE STABILITY OF POPULARITY FUNCTIONS ACROSS TIME AND ACROSS VOTERS

To test the stability across time of popularity functions, movements in voting intentions in Britain were correlated with corresponding movements in the inflation rate, the unemployment rate, the balance of payments and growth in real incomes; in the choice of variables I followed Kaldor (1971) who argued that price stability, full employment, external stability and growth were the four main objectives of post war British economic policy. The estimation period 1955–79 was sub-divided into three sub-periods 1955: Q3 – 1964: Q4; 1964: Q4 – 1970: Q2; and 1970: Q3 – 1979: Q1 with period I being one of Conservative rule under Eden, Macmillan and Home, period II of Labour rule under Wilson, and period III of both Conservative rule under Heath and Labour rule under Callaghan. The popularity function was then estimated over each sub-period separately and the results provide some insight into the apparent instability of such functions found previously in the literature (see Stigler, 1973; Arcelus and Meltzer, 1975).

The main conclusion that emerges was that the results were stable within each sub-period but unstable between sub-periods. This paradox of stability of popularity functions *within* a period relating to a particular government and of instability *between* different governments is not really surprising. The economic problems that are highlighted – and by implication the problems that are underplayed – differ between governments. This may be partly due to genuine differences in ideology and partly to a desire to take advantage of existing economic conditions (witness Mr Wilson on the balance of payments). To some extent this alters voters' perceptions of what is important; to another extent voters judge governments by the criteria the governments themselves set. Both these factors combine to produce what I term the 'changing criteria of economic success'.

However once a set of criteria has been established for a particular government, it remains unaltered until a change of government leads to a change in the tone of the political debate, and hence to a change in the criteria. To take an example: it is not difficult to imagine a Labour government, elected on a platform of ensuring near-full employment, paying a heavy electoral price for three million unemployed. Mrs Thatcher has not paid such a price because she has altered the nature of the economic debate by downgrading high employment and upgrading low inflation rates as objectives of economic policy. In terms of her own criteria, the falling rate of inflation would indicate that she is succeeding, and her strong performance in the recent elections bears witness to this.

The results also show that the nature of these changing criteria was two-fold. First, the behaviour of certain variables is a consistent source of concern to the electorate. Unemployment is such a variable. However it is not levels so much as changes in the levels of unemployment that worry the electorate. Unemployment becomes an election-losing issue – particularly when it has already been downgraded to a price one has to pay for a better future – only through the insecurity that high and rising levels of unemployment communicate to those already in employment. Remove the 'rising' part of unemployment and you remove a large part of the insecurity. Second, the behaviour of some variables was a source of concern to the electorate in certain periods but not in other periods. The outstanding example of this is Britain's balance of payments performance which significantly affected the government's electoral popularity in the 1964–70 period but did not exercise much influence either before or after this period.

I turn now to the differential impact of economic changes across voters and since this chapter is written at a time when numbers out of work are unprecedentedly high, it is perhaps appropriate to begin by examining the effects of unemployment on society's sub-groups.

The characteristics of individuals comprising the unemployment stock are determined by two distinct selection processes: the ease with which people lose their present job and thus join the unemployed pool and the ease with which they find a new job and thus leave the unemployed pool. Daniel (1981) using survey data demonstrated that people becoming unemployed tended to over-represent (in relation to the overall working population) the young, the less skilled and the low paid. Thus in May 1980, 40 per cent of the unemployed in Britain were unskilled or semi-skilled while only 27 per cent of the male working population in Britain worked at these levels. Even more significantly, this picture had not altered over the past decade. Thus Hibbs (1982), using the *General Household Survey* of 1971 and the Department of Employment's survey of the registered unemployed in 1973, calculated that the incidence of unemployment among manual workers was nearly twice that among non-manual employees.

In terms of the ease with which new jobs could be found, a lack of skills again proved to be a major handicap. Thus Mackay and Reid (1972), while examining the unemployment experiences of male employees made redundant from twenty-three engineering plants in the West Midlands of England over the period 1966–68, discovered that the average duration of unemployment was highest for unskilled workers (20.45 weeks), next highest for semi-skilled workers (12.56 weeks) and lowest for skilled workers (9.70 weeks). Skilled workers of course have the option of resuming employment at a lower point in the occupational scale and this further aggravates the position for the unskilled job-seeker. These conclusions are reinforced by the Royal Commission on the Distribution of Income and Wealth (1978). Using data for 1975 they demonstrated that unskilled and semi-skilled workers had longer durations of unemployment than skilled workers. At the same time they confirmed earlier evidence that unskilled and low-paid workers were more likely to become unemployed than other categories of workers.

The effects of unemployment would therefore appear to fall most heavily upon certain clearly identifiable groups. The young, the unskilled, the low paid and the disabled – who collectively form the weakest and poorest sections of the community – are particularly vulnerable to unemployment. The fact of being unemployed is of course made worse by the economic, social and psychological costs of enforced joblessness. Thus the Royal Commission (1978) for a 1972 sample of the unemployed found that after taking account of all benefits and tax refunds, the average shortfall of household income for the unemployed was 25 per cent. At the same time 40 per cent of the unemployed were losing more than 30 per cent of their net income as a result of being unemployed. In addition of course the income loss would be greater the longer the duration of unemployment.

Compounding the economic costs are the social and psychological miseries of being out of work. In a survey analysed by Daniel (1974), 71 per cent of unemployed respondents said that being out of work had been a 'bad' experience. Although the chief source of hardship was economic, psychological and social costs also featured prominently. The most common complaint was 'boredom' followed by depression or apathy. Third came feelings of inadequacy and a sense of failure. Thus, given the economic and other costs of unemployment and the particular vulnerability of the weak and disadvantaged to unemployment, it follows that a rise in unemployment levels exacerbates inequality.

The differential effects of inflation on the different social sub-groups are more intangible and harder to ascertain. Hibbs (1976) pointed out that the real wage of British manufacturing workers had not been significantly eroded by inflation. On the contrary it was corporate profits which suffered relative declines in inflationary times. Piachaud (1978) argued that it was investment yields that did not keep pace with inflation thereby disadvantaging the relatively well-off and those dependent on unearned income.

In terms of the perceptions of individuals of the deleterious effects of inflation the best evidence is provided by a survey of 2364 adults analysed by Daniel (1975). The results of this survey indicated that the expression of concern about inflation as an economic problem and the feeling that it was personally harmful was common to all sections of the community irrespective of social class, employment status or sex. Thus 73 per cent of the total respondents felt that they had suffered personally from inflation and this varied from 78 per cent for respondents who were in the managerial/professional category to 70 per cent for respondents in the semi-skilled/unskilled manual category. (These figures should be used in conjunction with the fact that the lower the social grade the higher the proportion unable to make an assessment.)

A more interesting picture emerges from the survey when respondents were confronted with the proposition that higher levels of unemployment would be desirable as a means of reducing the inflation rate. Although 77 per cent of the respondents rejected the proposition, the degree of rejection differed markedly between social groups. The proposition was most vehemently rejected by the households of manual workers while among the professional and managerial groups the proportion rejecting the proposition dropped below half.

The conclusion that emerges from the above discussion is that it is the weaker sections of the community – the unskilled and the low paid – who are particularly vulnerable to unemployment and to long durations of unemployment. On the other hand, no significant differences would appear to exist between the different social groups in the perception of their vulnerability to inflation. However, the groups most at risk through rising unemployment would most strongly reject the idea of using unemployment as a means of controlling inflation. The implication for studies of voter behaviour is therefore that the assumption of voters reacting identically to changes in economic variables is a very limiting one and that a realistic appraisal of voter reactions must take into account their social and class backgrounds.

With these observations I now turn to the second part, which concerns the possibility of governments manipulating economic events in order to secure an electoral advantage.

4. THE POLITICS OF ECONOMIC POLICY

Neither Marx nor Kalecki were strangers to the idea that the functioning of an economy can, and does, have a political basis. By emphasising the role of class conflict, in the Marxian *schema*, the economy would be characterised by booms and slumps calculated 'not only to leave intact the foundations of the capitalist system, but also to secure its reproduction on a progressive scale' (Marx, 1967, vol. 1, p. 620). Kalecki argued that 'the class instinct of business leaders tells them that lasting full employment is unsound from their point of view' and that therefore a government's economic policy would be directed towards ensuring that 'unemployment is an integral part of the normal capitalist system' (Kalecki, 1943).

The existence of class conflict in society and its possible influence on economic policy and performance has however been studiously ignored by the dominant paradigm in economics. Indeed this paradigm, has examined questions of a purely normative nature, namely the principles that ought to underlie the making of policy, and has eschewed an investigation of the positive, and empirically relevant, issues, namely the principles that actually underlie, the making of policy.

In this normative, optimising tradition, the work of Tinbergen (1952) was seminal. In the Tinbergen approach the government was viewed as a benevolent dictator acting in the best interests of the governed and in operational terms its problem was to choose levels of policy instruments that would maximise a given social welfare function. Although this approach to economic policy was subsequently refined in several respects, the view of government acting for the greatest good of the governed remained unchanged until Nordhaus (1975) investigated the optimum policy required to maximise a government's re-election prospects subject to the constraint of an inflation–unemployment trade-off. However this attempt by Nordhaus to inject a degree of political realism into an analysis of government behaviour remained rooted in the normative, optimising tradition (i.e. what should a government do to maximise its re-election prospects) and it was dissatisfaction with this tradition that led others (Frey, 1978a, b; Frey and Schneider, 1978) to seek an explanation of what governments actually do, in terms of 'satisficing' rather than optimising behaviour.

Almost a century after Marx, therefore, the wheel has turned full circle, and mainstream economists are expressing an (albeit peripheral) interest in the motivations that underlie the making of economic policy. With this renewed interest however, the insights provided by Marx and Kalecki in terms of societal conflict continue to be ignored and the analysis remains one of a situation in which a homogeneous entity governs a homogeneous society. It is the contention of this part of my lecture that no proper understanding of the behaviour of government, in its role as economic policy maker, is possible without taking account of the differences in interests between the various groups in society and that therefore, our understanding in this area has not been greatly advanced by either the 'optimising' or 'satisficing' approaches to the making of economic policy.

In developing this, I argue on the basis of British evidence for the period 1964–81, that policy is not the output of a homogeneous entity, but instead is the result of a reconciliation of a number of competing and contradictory interests within a government. Furthermore, the ability of a government to vary its policies so as to promote its ideology or to improve its electoral chances is severely limited by the state of the economy and hence the scope for such 'political' policy changes lies at the micro rather than macro-economic level. Finally, where such variations are possible, the role of interest groups in society is very important, with the ruling party altering policy so as to favour the groups with which it is most closely allied.

5. THE ORGANISATION OF BRITISH ECONOMIC POLICY

The making of economic policy in Britain is not the prerogative of any single department, and several ministries have economic functions and contribute to the formulation and implementation of policy in their areas of responsibility. Thus, to name but a few, there are the Departments of Energy, Trade, Industry, Employment, each dealing with a specific area of economic life. However, standing above this welter of economic ministries, through its overall responsibility for government expenditures and its inter-departmental allocation is the Treasury.

On the political side, the Treasury is headed by the Chancellor and he is assisted in his tasks by two, sometimes three ministers, one of whom, the Chief Secretary to the Treasury, usually has Cabinet rank. On the civil service side, the head of the Treasury is the Permanent Secretary and he is assisted by a range of second secretaries, below whom are deputy secretaries and under secretaries. The division of the Treasury, as indeed of every ministry, into the political and the non-political raises the possibility of conflicts between politicians and civil servants over the making of policy.

At the risk of caricature, this conflict may stem from two sources. Firstly, ministers and civil servants may believe in the same economic paradigm but may differ as to the degree to which a particular policy, on the need for which they are both agreed, should be followed. An example of this would be the Butskellite consensus of the 1950s and 1960s according to which demand management, through the regulation of public expenditures and taxes, was the instrument of policy and the maintenance of full employment, constrained by balance of payment considerations, its objective. In the second scenario ministers may come to power with a view of the economy which is at variance with the established civil service view. This situation might give rise to disagreements about the appropriate instruments of economic policy and perhaps even about its objective. An example of this sort of conflict would be the 'monetarist experiment' of the post-1979 Conservative governments. Mrs Thatcher's government of 1979 was the first post-war British government which was not committed to full employment policies. Indeed by downgrading high employment and upgrading control of inflation as objectives of policy, Mrs Thatcher reversed the post-war consensus on the economic role of government. Concomitant with this reversal of objectives was also the spurning of traditional demand management policies in favour of an almost exclusive reliance on policies designed to control the money supply. Attempts to reduce the money supply would of course have fiscal implications, since the government's borrowing requirements would have to be reduced and this in turn would require cuts in public expenditure and perhaps therefore a smaller public sector.

The manner in which these conflicts are resolved would of course depend on their origins. When disputes arise in the context of an agreed view of the economy it is possible that the civil servants in the Treasury would have the dominant say. This is because the Treasury deals with issues more technical and abstract than those dealt with by other departments. This would place the conventional type of politician at a disadvantage *vis-à-vis* Treasury officials. According to the doctrines that prevailed in the Treasury in the late 1960s, described in Brittan (1969), a rate of unemployment of 2 per cent was regarded as satisfactory. If the balance of payments position was reasonable, politicians would be allowed the political kudos of an unemployment rate lower than 2 per cent. If, on the other hand, the balance of payments was not satisfactory, the Treasury was prepared to countenance rates of unemployment in excess of 2 per cent, with the proviso that devaluation would be recommended if unemployment rose considerably.

When the basis for conflict is more fundamental, the government could try to alter the power structure within the civil service either by injecting new talent from outside or by upgrading civil servants more in harmony with the government's view. The appointment of outside advisors to economic ministries on a large scale was a feature of the Labour government of 1964 and was prompted by the fear that the civil service, after more than a decade of uninterrupted Conservative rule, would thwart a 'radical' government. The utility of such outside appointments is however diminished by the fact that though such appointments might contribute to the making of policy, the execution of policy would depend upon the cooperation of other departments and this they would not know how to obtain. The post-1979 Conservative governments have adopted the alternative strategy of restructuring the Treasury more to their liking. This has been effected in a variety of ways – through the appointment of a sympathetic Chief Economic advisor, through the appointment to key positions of Treasury officials who are sympathetic to the government's economic thinking and finally through a reallocation of influence between Treasury departments so that more traditional groups (like the forecasting group) are downgraded in terms of importance with a corresponding rise in the importance of officials dealing with monetary policy.

Turning one's attention outwards there is also the complexity of the Treasury's relationship with the other economic ministries and here too there is scope for conflict. The involvement of both the Treasury and the Department of Employment in the formulation and implementation of incomes policies illustrates the scope for this conflict. The Department of Employment has, as its natural constituency, the labour force and, in the past, in deciding on appropriate wage settlements, was more inclined to countenance exceptions to the incomes policies' norm. The Treasury, on the other hand, without any such interests, was less inclined to make exceptions.

Conflicts may also arise in the Treasury's relationship with the Bank of England. These conflicts are partly institutional. The Bank enjoys an independent income from the interest on securities held by its Banking Department and is therefore more generously staffed than the Treasury. Moreover, the Governor of the Bank of England, unlike the Permanent Secretary to the Treasury has the right to publicly express his views on economic affairs. However, conflicts may also arise through genuine differences in objectives between the Treasury and the Bank. Just as the Treasury is primarily interested in the government's expenditures and revenues, the Bank wishes to ensure the smooth functioning of the foreign exchange market and the market for government securities. Consequently the Bank, in the days of pegged exchange rates, was anti-devaluation and, with floating exchange rates, is more anxious to smooth out fluctuations in the foreign exchange market. On the domestic front the Bank would pay close attention to the government's borrowing requirement and this might bring it into conflict with the Treasury's demand management policies (see Brittan, 1969, pp. 48–9).

The preceding paragraphs indicate that a government's economic policy is not the output of a homogeneous entity but instead evolves through the resolution of conflict both within a central policy-making department like the Treasury and also between the central department and other departments. I now proceed to consider two instruments of British government policy – government expenditures and revenues– – with a view to examining what politically motivated changes, if any, have been effected, in the past two decades, with respect to these instruments.

6. ECONOMIC POLICY IN BRITAIN: GOVERNMENT EXPENDITURES

A problem with discussing the role of government expenditures as an instrument of economic policy is the control of the many agencies responsible for implementing the programmes which constitute the government's expenditure policy. This, in the British context, provides a good example of policy evolving through the resolution of conflict between different branches of government. When the central government expands expenditure, it has to suffer the economic and political consequences of the adverse effects of such expenditure increases on the balance of payments and the rate of inflation. The adverse macro consequences of expenditure increases do not however rebound on local authorities. On the other hand, increases in local taxes (rates) to finance such expenditures do make local authorities unpopular with their constituents. This lays the basis for a conflict of interests with local authorities wishing to maximise their expenditures, to maximise the amount of the rate support grant from the central government and hence to minimise the level of local taxes. The central government would have, of course, precisely the opposite interests. Although the above discussion caricatures the intensity of conflicting interests between central government and local authorities, it does provide another example of the difficulty of regarding a government's expenditure policy as a homogeneous entity being smoothly implemented towards a definite end.

A striking feature of the period 1964–81 is the stability of the ratio of current government expenditures to GDP. Between the peak years of 1975–76 and the trough years of 1964–65, in this respect, there was no significant change in the government's claim on national resources. This stability could of course be due to the offsetting movements in the volume and relative price effects and Table 2.1 examines the volume growth of government expenditures relative to real growth in GDP for the four governments (Wilson, Heath, Wilson/Callaghan, Thatcher) of the period 1964–81.

The smallest expansion of government relative to national output occurred under Wilson and the largest (if one ignores the recent recession) under Heath. This was in spite of the Heath government's intention to substantially reduce previous plans for public spending and to permit taxation to be reduced. By the budget of 1971 however,

TABLE 2.1 *Growth in current general government expenditures on goods and services and in GDP (all at 1975 prices). Percentage change over sub-periods*

	Wilson 1964–70	Heath 1970–74	Wilson–Callaghan 1974–79	Thatcher 1979–81
Current government expenditures	8.4	12.3	7.6	2.2
GDP	13.6	11.8	7.7	−4.3

SOURCE: *Economic Trends Annual Supplement*, 1983.

the Chancellor, worried by rising unemployment, (the numbers unemployed rose by over 12 per cent between the first quarters of 1970 and 1971) proposed a reflationary budget, and the desire to use public spending as an instrument to control the rising levels of unemployment gained further strength as the life of the government progressed. This was of course a classic instance of a government of a particular ideological persuasion following policies that negated its ideology, for economic and political reasons.

On the other hand the early Wilson administration pursued a policy of relative deflation, despite its ideological commitments to expansion, in order to solve the balance of payments crisis. One could interpret such actions as being motivated either by a re-election constraint or more simply, by a balance of payments constraint. Both the early Wilson and the Heath administrations therefore provide examples of frustration of ideology due to re-election constraints.

The Labour administration of 1974–79, provides an instance of a government ideologically committed to high employment levels but forced to follow deflationary policies through pressures exerted on it through an outside agency – the IMF. Finally the Thatcher government represents an administration which, for better or for worse, follows policies which are broadly consistent with its ideological position of reducing the role of the state in economic affairs. Many factors combine to explain Mrs Thatcher's persistence with ideology. Firstly, there is the personality factor – Mrs Thatcher has disowned the existing tradition of consensus politics and, to a far greater extent than her predecessors, has projected herself as a strong-willed leader pursuing a well-defined ideology. Secondly this strategy has not been electorally damaging both because the Labour party, in its present state of disarray has not been able to exploit the unemployment issue and because Mrs Thatcher – with the assistance of a Conservative biased media – has been able to alter the substance of the economic debate and thereby to upgrade control of inflation and down-grade the maintenance of high employment levels as priorities of economic policy.

Further insight into the behaviour of the different governments is provided by examining the composition of government expenditure (see Table 2.2). Irrespective of party affiliation there has been a trend towards reducing expenditures on military defence as a proportion of total government expenditures. This trend has coincided with the decline in Britain's own position in international affairs, along with the granting of independence to former colonies and the gradual reduction in military commitments abroad. However it could be plausibly argued

TABLE 2.2 The composition of current general government expenditure on goods and services at current prices as a percentage of total expenditure

	Wilson 1964–70	Heath 1970–74	Wilson–Callaghan 1974–79	Thatcher 1979–81
Defence	30	26	23	23
Health	20	20	22	23
Education	19	20	21	20
Other	31	34	34	34
	100	100	100	100

SOURCE: *National Income and Expenditure*, successive issues.

that expenditures on health and education are determined by social and demographic factors and that such marginal changes in these expenditure shares that have occurred between governments have been relatively free of ideological overtones.

There is much more evidence that the government has, to an extent, used its capital expenditures as an instrument of policy. This usage shows up first of all in variations in the level of public investment relative to GDP (Table 2.3). A casual inspection of Table 2.3 shows some counter-cyclical pattern to general government investment so that it moves in a direction opposite to that of private investment. No inter-party differences in preference for public investment emerges from the figures. The halcyon days of social capital formation appeared to be the years of Wilson and Heath and under the most recent Labour and Conservative governments public investment (as a proportion of GDP) has gone into decline. This proposition can be examined more closely by looking at the growth of public-investment in volume terms, under the different governments of 1964–81. Table 2.4 illustrates very dramatically the cuts in social capital formation that have occurred since 1974.

In many respects social capital is a very tempting target for governments concerned with reducing public expenditure as the Labour government of 1974–79 was, and the present Conservative government continues to be. In the first place there is no obvious reduction in level of services provided to the public through cuts in capital expenditure and in the second place, due to the practice of contracting out work to private operators, there is a minimal loss of public sector employment. An interesting feature of the Labour administration's cuts is that investment in dwellings got off relatively lightly whereas under the present Conservative government, investment in dwellings had come in

TABLE 2.3 Public and private investment as a percentage of GDP

	Year	General government investment	Public corporations investment	Private investment
	1964	4.8	4.1	11.8
	1965	4.8	4.1	11.9
Wilson	1966	5.1	4.4	11.4
	1967	5.6	4.8	11.1
	1968	5.8	4.3	11.7
	1969	5.7	3.8	12.2
	1970	5.6	3.9	12.3
Heath	1971	5.2	3.8	12.3
	1972	4.9	3.2	12.8
	1973	5.7	3.2	13.2
	1974	5.9	3.8	13.0
	1975	5.3	4.2	12.3
Wilson/Callaghan	1976	4.9	4.2	12.1
	1977	3.8	3.8	12.8
	1978	3.2	3.4	13.9
	1979	3.1	3.4	14.0
Thatcher	1980	2.8	3.5	14.0
	1981	2.2	3.3	13.2

SOURCE: *Economic Trends Annual Supplement* 1983.

TABLE 2.4 Growth in the volume of general government investment. Percentage change over sub-periods

	Wilson 1964–70	Heath 1970–74	Wilson–Callaghan 1974–79	Thatcher 1979–81
General government investment	30.2	5.8	−35.0	−37.0
of which:				
Dwellings	17.0	−10.0	−4.0	−43.0
Other new building	40.6	11.5	−52.2	−40.0
Plant and machinery	42.0	22.2	−17.5	−4.8
Vehicles	47.8	12.2	0	−13.3
Growth in GDP	13.6	11.8	7.7	−4.3

SOURCE: *National Income and Expenditure*, successive issues.

for the heaviest punishment. It is clear that the construction of public sector dwelling is very much determined by ideological forces rather than by re-election or economic considerations, since the early Wilson government expanded dwellings *despite* a popularity and balance of payments crisis, and the Heath government cut expenditures on dwellings *despite* a fall in popularity due to rising unemployment. However, we have the additional reason that the greater provision of public housing in meeting housing needs promotes the electoral chances of the Labour party, and the spread of owner occupation benefits the Conservative party.

Grants and subsidies by the government however showed an increase (as a percentage of GDP) over the period 1964–81. This increase can be traced to reasons of social and economic policy. Social security benefits have been a method of redistributing income while subsidies combine the further use of combating inflation. Variations in the real value of the weekly rate of the principal National Insurance benefits are shown in Table 2.5.

If any pattern can be discerned in the numbers of Table 2.5 it is that both the Labour governments that succeeded Conservative administrations began by disbursing large increases in the real value of benefits. Thereafter they allowed the real value to decline, but never for more than a year, before resuming a mere modest growth. The largest step increase in the standards of living of those on social security occurred with the advent of the first Wilson government when the real value of unemployment and sickness benefits, widows' pensions and retirement pensions rose by over 13 per cent. Subsequently however the real value of benefits was allowed to decline and in November 1969 unemployment benefits stood at the rates prevailing (in constant prices) two years earlier while the retirement pension actually was lower than the October 1967 rate. The Heath government saw modest rises in the value of benefits and these benefits were magnified by the incoming Labour government which awarded real increases of 6 per cent to the unemployed and almost 17 per cent to the retired. Thereafter the pattern of the Wilson government of 1965 was repeated with the real value of benefits being allowed to fall sharply before resuming a moderate growth. Under the Thatcher government the real value of unemployment benefits was allowed to fall for two successive years so that an unemployed man enjoyed a lower level of benefits in November 1981 then he would have over a decade earlier.

TABLE 2.5 Weekly rate of the principal National Insurance benefits (1975 prices)

		Unemployment[1] benefit	Retirement[2] pensions	Family[3] allowances	Sickness benefit	Widow's pension
	March 1964	8.31	13.76	0.99	8.31	8.31
	January 1965	9.43	15.63	0.94	9.43	9.43
	October 1967	9.65	16.11	0.86	9.65	9.65
Wilson	April 1968	9.30	15.60	1.55	9.30	9.30
	October 1968	9.15	15.30	1.83	9.15	9.15
	November 1969	9.67	16.07	1.74	9.67	9.67
	September 1971	9.98	16.49	1.49	9.98	9.98
Heath	October 1972	10.31	17.00	1.37	10.31	10.31
	October 1973	10.17	17.43	1.24	10.17	10.72
	July 1974	10.79	20.36	1.13	10.79	12.54
	April 1975	9.88	18.57	1.51	9.88	11.7
Wilson/Callaghan	November 1975	10.37	19.76	1.40	10.37	12.43
	November 1976	10.48	19.38	1.22	10.48	12.44
	November 1977	10.58	19.59	1.80	10.58	12.58
	November 1978	10.48	20.39	3.99	10.48	12.97
	November 1979	10.50	21.04	4.54	10.50	13.22
Thatcher	November 1980	10.16	21.52	4.68	10.16	13.36
	November 1981	9.89	21.04	4.62	9.89	13.02

1 Men, single women and widows.
2 Married couple; deflated by pensioners index, all other items deflated by retail price index.
SOURCE: *Economic Trends Annual Supplement*, 1983.
3 Two children.
SOURCE: *Annual Abstract of Statistics*, successive issues.

7. ECONOMIC POLICY IN BRITAIN: GOVERNMENT REVENUES

The development of British economic policy with respect to the government's control of its revenues can be analysed in terms of revenues from direct taxation and revenues from indirect taxation. Direct taxation can be further considered in terms of personal taxation and company taxation.

As regards personal taxation there is the possibility of genuine ideological differences between the Labour and Conservative parties. The heart of this difference would appear to lie in disagreements about the disincentive effects of higher tax rates. Thus, while on the one hand, an increase in the marginal rate of income tax may reduce incentives to work, on the other hand the consequent increase in average rates may induce people to work more in order to maintain a given post-tax income. Price (1978) notes that there was a marked difference in income tax policy in the Labour years of 1964–70 and the years before and after. In general, Conservative policy was characterised by reductions in income tax rates and higher tax thresholds while the Labour policy of a buoyant public sector required increases in the standard rate of income tax and an erosion of the real value of allowances. These details are set out in Table 2.6.

Under the Wilson (1964–70) government, the real value of tax allowances declined steadily for the first four years. Accompanying this were a rise in the basic rate of tax in the 1965 budget and two successive rises in the highest rate of tax in the 1965 and 1966 budgets. However the pre-election budget of 1970 saw a 7 per cent rise in the real value of allowances over the 1969 budget levels. The Heath government began in the 1971 budget by increasing the real value of allowances, cutting the basic and lowest rates of income tax by 1.94 percentage points and by cutting the highest rate of income tax by almost 16 percentage points. Although the rates of income tax were left unchanged, substantial increases in the level of allowances were awarded in the reflationary budget of 1972. The Wilson–Callaghan government of 1974–79 continued the Labour tradition of eroding the real value of allowances (between the 1974 and 1978 budgets this fell by 31 per cent) and raising tax rates, although the pre-election budget contained the substantial concession of a 25 per cent rate of tax for lower income bands. Mrs Thatcher's government lowered the basic rate, increased the rate of tax on lower incomes and substantially reduced the rates on high incomes. Since in the Conservative philosophy there is an inverse relation

TABLE 2.6 *The real value of allowances and statutory rates of tax*

		£ (1975 prices) Threshold	Personal taxes			Company taxes		Indirect taxes
			% lowest rate	% basic rate	% highest rate	% On retentions	% On distributions	% Purchase tax/VAT
	1964–65	1862	15.60	30.14	88.75		56.25	10–25
	1965–66	1836	15.60	32.08	91.25	40.00	64.75	10–25
	1966–67	1767	15.60	32.08	96.25	40.00	64.75	11–27.5
	1967–68	1725	15.60	32.08	91.25	42.50	66.22	11–27.5
Wilson	1968–69	1647	15.60	32.08	91.25	45.00	67.69	12.5–50
	1969–70	1650	23.33	32.08	91.25	42.50	66.22	13.75–55
	1970–71	1767	32.08	32.08	91.25	40.00	64.75	13.75–55
	1971–72	1789	30.14	30.14	75.44	40.00	63.25	11.25–45
Heath	1972–73	1940	30.14	30.14	75.44	40.00	63.25	11.25–75
	1973–74	1794	30.00	30.00	75.00	52.00		10
	1974–75	1758	33.00	33.00	83.00	52.00		10
	1975–76	1505	35.00	35.00	83.00	52.00		8
Wilson–Callaghan	1976–77	1506	35.00	35.00	83.00	52.00		8
	1977–78	1381	34.00	34.00	83.00	52.00		8
	1978–79	1234	25.00	33.00	83.00	52.00		8
	1979–80	1094	25.00	30.00	60.00	52.00		15
Thatcher	1980–81	1097	30.00	30.00	60.00	52.00		15
	1981–82	980	30.00	30.00	60.00	52.00		15
	1982–83	1027	30.00	30.00	60.00	52.00		15

SOURCE: Price (1978) and *Annual Abstract of Statistics*, 1983.

between tax rates and work incentives, this might mean that, in the Conservative view, the importance of work incentives was confined to people in the higher income brackets and the benefits accruing to such persons was, to an extent, paid for by imposing higher tax rates on lower incomes and by allowing the real value of allowances to decline considerably. Indeed, in the 1981–82 financial year, the real value of allowances stood at their lowest value for the period 1963–83. It could be argued that, from a political point of view, the problem is one of visibility. The hand that takes away by cutting the real value of allowances operates stealthily whereas the hand that gives by cutting rates of income tax is clearly visible to a grateful public.

The influence of political ideology is also apparent in the sphere of company taxation, though perhaps this influence is not so obvious as it is with regard to personal taxation. Up to the budget of 1958 profits retained by companies were taxed at a lower rate than profits distributed to shareholders. This discrimination in favour of retained profits was ended in the 1958 budget when a single tax on profits was introduced, and this reform followed from the majority recommendation of the Royal Commission on Taxation of Profits and Income.

The Wilson government of 1965 introduced changes which were ideologically consistent with the Labour government's socialist position. The old system of discriminating against distributed profits was revived although under a different guise. There was now to be a uniform rate of Corporation Tax which applied to all company profits, whether distributed or not. However dividends, having already been taxed as a part of total company profits, were to be taxed again at the standard rate of income tax with companies responsible for deducting this at source. At the same time both long-term (on assets held for more than a year) and short-term capital gains were made subject to a capital gains tax of 30 per cent. The Labour reforms therefore hurt the 'rentier' class in two ways – through the system of double taxation of dividends, and through the taxation of long and short term capital gains.

The Conservative government of 1970 announced, on its return, that it would end discrimination against distributions, though the system for doing so was introduced, after considerable debate and discussion, in 1973. Under the new system of Advance Corporation Tax (ACT), companies make an advance payment, at the standard rate of income tax, on their distribution of dividends. This advance payment was to be essentially an income tax payment by companies on behalf of their shareholders for the Corporation Tax paid in advance counted against the companies' eventual Corporation Tax liabilities. These reforms of

1973 achieved two objectives. Firstly, the separation of the company and the personal tax systems, initiated by the 1965 budget, was confirmed. Secondly, because companies could set the advance Corporation Tax against their mainstream tax liabilities, the discrimination between distributed and undistributed profits was removed.

The preceding paragraphs described the different attitudes (and consequently the different legislation) of the Labour and Conservative governments to company taxation. Mayer (1982), in examining how the average corporate tax rate (Corporation Tax liabilities divided by historic cost accounting profits) have varied for a sample of 276 firms over the period 1965-76, finds that they fall from a peak of 40 per cent in 1965 (start of the Wilson government) to around zero per cent in 1974 (end of the Heath government). Since these changes may be due to either changes in the tax system and its associated rates and reliefs or to the performance of the companies in the sample, he decomposes the changes in the average rate into changes due to each of these factors. Mayer's conclusion is that the dramatic falls in the average Corporation Tax rate paid by his sample of forms can be traced to the set of reliefs and incentives introduced between 1971 and 1974 by the Heath government. The rise in investment allowances in 1971 and 1972, the introduction of stock relief and the small companies rates in 1973 and the Advance Corporation Tax system of the same year meant that the average rate of Corporation Tax fell from just under 40 per cent in 1970 to about zero in 1974.

What emerges from the above discussion is therefore a clear difference in attitudes of Labour and Conservative administrations towards company taxation. Conservative policy has been to minimise the tax liabilities of companies – particularly smaller businesses – whereas Labour policy has been to ensure that companies made a positive contribution to government revenues. In terms of appealing to interest groups, this means that the Conservatives (Labour) give rather more (less) weight to business corporations and the rentier class.

Turning to the question of indirect tax rates, prior to the introduction of Value Added Tax (VAT in 1973, there existed a number of purchase tax rates and Table 2.6 shows the lower and upper limits of these rates. As Price (1978) notes that though purchase tax increases were occasionally used in contractions, its absolute and relative impact on a restricted range of goods was a drawback recognised by all Chancellors; thus 'in Conservative periods this acted as an incentive to reduce and standardise rates and in Labour periods as a disincentive against increases'. The Wilson government introduced, in its 1966 budget, the Selective Employment Tax, levied as a flat-rate surcharge on employers' National Insurance contributions. This tax was to be refunded to all industries except services and construction, the logic being to transfer manpower from the service industries into manufacturing. This tax was abolished by the Conservative government (in two steps, in 1971–72 and 1973–74) as a part of a wider programme to introduce VAT. In 1973–74, VAT, at a rate of 10 per cent was introduced with a broader and more uniform tax base than the earlier purchase taxes which were more selective in their impact. The rate on VAT was reduced by the Labour government from 10 per cent to 8 per cent thus demonstrating a Labour party preference for raising revenues from direct rather than indirect taxation. A preference in precisely the opposite direction was revealed by the Conservative government of 1979 who raised the rate on VAT from 8 per cent to 15 per cent. This may be interpreted as the Labour party representing the interests of the unemployed and lower income groups in society, since these groups typically consume a much greater proportion of their income than other groups in society.

8. CONCLUSIONS

This chapter has attempted to examine, in the British context, the interaction between the government's economic performance and its political popularity. It was pointed out that studies of the effect of performance on popularity were limited by the two assumptions that the reactions of voters did not change over time and that voters were alike in the sense of having identical reactions to changes in the economic environment. Many reasons can be found for such self-imposed constraints and among them must surely be the fact that modern economics is, and has been for some time, a curiously ahistorical and impersonal subject which does not cast its analysis within the framework of social history.

Studies of the effect of popularity on policy also tell a similar story. Modern theories of the behaviour of governments, by ignoring the role of conflict (emphasised strongly by Marx and Kalecki) have not advanced our understanding in this area. Reasons for this lack of progress are not hard to find. Theories constrained by the principle of optimising behaviour have been forced to examine normative rather than positive questions. Theories that have not employed the optimising principle, have been constrained by the use of econometric methodology for uncovering their evidence. This methodology has forced them to examine the question of government behaviour in a broad, aggregative, macro-economic framework which is quite misleading, firstly because it ascribes to government the quality of homogeneity which it does not possess, secondly because it ascribes to government policy instruments that it does not control, and finally and most importantly, because the most interesting questions relating to government behaviour are to be answered at a micro- rather than a macro-economic level.

REFERENCES

Arcelus, F. and A. H. Meltzer, 'The effects of aggregate economic variables on congressional elections', *American Political Science Review*, vol. 69 (1975), pp. 1232–40.
Brittan, S., *Steering the Economy* (London: Secker and Warburg, 1969).
Butler, D. and D. Stokes, *Political Change in Britain* (London: Macmillan, 1974).
Converse, P. E. 'The Shifting Role of Class in Political Attitudes and Behaviour', in E. E. Maccoby, T. M. Newcomb and E. L. Hartley (eds), *Readings in Social Psychology* (London: Methuen, 1958).
Daniel, W. W., *A National Survey of the Unemployed* (London: Political and Economic Planning Broadsheet, 1974).
Daniel, W. W., *The PEP Survey on Inflation* (London: Political and Economic Planning Broadsheet, 1975).
Daniel, W. W., *The Nature of the Current Unemployment* (London: British-North American Research Association (Occasional Paper 6), 1981).
Downs, A., *An Economic Theory of Democracy* (New York: Harper and Row, 1957).
Frey, B. S., 'Politico-economic models and cycles', *Journal of Public Economics*, vol. 9 (1978a). pp. 203–20.
Frey, B. S., *Modern Political Economy* (Oxford: Martin Robertson, 1978b.
Frey, B. S. and F. Schneider, 'A politico-economic model of the United Kingdom', *Economic Journal*, vol. 88 (1978), pp. 243–53.
Goodhart, C. A. E. and R. J. Bhansali, 'Political Economy', *Political Studies*, vol. 18 (1970), pp. 43–106.
Hibbs, D. A., *Economic Interests and the Politics of Macroeconomic Policy* (Cambridge, Mass: MIT Center for International Studies, 1976).
Hibbs, D. A., 'Economic outcomes and political support for British governments among occupational classes: a dynamic analysis', *The American Political Science Review*, vol. 76 (1982), pp. 259–79.
Kaldor, N., 'Conflicts in national economic objectives', *Economic Journal*, vol. 81 (1971), pp. 1–16.
Kalecki, M., 'Political aspects of full employment', *Political Quarterly*, October/December (1943), pp. 322–31. Also reprinted in *Essays on the*

Dynamics of the Capitalist Economy, 1933–1970 (Cambridge: Cambridge University Press).
Mackay, D. I. and G. Reid, 'Redundance, Unemployment and Manpower Policy', *Economic Journal*, vol. 82 (1972), pp. 1256–72.
Marx, K., *Capital*, Volumes I, II, III (New York: International Publishers, 1967).
Mayer, C., 'The structure of corporation tax in the UK', *Fiscal Studies*, vol. 3 (1982), pp. 121–41.
Miller, W. L. and M. Mackie, 'The electoral cycle and the asymmetry of government and opposition popularity: an alternative model of the relationship between economic conditions and political popularity', *Political Studies*, vol. 21 (1973), pp. 263–79.
Nordhaus, W. D., 'The political business cycle', *Review of Economic Studies*, vol. 42 (1975), pp. 169–90.
Piachaud, D., 'Inflation and income distribution', in J. H. Goldthorpe and F. Hirsch (eds), *The Political Economy of Inflation* (Cambridge, Mass: Harvard University Press, 1978).
Pissarides, C. A., 'British government popularity and economic performance', *Economic Journal*, vol. 90 (1980), pp. 569–81.
Price, R. W. R., 'Budgetary policy', in F. T. Blackaby (ed.), *British Economic Policy 1960–74* (Cambridge University Press, 1978).
Royal Commission on the Distribution of Income and Wealth, *The Causes of Poverty* (London. HMSO, 1978).
Stigler, G. J., 'General economic conditions and national elections', *The American Economic Review*, vol. 63 (1973), pp. 160–7. (See also subsequent discussion by MacCracken, Okin and others.)
Tinbergen, J., *On the Theory of Economic Policy* (Amsterdam: North-Holland, 1952).

3 The Prisoners' Dilemma and Coase's Theorem: A Case for Democracy in Less Developed Countries?

MICHAEL LIPTON

I

There are many situations in a society, of the following type. A freely usable common resource, such as grazing land, exists. Each private herd-owner, if motivated only by short-term net income, will increase it by placing more beasts on this common resource, until the extra private return to him (MPR minus MPC) from his herd expansion declines to zero. But the expansion of grazing by *each* herd-owner reduces the available pastures for *all* graziers, and thus the condition of their herds. Soon, 'the tragedy of the commons' is upon them: each herder, in rationally expanding his private claim on grazing, may reduce the total value of other people's animals much more than he increases the value of his own.

There are two extreme accounts, parables really, of how this situation might be resolved: Coase's Theorem and Prisoners' Dilemma (PD). According to Coase's Theorem – on one set of apparently plausible assumptions – all herders will transact contracts that maximise the benefits of grazing to them all, taken together. A corollary to Coase's Theorem is that the rules, by which any gainer from extra grazing must (or need not) compensate losers with existing herds whose feed is reduced by his extra beasts, will not affect that optimal outcome, which I call Coase's Outcome (CO).

According to the standard exposition of PD – on another set of apparently plausible assumptions – each herder will decide on his grazing level in his own short-term self-interest. He will thus increase his own herd, on common land, as long as private gain exceeds private cost – because self-restraint would leave him worse off than greed, whether the other graziers show self-restraint or not. So all overgraze greedily, and all lose.

PD and CO are parables (ideal types, extreme cases). A society where all relations followed the non-cooperative PD pattern could not be governed; except to 'improve' distribution, a purely CO society would not need to be governed.[1] In practice, because very many cases lie between PD and CO, a major task of government is to edge them from the former towards the latter.

Oddly, the two approaches – CO and PD – are analysed in separate literatures, with little mutual awareness. Since a major task of governments is to convert PDs into COs, this is unfortunate. It is especially unfortunate in less-developed countries (LDCs). There, both existing circumstances and patterns of change tend systematically to convert COs into PDs, cooperative optimising into non-cooperative externalising, and hence to set tasks for government that require analysis of PD and CO together.

This Third World drift towards PD non-cooperative outcomes occurs for several reasons. The first is *population growth*, which increases the number of transactors who – if a CO is to be stable – have to agree and then trust each other (or be made) to stick to the agreement; genuine PDs are much commoner,[2] and COs much less common,[3] in many-person than in few-person contests. The second is *developmental change*, which reduces the similarity of circumstances in which an individual makes successive decisions, and therefore reduces the number of times that essentially similar PD games are replayed by the same participants; and repeated PD games – which are really pseudo-PDs because the non-cooperative solution is not strictly dominant (see note 2) – are likelier to home in on COs than are true PDs (viz. distinct single games). The third reason is *risk aversion*. Can I be sure that CO strategies will be adhered to by others as promised, or made binding on them? If I am unsure, my risk-aversion will incline me towards a choice that – if they are not – keeps my loss down. And the great poverty and high risk of developing rural areas increases risk aversion there.

The fourth reason why poor but growing rural areas increasingly feature non-cooperative PD rather than CO outcomes is the most important for the subject of these sessions, Economics and Democracy. Development, by integrating small societies into larger and less personalised markets, involves a *transition of trust*.[4] Either a chiefly hierarchy, or a clan-like view of the common good, could in a small localised society restrain, towards a total use reflecting that society's optimum, each individual's use of common resources – grazing land; fishing rights; irrigation water; the confidence of a credit cooperative; even the 'maintained' price of an item with a gluttable nearby market.[5] As the nexus of government widens – as cities or 'capital' or transport integrate and strengthen the State – old chiefly authorities and clan-like decisions are challenged by central governments and codified laws. Each grazier or irrigator feels less bound than before to obey chief or clan, and more tempted to seek short-run self-interest out of fear that neighbours too will disobey. Yet the new authority has not yet acquired the information, the power to reward or penalise, or the powers of moral suasion, permitting it to replace the old authority's lost powers: to guarantee, by force or by appeal to a sense of moral community,[6] that all (or sufficient[7]) graziers or irrigators avoid short-run self-interest and home in on COs rather than PDs.

Population growth, developmental change, high risk-aversion, transition of trust: all hit today's often still risk-averse developing rural societies together. In Sri Lanka, the Kandyan kings had the power to enforce Draconian laws against any 'head-ender' (farmer near the irrigation source) who did not restrain his use of irrigation water. Almost all head-enders, therefore, did exercise restraint; and total output, from head and tail users in both crop seasons, benefited as a consequence. Today – with more irrigators (due to *population growth*), competing for water in sequences of increasingly unfamiliar situations (due to *developmental change*) – hegemony has often been replaced by weak local officialdom (*transition of trust*); and both this and the stresses of change increase the risk of non-delivery of water, and hence marginal *risk-aversion*. Increasingly, each head-ender cuts sluices in the main season, to assure himself of ample water; thus head-enders taken together produce less in the subsequent second season, because they used up too much irrigation water in the main season; and all head and tail users taken together produce less in each season than would be the case if each head-ender restricted water use in the main season. What can restore trust; or render change manageable; or reduce (or compensate for) risk aversion; or possibly internalise the will to regulate population growth?

The main answer lies in *side payments*; and they are feasible only if we reconsider the view, central to Coase's Theorem, that the rules of compensation are irrelevant to the efficiency of an outcome. Consider Pigou's case of a smoky factory setting up near a laundry. For Coase, the existence and output of the two activities is not affected by the *attribution of benefit* through a rule of side-payments (compensation). But COs *do* depend on existence and enforcement of *some* rule. Suppose there are three options: factory plus laundry (FL), laundry alone (L) or factory alone (F). If net output is more from FL than from either F or L, then F and L negotiate, and (according to the compensation rules) F pays L not to object, or L pays F to control smoke or to restrain output. Agreements to make side payments, and justified trust that such agreements will be adhered to, are central to a society's chances of turning PDs into COs.

Such agreement and trust, however, are usually dependent on a sense that side payments, outcomes, and resulting income-distributions are just. This is why a distinction between efficiency (unaffected by compensation rules) and equity (affected) is too sharp. Unless there is an all-powerful autocrat, rules perceived as very inequitable will be widely broken; promised side payments will not be made; later, confidence in them will erode; COs will give way to PDs; and efficiency too will suffer. Coase is right that efficiency is not affected by society's decision to make this or that *choice among* rules about side payments (e.g. compensation rules). But efficiency does depend on general trust in *adherence to* whichever rule about side payments has been chosen. Laundry must *know* that Factory, if bribed, will (as promised) either operate smokily only while L is not drying clothes or pay L for the extra cleaning costs; or else, under a different compensation rule, F must *know* that L, if bribed, will (as promised) not exercise its rights to prevent smoky operation, or will pay F to the extent that it does. As Coase states, whichever rule prevails, costless information and negotiation should permit optimisation of volume and composition of GNP; the rule affects 'only' its distribution among persons[8] (F, L; and users of F and L if cost changes are partly or wholly passed on as price changes). But that *some* law prevails is essential for such optimising to work. It depends on trust. That, in turn, except in Pharaonic societies, depends on perceived equity.

As the example of 'tragedy of the commons' (Section V) makes clear, equity implies not only fair application of laws, but construction of laws so that, to the extent possible, reasonable expectations are not subsequently invalidated by such laws. 'Expectation' is a concept involving time. If L was there first, and had no reason to expect F to arrive later, equity demands *ceteris aribus* laws that F compensates L for smoke, not that L bribe F to avoid smoke. If F was there first, operating in a particular way, L cannot arrive long afterwards and expect smoke compensation. Unless such equity prevails, it is unlikely that both L and F will be prepared to settle by negotiation. We shall move from side-payments to conflicts, from CO to PD.

How does this relate to our theme of *Economics and Democracy*?

(a) Social efficiency requires a tendency to home in on outcomes like COs, not on outcomes like non-cooperative 'solutions' to PDs.
(b) This tendency requires that the parties generally trust in adherence to, for example, laws on side payments.
(c) This requires a sense that such laws are equitable.
(d) It may well be that 'democracy' helps to create that sense.

The link is through the *operation* of the law. Consider the expression, 'The law is no respecter of persons'. In traditional societies, this meant: 'Laws are not bent to help the rich and powerful'. The protestation had to be made exactly because laws were, in reality, often so bent. But such bending will not secure general assent to laws about side payments that move society from PD to CO solutions. Nowadays, in the rich world, the expression 'The law is no respecter of persons' means, instead, 'Laws are not bent to help the poor and weak – to temper the wind to the shorn lamb; hard cases make bad law'. This protestation, too, arises because laws do tend to be bent: in rich developed democracies, to help the weak. The logic is then as follows. Economic efficiency requires moves from PD-like to CO-like solutions. Such moves require stability of trust in general adherence to agreements and procedures about side payments. This trust usually requires a widespread sense that laws are equitable and hence should be observed. Where most people are poor, that means that laws should move from 'respecting' (i.e. making concessions, if any, to) rich minorities to respecting poor majorities.[9] Democracy is *one* way to speed up that transition in the Third World, where majorities are poor (and those whom laws 'respect' are not).

This paper proceeds as follows. Section II considers the scope and limits of Coase's theorem. Section III looks at some of the factors impeding COs in Third World environments. Section IV discusses the scope and limits of PD. Section V considers some celebrated examples of non-cooperative PD-like outcomes in the Third World, in the light of factors that might appear to induce COs – the 'tragedy of the commons' in some detail, several others far more briefly – and enquires what combinations of rules, attitudes (e.g. moderate altruism), procedures (e.g. 'participation'), and above all laws about side payments, might shift these environments from PD to CO outcomes. Section VI briefly asks what role democracy has in encouraging or discouraging enforcement, or voluntary acceptance, of such remedies.

II

In his celebrated paper, Coase presented an argument, seemingly watertight, that if behaviour is rational and transaction-cost negligible (a) external costs and benefits do not affect resource allocations, (b) neither do judicial decisions (or government actions), assigning liability for external costs – or reward for external benefits – as between the causes of the externality and the gainer or loser from it. The argument is most simply put by Reder (1982, p. 22): if 'everyone is optimising, and in the absence of transaction cost, failure of' a person or firm injured by an externality to pay 'his injurers to desist implie[s] that the marginal cost, to the injurer, or desisting' exceeds 'the marginal benefit (of non-injury) to the injured'.[10]

In other words, if commitment of resources to make [a product plus its negative externality] yields a benefit/cost ratio above that earned in the next-best use of resources, there are four Coasean paths to allocative optimality.

(1) It may pay the direct gainer to bribe the direct losers to permit production up to optimal level – then, the factory owner compensates the farmers for smoke damage (or, if cheaper, pays to control his smoke) and still makes adequate profit.
(2) It may pay the direct loser to bribe the gainer – then, the farmers pay the factory owner to install smoke-control devices (or, if cheaper, the farmers adopt smoke-resistant grain varieties).
(3) If neither of these pays, so that some farmers go out of business because neither can be agreed upon, it is by definition because the extra factory outputs exceeds in value the lost farm output.
(4) If there are indirect losers – if third parties find the long-run effects of this changed output-mix sufficiently damaging – it will pay them to 'bribe' farmers to grow more, and/or the factory to produce less and/or to install smoke-control devices. Coase, in essence, argues that the four paths to optimality are the *only* ways an economy, with zero transactions costs (and no Bickerdike effect – see note 10), can respond to externalities.

The implication goes far beyond external costs. 'If one assumes rationality, no transaction costs, and no legal impediments to bargaining, *all* misallocations of resources would be fully cured in the market by bargains', because misallocations exist if and only if there exists 'a possible reallocation in which all those who would lose from [it] could be fully compensated by' gainers, leaving nobody worse off and somebody better off (Calabresi, p. 68). Consumers would bribe monopolists to produce at the minimum of their average cost curves; pedestrians would pay drivers to minimise joint costs from potential accidents; and anti-trust laws and road-safety laws would be as superfluous as State or judicial action to compensate the victims of factory-smoke or Agent Orange. Crucially, if only prisoners could negotiate and enforce agreements, all PDs would home in on the outcome that maximised *joint* welfare; no prisoner would confess.

Something has gone wrong somewhere. Such expressions as 'rationality' (Calabresi) or 'everyone is optimising' (Reder); such conditions as 'zero transaction costs'; such assumptions as that the static impact on resource allocation can be separated from the impact on income distribution: these carry unsustainably heavy weight. Many people conclude, from Coase's Law, that on *perfectly reasonable* assumptions – rational behaviour, low-cost transactions, entry into these in order to secure one's potential gains – externalities, and hence *assignment of responsibility for their costs*, simply *don't matter*. All that can really be concluded is that on *extreme* assumptions – a world of pure risk-neutral profit maximisers, with perfect knowledge of guaranteed outcomes, operating in a legal context that both lays down and *enforces precise and predictable assignments* of liability for externalities – externalities don't affect *resource allocation* if relative output prices are independent of income distribution, i.e. in small open economies with no transport costs.

III

Nothing in Coase's paper goes beyond the latter claim. Both he and Calabresi carefully deny that 'Coase's Law' provides any presumption against Government action to assign liability for externalities – or to legislate against activities causing them, if establishment of who is liable, or of what he owes to whom, is too costly. But many students of economics seem to grossly over-interpret Coase. In particular, the rural Third World is a world of externalities, with few Coasean solutions

– despite perfectly rational (though not at all profit-maximising) behaviour and quite well-functioning markets. This is due to uncertain and shifting (and politicised) assignments of responsibility for external costs; heavy interdependence of income distribution and resource allocation; and therefore large, but not reliably assignable or readily negotiable, social costs due to externalities.

In other words, it is probable that there exist certain features of Third World life that – while in no way refuting Coase's logic – violate the extreme assumptions needed for that logic to imply optimal results despite unregulated externalities.

(1) In LDCs, poor people find risk-aversion necessary for survival. So not all the parties, supposed to contract in a profit-maximising manner in order to assume optimal resource use despite externalities, would be 'rational' (let alone 'optimising') if they did so. Moreover, the distance between reasonable and profit-seeking behaviour varies according to the way in which the costs of the externality are initially assigned.

(2) In LDCs, when the 'transition of trust' is combined with rapid change, rules of assignment are shifting and uncertain. On Coase's assumptions, *any one* certain assignment of liability for external costs (or reward for external benefits) is as sure to produce optimal resource allocation (by profit-maximisers) as *any other*. But a solution where there is *no* certain assignment – the typical LDC situation – is worse than *any particular* assignment by law, claim, or market.

(3) In particular, extra-economic power can lead one party to disregard, without penalty, promises to abide by a socially optimal solution. Suppose I agree to adopt, in a 2-person variable-sum game, the strategy 1, maximising *joint* net income if you adopt 1, and to make side payments reflecting the value to me of your not adopting another strategy 2, better for you but worse for me by more (Table 3.1). I may (a) refuse the side payment after the event, or (b) adopt 2, better for me but worse for you by more. Only legal or customary constraint can stop me thus abusing my power. There is a sense in which Coase's theorem asserts that variable-sum games always settle upon strategy sets that maximise total returns to all participants together. Market-power, coalitions, and mistrust prevent this (see Section V).

(4) The rate of time-preferences (as of risk-aversion), and access to credit-markets to 'defray' time-preference, varies hugely in LDCs

TABLE 3.1 *Cheating or sanctions?*

Your strategies

	1.	2.
My strategies 1	$5_I, 2_U$	$-1_I, 6_U$
2	$8_I, -5_U$	$-5_I, -7_U$

between poor and non-poor agents. Therefore the pattern of resource allocation is greatly affected according to whether liability for 'costs now and returns later' rests with rich or poor agents.

(5) Not only do individual firms or consumers, by virtue of different time-preference or risk-aversion, as optimisers allocate resources differently *ceteris paribus*. 'Different systems' (e.g. sharecropping v owner-occupancy; self-financing of investment v moneylender-saving-dissaving networks) also do so. Individualist comparative status often overlook this.[11] Transitional LDCs feature prolonged co-existence of 'different systems'. If the impact of alternative assignments of external-cost liability shifts output or power between, say, sharecropping and owner-occupant *villages*, such alternatives will produce different resource allocations.

(6) Transaction costs are increased by population growth. A population of n has $\frac{1}{2}[n(n-1)]$ potential dyadic relations to worry about.

Before going into the examples, I'd like to stress that they are not in the usual sense examples of 'market failure'. People and firms know their options fairly well, and in transacting they each choose options such as to best fulfil their goals. Studies of one after another LDC market – credit, labour, sale of farm products – reveal few signs of 'market failure'.[12] What they reveal is far worse. Market *success* produces slow growth, and limits the benefits of such growth largely to better-off, less risk-averse, less present-time-preferring transactors. Such transactors tend to be from bigger, more capital- (and import-) intensive firms, who use their power to persuade State agents to set prices, roads, market conditions, research priorities, etc. in ways that favour size and capital-intensity. Because LDCs are relatively short of savings and foreign exchange, but have (increasingly) ample spare labour, this is bad for efficient growth, as well as for the share of the poor in what growth does exist. Ultimately the conflict is not between neo-classical or Coasean perceptions of efficiency, and radical perceptions of equity. It is between *both* and the realities of State power, captured to entrench economic rent. Whether it is private or State power makes a difference, but not to that fact.

IV

In the conventional PD, two prisoners, *I* and *II*, known to have committed a minor crime together, are separately interrogated about a suspected serious joint crime. If both confess to it, both get a longish sentence. If both hold out, both get a short sentence for the minor crime. If only one confesses, he goes free, and the hold-out gets a very long sentence. If we enter 'years in prison', *I*'s first and *II*'s second, as minuses (to reflect disutilities, or income compensation required to avoid an outcome) in each box, the table looks like this:[13]

TABLE 3.2 *Classic PD*

		II's strategies	
		1. Confess	2. Hold out
*I*s strategies	1 Confess	−10, −10	0, −12
	2 Hold out	−12, 0	−2, −2

I and *II* cannot communicate, and know nothing about each other's likely choices, though both know the above table. *I* may well reason: 'Given *II*'s decision, how do I do best? Suppose *II* confesses; I then do better by confessing, because 10 years in jail are better than 12. Or suppose *II* holds out; still I do better by confessing, because freedom is better than two years in jail. So I confess, as whatever *II* does that is my better strategy.' *II* may well reason identically, and also confess. Thus *I* and *II* home in on (−10, −10), the non-cooperative PD outcome. The 'society' of *I*-plus-*II* gets *minus twenty*. Could they not instead hold out – implicitly cooperate – and get *minus four*, the CO?

The analogy is with two private herd-owners grazing common land, or two crop-farmers drawing on common water, each deciding whether to maximise resource use now (and, if the other does likewise, leave too little for a good result for either user next season), or to trust the other user to exercise restraint, so that total output is more in both seasons combined. Such two-person analogies – depending as they do on instantaneous decision, no mutual knowledge of the other party's likely choice, and no communication – are implausible, but if for *I* we read 'any one herder (or irrigator)' and for *II* 'all other herders (or irrigators)' plausibility returns.[14]

In all PD cases, it is convenient – and makes no difference to the discussion – if the whole table's *absolute* values in the boxes or 'utilities' (the incomes) are linearly transformed by adding or taking away enough to make the smallest number zero. So, in Table 3.2, all are made positive by adding the largest negative number, if any, in the array. We call this 'normalising' the array (see Table 3.5). (In the above table, for instance, each prisoner could be assumed to have secured from the major joint crime a cache of gold, which neither would gain by confessing, and which is safe for recovery and use after release, and worth exactly as much to him as 12 years' jail.[15]) Also, the exact *relative* values in the above table need not hold, and carry certain structural implications – not only symmetry, but also, for example, that *I* and *II* taken together necessarily do better from holding out, than if one confesses and the other holds out (-2 plus -2 exceeds -12 plus 0) – not needed to generate PD, but in fact very important to the prospects for successful institutions to turn non-cooperative PD outcomes into COs. Hence we seek a more general array to reflect, in positive units of income (or welfare or utility) relative to some arbitrary origin or zero, Table 3.3:

TABLE 3.3 *General form of PD*

	II's strategies	
	1 (Confess, graze heavily, take lots of water now ...)	2 (Hold out, graze lightly, take moderate water now ...)
I's strategies 1 Confess, graze heavily, takes lots of water now, don't replay village credit coop, free-ride ...)	Third-best for each	Best for *I*, worst for *II*
2 (Hold out, graze lightly, take moderate water now ...)	Worst for *I*, best for *II*	Second-best for each

The array reflecting the above set of pay-offs is:

TABLE 3.4 *Outcomes of general form of PD: $0<a<b<c$; $0<a_1<b_1<c_1$*

II's strategies

		1	2
I's strategies	1	a, a_1	$c, 0$
	2	$0, c_1$	b, b_1

In Table 3.4, what can be said about the ranking of outcomes to society? Suppose that society is – prior to each 'play' of PD – indifferent to the distribution of potential 'income', 'utility', or 'benefits' between *I* and *II*. Then outcomes are ranked socially in the same order as the box sums $(b+b_1)$, $(a+a_1)$, etc. However, Table 3.5, the normalised form of the classic PD in Table 3.2, is only one possible box-sum ranking. Implied by Table 3.4 – the generalised PD – is only that $(b+b_1)$, which occurs when both *I* and *II* adopt strategy (2), exceeds $(a+a_1)$, which occurs when they both adopt strategy (1). In Table 3.4, unlike Table 3.2, c or c_1 might be so big as to exceed $(b+b_1)$ – one or both prisoners might be offered an enormous reward, as well as freedom, for being the only confessor (but none if his partner in crime confessed too[16]); this produces a structure like Table 3.7. Alternatively – and the alternatives are mutually exclusive – in Table 3.4, unlike Table 3.2, c or c_1 (although bigger than b and b_1 respectively, and *a fortiori* than a and a_1 respectively) might be *smaller* than $(a+a_1)$; this produces a structure like Table 3.6. The three outcomes are shown in normalised form in Tables 3.5–3.7, assuming symmetry still ($a=a_1$, $b=b_1$, $c=c_1$).

TABLE 3.5 *Normalised classic PD (Table 3.2: all entries plus 12)*

II's strategies

		1	2
I's strategies	1	2, 2	12, 0
	2	0, 12	10, 10

TABLE 3.6 *Normalised PD amended: shift from [1, 1] to [1, 2] or [2, 1] socially harmful*

		II's strategies	
		1	2
I's strategies	1	8, 8	12, 0
	2	0, 12	10, 10

TABLE 3.7 *Normalised PD amended: [2, 2]-strategies miss social optimum*

		II's strategies	
		1	2
I's strategies	1	2, 2	25, 0
	2	0, 25	10, 10

Apart from such structural shifts, affecting the desirability for the 'society' of the relative outcomes, even different *absolute* numbers (preserving *ranking* of all numbers) in Table 3.5 would change the answer to a crucial question: how much would people like *I* and *II*, likely to be faced at times with true non-repeatable PDs, be willing to pay for social institutions to ensure an optimal social outcome – in the case of Table 3.5, an outcome where both 'players' adopt the second strategy? (Let us write these *strategies* [2, 2], and (10, 10) for the *entries* there.) We revert to this crucial matter in discussing the shift from 'Phase 3' to 'Phase 4' in the tragedy of the commons (see p.69) and the misincentive argument (p.64); in both cases, asymmetry between *I* and *II* in the above tables – unequal capacity to expand herd or irrigated land size, for example – brings further complications.[17]

The general PD problem is: since in Tables 3.2–3.7 strategy [1] is dominant for each party – that is, it does better for him not only if the other party adopts [2], but also if the other party adopts [1] – how can 'societies' – sets of persons like *I* and *II*, reach the CO, an outcome other than [1, 1],[18] and thus maximise social gain? We look below at several possible answers, each suggesting a distinct way for 'society' to make or encourage a PD-to-CO transition. The first three proposed answers rest entirely on 'improving knowledge' (markets?) and demonstrably do not suffice to resolve PD or achieve CO. The other answers, or *arguments*, involve claims that real-world conflicts of interest, allegedly analogous to Table 3.4, are not truly analogous, or need not be if appropriate policies are adopted by 'society'. These answers, taken together, amount to a protest against some discussions, which seem to cut or stretch almost every sort of externality, or even of conflict, into a Procrustean bed of irresoluble PD.

1. Communication argument

'The trouble is that *I* and *II* cannot communicate before each chooses his strategy.' (But, if they could, why should either stick to any agreement reached? If *I* trusts *II* to stick to an agreement to hold out in Table 3.2, why should not *I* break the agreement, confess, and go free? If *I* does not trust *II* to stick to the agreement, but expects *II* to confess, why should not *I* confess also and get 10 years' jail instead of 12? Only if there are side-payments, or societal control, altruism, sanctions against agreement-breaking, etc., will communication help.) An important analogy is the attempt to define some important real-life PDs in poor countries as *isolation* paradoxes.[19]

(a) Are savings-rates 'too low' there because, as A. K. Sen argues, each household – while preferring higher total saving – cannot communicate with its fellow-households to ensure that they save more if it does? Warr and Wright object that such a pattern would not justify a below-market social rate of discount, or therefore higher public saving, because this crowds out private (isolated) saving and leaves the 'paradox' unresolved. But truly this is not a paradox of isolation, but of 'assurance', viz. trust or enforcement: if all agree to save more (privately or publicly), what sanctions or ethics ensure that others will adhere to the bargain if I do? *If* this were assured, each would gain by saving more (privately or via public taxes) and be happy afterwards.

(b) Cassen similarly rejects any use of the 'communication argument' to present overpopulation as a PD that is simply remediable by ending isolation. *Each* couple has many children to raise its prospects of support in old age, but thereby raises unemployment and worsens *all* couples' prospects – a non-CO solution to a PD. But a 'social contract' to have fewer children – an end to isolation – would not help unless changed incentives, income-expectations, means to family planning, or (implausibly, and undesirably) direct enforcement, rendered it plausible to *each* couple that most *others* would abide by the 'contract'. And, if it were, the contract would not be needed to secure compliance.

2. Probability argument

'The trouble is that neither player knows the probability that the other will adopt strategy [1] or [2].' (But, for each player, [1] dominates, whatever the other does. Even certain knowledge of the latter would not get the former to switch to [2]. So why should knowledge of its probabilities help?)[20]

3. Simultaneity argument

'The trouble is that the two prisoners, graziers, irrigators, duopolists ... have to decide strategies at the same moment; if one knew the other's decision before choosing strategies, all would be well.' (Not at all; the second decider in any of the Tables 3.2–3.7, knowing what the first had decided, would choose [1]; the first decider would work this out and also choose [1] – unless there were the sorts of reason to do otherwise considered below.)

4. Single-play argument

'The trouble is that the game is played only once. With many plays, each player (prisoner, grazier, irrigator, contributor to the finance of a public good, duopolist, borrower...) will come to learn the advantages of homing in on [2, 2] – or in Table 3.7, even better, on [1, 2] or [2, 1] – and avoiding [1, 1]. The other player can "penalise" him if he does not, by adopting a tit-for-tat strategy, for instance in Table 3.5 by playing [1] if and only if his rival has played [1] on the previous play;[21] or the "society" of all potential players can impose sanctions or side-payments, teach altruism, etc.' This answer to PD has at least three variants:

(a) Retaliation avoidance So-called repeated PDs are likelier than single PDs to home in on COs. If Table 3.5 were to be repeated several

times, each player's implicit threat of retaliation at the next play, if the other player adopts [1] this time, amounts to a side payment for adopting [2]. This may mean that the long-run game structure is not a true PD – is not a situation where it is, even in the long term, 'worse for both if each, rather than neither, does what will be better for himself'.[22] Then, the 'cross-section' of a single play looks like, say, Table 3.5, but the 'integral' of all cross-sections does not.[23]

(b) Trend-spotting So-called continuous or adaptive PDs – which may be single or repeated – allow each player to see the trend created by his strategy and the other player's, and to change strategy if he dislikes that trend. Such games may or may not be true PDs (see note 20), but – again assuming both players 'know the table' at each moment – do give some force to the remedies, bogus in a one-play non-continuous PD, suggested in Arguments 1 to 3 above: communication, knowledge of probabilities, or non-simultaneous decisions.

(c) Threshold anticipation In particular, either repeated or continuous PDs, whether true examples or not (note 22), may contain a *threshold*, after which a string of – or persistence in – self-seeking actions [1, 1] causes pay-offs to one or both players to change drastically. The commons may suddenly, irretrievably degrade, damaging both graziers. Or one duopolist, irrigator, etc. may (especially in asymmetric PDs) get so poor that he must sell out cheaply to the other. Again assuming all outcome sets known to both players, the former threat might help turn PDs into COs, but the latter threat – typical of 'unfair competitive' practices, like dumping, or loss-leading that accept short-run losses in order to bankrupt a rival – makes non-CO outcomes for the 'society' of producers, notably in duopoly PDs, more likely.

It remains to be seen how frequent (a), (b) and (c) are. Back now to single, non-continuous PDs.

5. Misincentive argument

'The trouble is that incentive structures are so set as to create a PD. These are right if Tables 3.2–3.7 really relate to two prisoners in the situation described around Table 3.2, but wrong for the analogues. Around Table 3.2, the "society" that sets incentives is not a Prisoners' CO Society, but the larger society, represented by authorities and laws. This larger society wants to set incentives that encourage confession – not a cooperating prisoners' sub-society of holdouts. In the analogues (irrigators, graziers, etc.), "society" would set incentives to stimulate cooperation for all pairs of persons – even if playing a once-for-all, non-repeated, non-continuous, true PD – thus converting it into a pseudo-PD.' Three things may be being said here; that incentives are stimulating [1, 1] outcomes because:

(a) Box entries have the *ordering* of Table 3.3 – this 'answer' either begs the question ('PD produces a non-CO because the structure is PD') or else boils down to Argument 6 below;

(b) Box entries have *symmetry*: that is, because in Table 3.4, $a = a_1$, $b = b_1$, $c = c_1$ – asymmetry implies different gains by the players from a strategy switch, and changes the prospects for a solution via enforcement of agreements, via hierarchy, or via side-payments;

(c) Given ordering and symmetry, *relative values* in Tables 3.2 and 3.5–3.7 discourage a homing-in on the CO.[24] For example, without changing the structure of Table 3.5 in any way, 'society' – or Nature, in the case of an acute 'tragedy of the commons' near the threshold of herding capacity – might amend the entries as follows:

TABLE 3.8 *Normalised classic PD: incentive shift towards [2, 2]*

II's strategies

		1	2
I's strategies	1	2, 2	(10m. + 1), 0
	2	0, (10m. + 1)	10m., 10m.

The 'temptation of goodness'[25] upon each player – to go for the social optimum and choose [2] – is now greater; the risk of getting 0 if the rival is greedy is less of a deterrent, and the hope of getting 10m otherwise more of an attraction. This works especially well if the units are small – say pennies – so that the difference between winning 0, 1 and 2 is almost imperceptible, but that between 0, 1 and 2 and 10m is substantial.[26]

6. Side-payments argument

'The trouble is that side payments are impossible'. Back in Table 3.2, suppose that if either prisoner confessed and the other held out, the confessor had to compensate the hold-out with cash agreed by both to be 'worth' six years in jail. This, of course, destroys the PD structure of Tables 3.2–3.8, and ensures a CO. It is, indeed, a sort of Coasean negotiation towards a 'societal' optimum – assuming 'society' to comprise only the pair of prisoners, graziers, etc. But plainly the existence, enforcibility, and indeed value and incidence, of side-payments is vital to this CO. It appears to violate the Coasean theorem that the CO does not depend on compensation rules – but this is not really so. Back in Table 3.2, Coase would rightly assert that *I–II* negotiation before interrogation, to reach *any* contract enforcible subsequently, would cause them to select [2, 2], however they agreed to distribute gains afterwards. In brief:

> negotiation, plus side-payments, plus enforcible contracts regarding negotiated side-payments, leads to the CO, with Coase's theorem on irrelevance of liability rules working;

> enforcible side-payments above can ensure the CO, but without negotiation of contracts their size and assignment have to be right, so Coase's *theorem* does not apply; it depends, naturally enough, on his assumptions.

Note that 'big society' – not a micro-society of prisoners – does not, through its laws, allow enforcement of side-payments from confessor to hold-out, whether negotiated before the crime or claimed (or extorted) after the hold-out's release; indeed, such pre-crime negotiation would normally itself be illegal,[27] as would attempts by prisoners' 'microsociety' to enforce such payments later. That is in complete contrast to the *analogues* of PD; societies normally have laws to enforce contracts between graziers, irrigators, etc. to recover external costs. The difference between PD and its analogues is similar to that for the misincentive argument 5.

7. Altruism argument

'The trouble is lack of altruism.'[28] Suppose the numerical entries in all our tables are £ Sterling, and that £1 adds one interpersonally comparable util to any person. If both *I* and *II* are known to love their neighbours as themselves, both will maximise joint income. In Tables 3.2, 3.5, 3.6 and 3.8, this leads to a social optimum [2, 2] without any agreements or negotiations. (Table 3.7 is more difficult, because in seeking [1, 2] or [2, 1] isolated and unprepared prisoners could end up at [1, 1]; since prisoners may be mutually altruistic, Table 3.7 is a *better* PD than Tables 3.2, 3.5 or 3.6 for the 'macro-society' that wants prisoners to confess.) Indeed, milder altruism will often do. In Table 3.5, if *I* loves his neighbour *II* more than one-fifth as much as himself, then *I* will prefer the outcome of [2, 2] to that of [2, 1] – and that of [2, 2] to that of [1, 2] – because *I* in each case values *II*'s gain of 10 more highly than *I*'s loss of 2. Thus *I* adopts [2]. Even if *II* is totally selfish, the box sum [2, 1], at 12, is better than the PD box sum [1, 1], viz. 4. If *II*, like *I*, loves his neighbour more than one-fifth as much as himself, the outcome is the CO [2, 2], box sum 20.

8. Hierarchy argument

'The trouble is lack of a truly agreed, internalised hierarchy.' If all villagers agree on the relative values of extra income for Brahman, farmer-caste and ex-Untouchable, all will so act as to produce the outcomes, in two-person PDs, that maximise a weighted sum of box entries – and will home in on the strategy combination that does so. In Table 3.5, if *I* is Brahman and *II* is ex-Untouchable, and all agree (a) that Brahman income is worth more than five times ex-Untouchable income, both will home in on [1, 2]; or (b) *vice versa*, both home in on [2, 1]; or (c) that Brahman and ex-Untouchable income is less unequal in worth than a 1:5 or 5:1 ratio, on [2, 2]. The social pessimum [1, 1] never happens. The altruism argument, 7, ranking 'others' and 'oneself' rather than, say, Brahmans and other castes, is a sort of at-a-slant special case of this argument. So is egalitarianism, or internalised democracy, with respect to *extra* income.

9. Control argument

'The trouble is lack of societal control.' This control could take several forms: punishments for non-cooperative behaviour, rewards for behaviour moving towards COs, rules about side-payments, sanctions to ensure agreed side-payments, education to internalise altruism or other hierarchies, tax or subsidy incentives to discourage non-cooperation. Societal control can be against the interests of larger, or outside, societies: a society of criminals to mulct confessors, or a cartel, illustrate this.

10. Choice-of-cures argument

'The trouble is the combination of all the above absences: of societal control, of agreed hierarchies, of altruism, of side-payments, of socially apt incentives, of repeated similar plays, and of information.' Indeed, except for the last example – improving information alone *never* 'cures' one-off PDs – all the suggested improvements, viz. the implications of Arguments 4 to 9, appear to be substitutable. With a bit more altruism, we need a bit lower side-payments, or a bit less certainty that they will be enforced. Slightly lower gaps between the (12) outcomes in [2, 1] and [1, 2] in Table 3.5 and the (10) outcomes in [2, 2] – e.g. their alteration to (10, 5) and (10, 3) respectively – would substitute, in avoiding non-CO outcomes, for slightly higher expectations of a replay.

11. Murphy's Law argument

'All these things have to go wrong to create a true two-person PD, so it is in reality very unlikely – that is why we refer to the isolated-prisoner situation, where a "society" beyond that of *I* and *II* deliberately creates rules to produce PD, rules which (cf. the misincentive and side-payments arguments) have few plausible analogues.' True enough; but the imperfect information and isolation of two-person PD does have close analogues where there are many players (see note 2). Any *one* responsible grazier, irrigator, borrower considering repayment to a vulnerable local creditor, etc., is at great risk that half-a-dozen other villagers – whom he cannot sufficiently influence, observe or know – 'act irresponsibly' (being insufficiently moved by altruism, societal control, etc.). Two neighbours, sharing scarce water, are likely to reach a CO-like *modus vivendi* – perhaps, if one is much stronger, with very unequal sharing, but in any case without joint water overuse in one season leading to massive shared loss next season – and to observe and enforce the agreed solution. A hundred farmers are much less likely than two to avoid non-cooperative PD outcomes. Game theorists and empirical researchers into PD concentrate on two-person games: first, because these are difficult enough; second, because two-person games raise fascinating issues – for example, will pairs of men, pairs of women, or one of each show the greatest cooperative tendencies?[29] – that would be clouded by more players; third, because many 1-person games specifically confuse the issue by introducing the possibility of coalitions, frequently unstable ones. But the 'real life' of water-resource sharing, credit cooperatives, common grazing, etc. is many-person, and that is a necessary condition for its frequent approach to PD with non-cooperative outcomes.

This many-person reality – increasingly many as populations grow – increases the importance of social institutions of control. The key question is: will the required resources to pay for such institutions – resources which increase with the number, power, ingenuity, and hostility of those preferring non-cooperative strategies – be forthcoming?

Four phases can be separated. Let us concentrate on the classic dilemma of the commons – expanding private herd ownership, but a limited common grazing area. Assume population growth, but no sudden threshold at which the commons degenerates. In Phase 1, there is enough common land that the damage done by feasible expansion of some private herds to other herders' access to grazing (and hence herd wealth) is negligible. In Phase 2, with more beasts on the commons, each party has tangible losses from the expansion of all other parties' herds – but the *gain* to each individual, from herd expansion, exceed the *losses* to all others. In Phase 3, the *losses* to others exceed the *gains* to the herd expander – a PD has arisen; but the difference in 'total herd GNP' (box sum) between the many-person [2, 2, 2 ...] – between the CO where all graze lightly – and the non-cooperative PD outcome [1, 1, 1 ...] where all graze heavily, does not suffice to pay for social institutions that ensure that all[30] abide by the light-grazing strategy. In Phase 4, losses exceed gains enough that the light-grazing solution, if enforced on all, produces so much more total herd output than the heavy-grazing solution that the difference suffices to pay the cost of social institutions to ensure the light-grazing solution.

Population growth, with limited grazing land, carries societies inexorably into higher phases. In fact, many far-from-populous societies in Phases 2 and 3 do contain chiefly authority, or clan-like consensus, to restrict individual grazing (or deforestation or water-use or whatever) to near the social optimum. Unfortunately, development creates a transition – from these inexpensive, if often unjust, traditional institutions – alongside population growth, so that costly new social institutions of enforcement are needed, and not available, in Phase 3. So is the answer, on Boserup lines,[31] more population growth into Phase 4? Often not, for two reasons. First, if there is not enough trust, altruism, or control to secure a CO in Phase 3, why should each herder trust his fellows to pay their share of the costs of enforcing a CO in Phase 4? We consider this problem in Section V(7) below. Second, while neither necessary nor sufficient for the degradation of the commons, and while probably not very common (note 35) – there are sometimes *thresholds*, not anticipated as well as is suggested in argument 4(c). Herd expansion, accelerated by population growth, and during the 'transition of trust' from chiefs of clans to modern authority, then produces sufficient (true multi-person PD) overgrazing that the commons degrades – or rehabilitation cost rises – very sharply.

We now pass to consideration of some examples of situations where PD or CO outcomes seem feasible. How do the arguments of the last two sections affect the result? How can policies – or 'democratic' or other ways to operate policies – help push the results towards CO?

V

1. **Tragedy of the commons**

Many things have to go wrong for this tragedy to happen – for a move into the critical Phase 3. Necessary conditions are not merely (i) private herd ownership, (ii) common grazing land. Also (iii) the common grazing is (increasingly) not a true public good, because privately profitable extra use of it by one herd-owner (increasingly) reduces benefit from it to others.[32] (iv) No rational authority is clearly accepted by all herders – if rational, any such authority, however benevolent or self-seeking, would set rules and/or incentives[33] to optimise cattle/land ratio at each moment, assuming *some* selected social rate of time preference. Yet (v) lacking such an authority, herd-owners do not negotiate towards individual grazing that add up to such an optimum, or cannot enforce – or agree to have enforced externally – the outcome of such a negotiation. (vi) Nor do they accept common values, leading to attitudes, ethics, or education that 'internalise' the limitation of private herds on common land. Indeed, (vii) there is not even a sufficient 'core' of animal ownership – of beasts, and power to accrete beasts through breeding or acquisition – remaining with people who *do* negotiate (or accept authority, or internalise herd-limiting values), to make it worth while for enough cooperation to happen to prevent worsening of total net social income from herds on the commons.

For some writers,[34] there is an eighth condition for TC: a 'threshold of cumulative overgrazing beyond which the commons deteriorates very sharply or irretrievably. It is, as Kimber (note 34) points out, hard to believe that education or past experience would not prevent most groups of graziers from pulling up well short of such a threshold. The threshold assumption, however, is not necessary for a TC;[35] *steadily* increasing negative marginal social returns to private herd expansion, combined with still-positive marginal private returns, are 'tragic' enough, and observably common enough. Why? How do the Three Horsemen – not enough accepted rational authority; not enough binding negotiation; not enough internalisation of herd-limiting values – persist?

(a) *Population growth* pushes total numbers of herders, and/or each herder's private optimum herd size, steadily up. This growth steadily increases the costs of reaching and enforcing Coasean outcomes: more negotiations must be undertaken and their outcomes policed; and/or more people must be supervised and/or persuaded by authority; and/or more education costs must be incurred to internalise herd-limiting values.

(b) Not only does the transaction (or supervision or education) cost of reaching an optimum by negotiation (or authority or moral-community) increase with population. Not only does it increase more than in proportion (because the number of relationships, conflicts of rights, etc. does so – for dyadic relationships, see page 57. The importance of *temporal priority of claim,* the difficulty of determining it clearly, and the ferocity with which it will be defended, all increase – and with them the difficulty of reaching a CO. Coase tries to eliminate the issue of temporal priority of claim:

> The question is commonly thought of as one in which A inflicts harm on B ... how should we restrain A? But this is wrong. We are dealing with a problem of a reciprocal nature. To avoid the harm to B would inflict harm on A ... I instanced ... a confectioner ... whose machinery disturbed a doctor in his work. To avoid harming the doctor would inflict harm on the confectioner. The problem [is] whether it was worth while, as a result of restricting the methods of ... the confectioner, to secure more doctoring at the cost of reduced ... confectionery (p. 2).

Coase rightly defines the social optimum as an output-mix and (p. 54 and note 36) rightly asserts that rules of liability – upon confectioner to curtail output or machine noise (or compensate doctor); or upon doctor to curtail output or to insulate his surgery (or pay off confectioner) – will not impede that optimum mix. But is it right to assert, further, that such rules of liability will not affect the costs – and the moral acceptability – of negotiation, or of authority or 'internalisation of values' to enforce or replace it?[36] Commonsense morality suggests that if the doctor was there first, and had no good reason to expect any nearby machinery, he has a right to be compensated by the confectioner; but if the confectioner set up machinery before any reasonable expectation of damage to others could be formed, then compensation rights are the confectioner's.[37] This commonsense morality cannot be absolute, because – for instance – (i) 'reasonable expectations' may be secured by longstanding practices that have come to be regarded as corrupt, unduly restrictive, or otherwise unacceptable; or (ii) a social consensus has arisen that poor confectioners (or their poor employees or poor customers) should not be mulcted to secure the prior rights of much richer doctors, patients, and doctors' employees. But these exceptions merely illustrate, in a different way, the rule exemplified by temporal priority: the rule that assignments of liability depend on the general moral consensus for their acceptability, and thus for low enforcement costs and high reliability. If assignments are not thus acceptable, they will be undependable – and negotiations based on them will tend to fail.

All this bears critically on population growth as a cause of ever more insistent claims of 'prior rights' in the case of TC. As a herder's adolescent children, labour force, hands and mouths increase, so does the household's insistence upon its vested interest in community lands. This involves increased resistance to the claims of newcomers from other herding households, also affected by population growth, in the same community.[38] Moreover, the steadier (i.e. less discontinuous) and the faster is population growth, the harder does it become to establish clear priority of claim. It is not simply 'increasing scarcity' of common grazing that causes population growth to erode the sanctions that formerly made for COs; it is also the fact that population growth increases the number and ferocity of cases of insistence on prior claim, yet also the difficulty of deciding such cases, and hence the cost and difficulty of maintaining trust that *any* laws of assignment of liability will be enforced. In such circumstances, the danger of an individualistic TC increases.

(c) *Time preference* varies among herders. Very poor small herders need real income for consumption now; bigger ones discount later saveable income much less. It is perfectly feasible for either Coasean negotiations or perfect credit markets nevertheless to reach COs and avoid tragedies of the commons: feasible, but not plausible.

(d) As mentioned above, these much greater difficulties of setting and enforcing social frameworks for Coasean negotiations coincide, in increasingly populous LDCs, with largely exogenous *'transition of trust'* from old to new authorities.

These four deterrents to a CO – transition of trust, population growth, moral 'authority' of increasingly numerous and obscure prior claims, and varying time-preference – correspond to encouragements to a non-cooperative PD outcome. Before looking at possible solutions, we try to place these encouragements alongside the 'arguments against PD' listed at the end of sec. IV. (Arguments 1–3 – to avoid PD via communication, estimation of rival's probable strategies, and sequencing of strategies – will not do as they stand: pp. 62–3.)

(e) Argument 4(a) – that repeated 'plays' by herders will teach them to cooperate (graze lightly) so as to avoid 'retaliation' – performs badly. Because circumstances are changing, past experience of repeats of the PD play does not give reliable hints that a CO solution, even if appropriate once, remains so. For example, extra people (and high-yielding cereals) cause land marginal between crops and pasture to shift towards crops; so the pressure on others to overgraze is greater than in the past; so I feel I can trust them less than in the past to home in on a CO.

(f) The 'trend-spotting' Argument 4(b) does look relevant. The structure of TC differs essentially from PD only in that any herder can adapt behaviour continuously. A group of herders can announce readiness to take some beasts from common to private grazing, the action to be maintained only if enough others to form with them a 'core' sufficient to make cooperation pay (see (vii) on p. 70, at the start of sec. V (1)) did likewise within a stated period.[39] However, if there is weak authority in a period of transition, and/or new herder-entrants on to the commons, what can guarantee the adherence of members of the original group, of other cooperators afterwards, and of sufficient of the new herder-entrants to keep the 'core' big enough that cooperation continues to pay those who do restrain common herding? The very factors pushing from CO towards non-cooperative PD also render it harder for would-be cooperators to take advantage of the continuous features of the 'commons' PD.

(g) Threshold anticipation, Argument 4(c), is central to some critics of TC. With perfect information,

> at the moment just prior to the collapse of the commons, the self-interested individual, who is dependent on the commons for his survival, will not make the fatal addition to his herd, because he *knows* that, if he does, the commons will collapse entirely (because

the others are making the same calculation). [Without perfect information] as the commons declines, [he] would be expected to try to reduce or remove the uncertainty by contributing to the establishment of an agency 'to create such information'.[40]

Leaving until sec. V(7) the Olson problem that optimising peasants might individually do best to free-ride, to leave the financing of such an agency (just like the restraint of common grazing itself) to one another – and Kimber's attempt to deal with this problem – we must recognise other difficulties with Kimber's approach. Even 'perfect information' hardly ever reveals a sharp, recognisable threshold. Some range ecologists' notion of a critical limit to 'carrying capacity' has no economic content. The commons seldom suddenly 'collapse'. The tragedy is prolonged periods of overgrazing in which each herder gains by putting extra beasts on the commons for extra days, but other herders lose more. There is no 'fatal addition', but a growing number of private 'beast-days' on the commons, with steadily rising negative social effect.

(h) The incentive arguments do suggest a possible line of action. Argument 5(a) does not help; the ordering of box entries in TC is PD all right. As for 5(c) – while relative pay-offs like the extreme threshold of Table 3.8 are implausible (see last paragraph) – tax incentives can move some way towards it. However, herd size difference – and hence possible *asymmetry* of incentives, as in Argument 5(b) – is very important. The more beasts a grazier has, the more is he harmed by one extra beast placed on the commons by any other herd-owner; and the fewer beasts, the less. This applies also to one's own beasts. A new grazier, placing his first (and only) beast on common land, feels no negative externality at all; a dominant herder, initially owning (say) one in three of all the commonly grazed beasts, might already have no further incentive to private herd expansion on the commons. This disparity, unfortunately, greatly weakens the possibility that hierarchy – as opposed to Pharaonic autarchy – can control TC (see (k) below). For the 'big fish' in a hierarchy of graziers, those likeliest to be able to exert hierarchical influence, have least to offer by restricting their own herds (since everyone knows they don't get much out of their marginal beasts anyway), and have most need for herd restriction by other, smaller and weaker, graziers.[41]

(i) To create side-payments – Argument 6 on p. 23 – is probably the most generally relevant policy to turn PD into CO in the case of TCs. It is dealt with below.

(j) Careful altruism (note 28), the 'cure for PD' in Argument 7, would certainly help. But the circumstances of TC include population-induced sharpening of rivalries, and development-induced (and possibly desirable) weakenings of 'moral community' in favour of market incentives. These conditions do not favour the growth of altruism, but rather suggest increased attention to the claims of a growing immediate family, threatened by other growing families, with a declining community nexus among them.

(k) Transition of societal control (and of the society to which an individual looks for control) – from tribe, clan or village to State – is certainly a cause of weakened enforcement of COs (Argument 9). Hence it is very important to identify institutions which transitional societies develop spontaneously, usually confined to particular areas of decision, to reduce the dangers or tensions of PD outcomes. The hierarchical approach (Argument 8) is less promising in handling TC, partly because hierarchies are themselves in transition, partly because their sway is weakened by (h) above, but perhaps mainly because the likely distributional results of successful hierarchy – reducing poor people's claims to common grazing – could be seen as worse than the results of TC itself.

(l) The large, growing number of transactors in TCs, due to population growth, of course raises the chances of PD (rather than CO) outcomes. The cost of avoiding Murphy's Law (Argument 11) rises.

2. Preventing or curing TC

Seven possible policies exist. Two are radical: (1) to make herd ownership common (as grazing already is), or (2) to make grazing private (as herd ownership already is). Four are reformist: to use (3) physical controls or (4) incentives to reduce private herd sizes on the commons; or to use (5) physical controls or (6) incentives to increase the amount, quality, or forage yield given amount and quality, of common grazing land. One is structural: (7) to accelerate changes in structure of GNP, or of expenditure, away from products – such as animal products – likely, given initial structures of control and incentive and ownership, to generate TCs via 'perverse' combinations of private and public resource access or use. Policy (7) is unlikely to be much affected by TC alone, since it emerges from overall economic development. Below, policies (1) to (6) are discussed with reference to the specific issue of private herds on common grazing, but most of the discussion applies *mutatis mutandis* to other PD-v-CO issues, considered in subsections (3) to (7). The policy options relate closely to the reasons for CO failure, and to the arguments against PD conceptualisations, considered earlier in this paper.

Policies 5 and 6, for example, are generally unwise because, while providing temporary relief, they strengthen individuals' medium-term incentives to preserve PD structures and to behave non-cooperatively within them. For example, better grassland on African ranges, or better forest browse in SE Asia, while temporarily increasing privately costless feed availability from the commons (and thus current herd quality), by that very outcome increases the incentive to each grazier to expand his private herd size. The marginal external cost of such expansion may be concealed (as feed becomes more plentiful) or in favourable circumstances even reduced quite sharply (if your herd increases, my beasts can now feed elsewhere, on a more productive commons); but such reduction or concealment is temporary, and gives strong incentives to seek non-CO solutions that make herds bigger, and overgrazing worse, than ever.

Societal action, concurrent with policies 5 and 6, could in principle be taken to persuade people to home in on COs, so that the policies 'bought time' to achieve a long-run solution, rather like extra food production is supposed to buy time for population control. Unfortunately the analogy breaks down. Reliable, well-distributed extra food (and real income) changes incentives in ways that normally cut fertility, as the need to have children for old-age security declines. But policies 5 and 6 change incentives in ways that cut both incentives for COs and urgency about societal pressures to achieve them.

Policies 5 and 6 could make sense still, given some combination of very high time-preference; and/or confidence that the growth rate of available feed (at a given real price) would exceed that of beasts, despite the incentive to raise the latter rate given by this very excess itself; and/or consequent rises in grazing resources (net of private costs of obtaining them) sufficient to raise, in the long term, the box sum from the post-policy CO outcome relative to that from the post-policy PD outcome, so that misincentives from relative pay-offs are less, and the CO strategies more attractive (Argument 5(c), p. 65). But is 'enough' of these three desiderata likely to persist long enough to put in place other policies, notably societal controls over PD outcomes (such as are probably implicit in policies 3 and 4), during a transition of trust, and while population growth and the consequences of policies 5 and 6 increase pressures to private herd expansion? Surely very seldom.

The radical alternatives 1 and 2 – which could conceivably both be tried in different places in the same country – at least face the logic, and try to move from PD to CO. As for 1, common herd ownership with common grazing is practised by some transhumant groups, perhaps in part as a cure for overgrazing. Some such groups, indeed, depend for long enough on the same commons for overgrazing to be a real danger, especially as settled populations grow and encroach on the transhumants' former 'cyclical' commons. It is hard, however, to envisage a regeneration of transhumant 'primitive communism' (probably something of a golden-age myth anyway) where economic power has already become highly polarised. In more organised systems, State or collective ownership of both lands and herds carries familiar problems: lack of individual incentive, costs of bureaucratic control.[42]

An example of policy 2 is the series of enclosure laws in eighteenth-century England. It does destroy PD by uniting costs of grazing with benefits,[43] but the efficiency gain is achieved by means that do great damage to the very poor, since it is almost always the better-off who enclose the commons, and the poor who lack private grazing alternatives. The poor lose not only assets but also bargaining power, and are often left with no resources except labour-power, typically sold to big graziers. These, once enriched by enclosing the commons, often show the larger farmer's typical tendency to avoid supervision and labour search costs by selecting higher capital/land and land/labour ratios than family farmers, e.g. by replacing herding labour by fences.

Policy 2 – privatising the common grazing land – has nevertheless been much recommended, and sometimes tried, in LDCs. Inequities are supposed to be prevented by two methods. The first is the formation of group cooperatives, to enclose some farmland on behalf of the poor, and to secure COs with asset ownership for them also. The second is by identifying and retaining crucial areas of common land, from which 'big men's herds' are to be removed into new ranch developments on enclosed, but allegedly little used, commons elsewhere. Group cooperative ranching by the very poor (or anybody else), for familiar reasons, seldom works. Protection, and attempted confinement to the poor, of heavily-grazed commons suffers – as in Botswana's Tribal Grazing Lands Programme – as large and powerful ranchers choose to put back youngstock on to such commons; yet Policy 2 provides three incentives to do this. (a) The commons are now emptier, so there is more grazing (and water) for each beast. (b) Because of the better grazing on private ranches, cattle birth and survival rates increase. (c) This better grazing and these higher rates would both be threatened were youngstock to be kept on the private ranches. If, as in Botswana, the government limits stocking rates on private ranches – either to protect its subsidies on capital there, or to counter alleged 'irrational' tendencies towards private overstocking – a fourth pressure to degrade the commons arises.

The main effective policies against TC, therefore, are usually physical controls or incentives to cut private grazing on common land: Policies 3 and 4. These normally prevailed before transition of trust, population growth, and rapid developmental change (the latter breaking down confidence in learning from past repeated PD plays in regard to common grazing). Chiefly authority typically involved regular culling of herds, colonial authority cattle-taxes, if overgrazing threatened. Often, traditional authority undertook such measures for reasons partly or wholly unconnected with TC: to pay for administration, to enrich rulers, etc. Whatever the reason for such measures, they *did* reduce the risk of overgrazing. This must have increased incentives both to apply and to tolerate them. In turn, the measures – and the consensus for them – not only cut the private herds directly (or cut the private incentives to increase them), but also caused each herder to believe that restraint by him would be echoed by other herders.

What policies, within 3 and 4, exist? The reasons why COs are often not reached in LDCs (pp. 56–7), and the arguments against the realism of PDs (pp. 62–8), give many hints. In seeking to move outcomes towards conventional COs, a government aims to create conditions where negotiation, followed by enforcements of contract, is the norm. In seeking to avoid non-CO outcomes in PDs – assuming the structure cannot be changed to destroy the PD (policies 1 and 2) – a government aims to create conditions where sets of individual strategies, or acceptance of publicly-set rules, produces results analogous to COs, viz. the box sum maximising outcomes in Tables 3.1–3.8.

Let us, in the TC context, revert to the reasons why Coasean outcomes are often not reached in LDCs (pp. 56–7). The impact of *risk aversion* on herd-size-increasing tendencies can be cut by reducing either risk[44] or aversion from it; but it is emphatically not the risk of cattle holding that governments seek to cut, for this would – although reducing risk-aversion all round, because each increase in risk means more-than-proportionately increasing dislike of extra risk – directly raise the incentive to hold animals. The aim of governments in this area should be to cut, or to help private herders to cut, the risk (a) of adverse consequences if they curtail grazing but others do not, especially if others thereby break agreements; (b) of downward fluctuations in total, *especially non-cattle*, net real income per household member; (c) that such net real income (even if risks (a) and (b) materialise) could fall below the level needed for the household to maintain essential consumption without sale of fixed assets, or 'emergency' labour or credit contracts, or other desperate mortgagings of future prospects. Risk (a) is best cut by enforcing agreements on the level of each private herd placed on the common grazing lands – costly and difficult; far better for governments to do it properly over 20 per cent of the common-grazed area (perhaps via rewarded local authorities – see sec. VI), than to assert authority over 80–100 per cent and achieve 5 per cent. Risk (b) is effectively cut, not by crop-insurance (a near-universal failure in LDCs), but by policies to reduce real causes of sudden income cuts; reliable irrigation, or even health insurance, could have major hidden benefits via greater willingness to tolerate the risks of 'trusting one's neighbour' to accept (or the authorities to enforce) physical or price controls on TC actions such as private overgrazing – for such tolerance implies greater readiness to accept the controls oneself, in an upward spiral towards the desired CO. Risk (c) – really a restatement of the proposition that poverty increases risk-aversion – implies a policy to increase income; that implication is less useless than it sounds, because it suggests regions and groups where the task is more urgent.

Unspecified assignments of liability are becoming a major problem in many TC circumstances. This problem creates a general rule for governments seeking to control TC by controls or incentives over private herds (policies 3 and 4): to assert laws about incentives, compensation, physical controls, etc. only where long-term voluntary observation, or external enforcement, are fairly certain. Coase correctly states that *any* liability rule, fully enforced, plus zero transactions costs, should lead to a CO; but a shifting, unknown, or unenforced rule, plus any positive risk-aversion, leads to levels of social product below the CO.

Extra-economic power, permitting unpredictable non-performance of promised contracts (or side-payments) by the powerful only, is a specially harmful example. This means not only net product below the CO, but a more unequal distribution. The traditional authority of chief or clan or colonist, too, was extra-economic, but normally predictable; it could constrain both resources used and the distribution of power and income, but within those constraints a CO, and therefore maximum certainty, were in the authority's interests as well as those of the herders. If I do not know whether a chief or his client can or will invoke traditional authority, then I do not know how to optimise, nor what to negotiate for.

Poorer herd-owners' *higher time-preference* induces them to seek a higher rate of depletion of the commons than bigger owners. This would not be so if credit markets allowed all to borrow at similar interest rates. If it is a social goal to reduce the rate of depletion, governments advance that goal indirectly by improving the functioning of credit markets. Here, a CO is hard to define: rich herders might see a grazing capacity on a given commons of 100 beasts this year and 100 next year as worth more than 120 and 65 respectively, poor herders the reverse. If governments (as custodians of the future, or at least of future elections) incline to richer herders' views, the implication is either to set incentives (e.g. via better credit markets) that move poor herders towards those views, or to cause poor herders to obtain livelihoods in sectors where their high time-preference does less to degrade common property. The latter path may be infeasible, inhumane or – if small herders are relatively land-saving and labour-using in a land-scarce, underemployed economy – inefficient.

Population growth of humans and beasts – linked, because both the extra needs and the extra working-capacities of extra humans increase their labour supply to herding – is a severe intensifier of TC. Incentives and physical controls to keep herds off commons can include the inducement of smaller families by, respectively, tax concessions and vasectomy campaigns (for both men and bullocks).

Let us pass now to the PD-interpretation of TC. Can the dissimilarities between the non-cooperative outcome and the herding situation (pp. 18–26) be increased by policies 3 and 4? If cattle technology is improving, Argument 4(a) (p. 20) – learning that non-cooperation brings retaliation – is in the TC example is hard to revive; CO herders will keep learning that their 'sacrifice' was worth more than it seemed at the time, and non-cooperative herders – if aware mainly of other non-cooperators – that they did better than expected by being, in their PD framework, intransigent. Policies to 'revive' faith in a repeated PD (even if they do encourage COs) would moreover deliberately impede technical change in cattle farming. Argument 4(b) – trend-spotting – is more promising, since TC is by nature a continuous PD; each herder can, at each moment, vary his private claims on common grazing, measured in beast-minutes! Here, exogenous controls or incentives (as opposed to internalised community values, or village authorities) are more promising with the herding TC than with private claims on restricted water use: the latter has to be cut back at critical points in the growing season to avoid PD outcomes, whereas – though of course there are seasonal variations in grazing stress – any day of 'saved' private grazing is worth having. Argument 4(c), threshold anticipation, is less helpful; the ecological threshold, when the commons suddenly degrade much more sharply, is usually mythical (note 35).

Incentives to change the structure of PD (5a), or more plausibly to reduce the incentives to non-cooperation relative to the rewards for strategies simulating a search for a CO (5c, though much less drastically than in Table 3.8), are however highly relevant. (Just as a quota normally has an equivalent tariff, so there is normally a culling policy equivalent to a cattle tax.) Such incentives can take the form of legislatively enforced side payments (p. 65, Argument 6) to particular victims, or of taxes to a societal agency. A promising approach (given the difficulty of identifying particular culprits and victims in TC, and the need for social acceptance) is a tax that each community, with its own commons, collects from its herders for each animal on the commons – and, provided the community undertakes to use the receipts for extra support of non-cattle uses of agricultural resources, is allowed to keep. This uses the same tax twice: to lower private benefits from extra grazing, and to raise them for alternative activities. Altruism and societal control (Arguments 7 and 11) are complementary with incentives whether achieved by rules about taxes, side payments or culling; the stronger altruism and/or societal control, the less strict the rule needs to be.

Argument 8 – that absence of hierarchy prevents COs – raises especially difficult issues. To the extent that potential herders agree on a non-self-excepting hierarchy of values attaching to extra incomes for different persons – for example that an extra rupee for the Brahman is worth twice as much as for anyone else – concord about which (grazing) strategy each PD player should adopt is much easier. Altruism, by reducing (favourable) self-exception, increases the extent of agreement. Egalitarianism is one such possible agreed hierarchy; so is the set of relative values preferred by traditional authority. Collapse of, or growing disagreement about, hierarchies means that it becomes less likely that authorities can impose their own, or cause 'players' to internalise other than egotistical, relative valuations of income gains for different members of the community. But the issues raised are difficult because (a) Policies 3 and 4 – culling or taxing cattle – have no obvious purchase on the decline of hierarchy, (b) even if they had, the gains to society from reactivation of such hierarchy through a move from PD to CO outcomes must be set against the losses. Narrowly, these losses arise from GNP reduction or maldistribution through restrictive behaviour by persons high in the hierarchy. Broadly, the losses include 'freedom' and 'development'; these are, to a great extent, co-extensive with decline of hierarchical valuations of persons (and of extra income for them). Can the virtues of hierarchies in securing agreed moves from PDs to COs – often with elements of altruism (*noblesse oblige*) or insurance, especially in hierarchies connected with religions – be retained or regained by modern States, without attempting an undesirable or futile 'reactionary' reversion to those hierarchies? This is one of the ways in which democracy may be relevant to the PD–CO transition in developing countries.

Argument 11 – the more herders, the more can go wrong to turn CO into PD – raises fewer problems. The more people (herders, irrigators) are in PD-type situations, the smaller are the prospects for agreed values, trust, or control; the greater are the transactions costs of negotiation and enforcement; the less is the negotiators' assurance that a sufficient 'core' is included to justify cooperation despite the dangers from non-negotiators (plus defectors plus new entrants); and thus the higher are the risks of non-cooperative PD outcomes. The consequences for the plausible medium-term options, taxing or culling cattle (policies 3 and 4), however, may be subtle, especially if growth in the population of transactors is underway, increasing these problems. Should the attempt be made to reduce them by reducing the size of the defined 'community' to fewer contracting, or competing, parties?

A common grazing area, a watershed, or a water-table may or may not be, without loss, physically separable between, say, two communities. If it is, a CO in *each* community (such that policies 3 and 4 reconcile private actions to social goals) is also a CO for *both* communities. If not, binding agreements between them – village counterparts of the water-sharing agreements between Indian States – are needed. Otherwise, a sort of 'two-layer PD' can arise; each *individual* in a community may feel the non-CO (water-mining, heavy-grazing) solution is dominant; so may each *community*, in dealing with others. Indeed, if successful in achieving an inter-individual, first-layer CO, a community, by raising the value of common resources to all its members, may render them even less cooperative in their relations with nearby communities, let alone outsiders, claiming to share those common resources. Sharp moves by each of two communities sharing commons towards CO may thus raise the risk that the two will conduct a non-cooperative PD with each other. Also the overarching authority of the State may be an acceptable – or tolerable – guarantor of COs to each member of a community, where an internal authority would not be. Or there may be economies of scale in centralising enforcement; or insufficient cash or force at local level. All this is said in warning against overstating the neat – and I believe on balance right – conclusion that, as populations grow, it normally becomes more important to decentralise control over the commons from the State to the community, lest in practice, due to assorted transactions costs, such 'control' be decentralised to a horde of dilemma-ridden prisoners.

3. Some other PD–CO choices: irrigation examples

The history of surface water use in Sri Lanka typifies the collapse, in many LDCs, of conditions once consistent with COs. For almost two thousand years, Sri Lanka maintained water restraint in complex, sequential canal-tank systems. Yet today its undisciplined, low-performance irrigation systems are overrun with experts in 'water management' from countries that, even one thousand years ago, managed water by praying for rain.

Major tank-canal-sluice networks like that based on the Giant's Tank in Mannar, and smaller-scale canal-field irrigation systems as in Kandy, have always been vulnerable to PD-style problems. Each top-end water user, to ensure ample water (and to save labour by drowning weeds), is tempted to take as much water as could be stored on the paddies as soon as it is available; this leaves the tail-enders too little water for a second crop.[45] Individual farmers who need water, anywhere in a gravity-flow system, tend to resort to extreme means. Under the Kandyan kings, strict discipline was enforced. The rare farmer who took water before the scheduled time was punished. The very rare sluice-cutter might even, on some accounts, have a hand cut off in return.

Farmers tolerated this discipline, partly for Coasean reasons. Enough of them valued proper water control – a CO – as typically *increasing* the net product, to each, by more than enough to make up for the atypical *reductions* in a season or year when rain was especially scarce, illegally appropriable canal water especially accessible, or weeding labour (as opposed to canal water to drown weeds) especially costly. There was a sufficient 'core' of gainers to allow the imposition, on core and non-core farmers alike, of effective sanctions against use of non-cooperative PD strategies. The secular similarity of farming conditions (no rapid development) and the relatively slow changes in numbers or families of transactors (no rapid population change) enhanced the capacity of the Kandyan kings – and other traditional island rulers – to impose firm irrigation control with 'general consent', sometimes well into the nineteenth century. The extent to which such 'consent' was given by a majority among rural people, as opposed to merely the rural strong or rich, is not known, and is relevant to the role of 'democracy' in securing transitions from PD to CO outcomes (sec. VI).

During most of the British rule, and in early Independence, water was controlled with less extreme punishments, but still firmly, by a local irrigation official called a *vel vidane*. His sanctions again worked mainly because backed by a 'core' of farmers *and* ultimately supported by State power. Since the mid-1950s, a series of rural experiments – short-lived, underfinanced, sometimes ill-considered, and very patchily implemented – sought to replace the *vel vidane*: with participatory institutions for water control, in the context of 'land reform', in traditionally irrigated villages; with system-level irrigation bureaucracies, in the new modern gravity-flow systems in Dry Zone settlement areas. However, many an individual farmer lacked trust in the capacity of the new authorities – whether participatory or bureaucratic-centralised – either to control overuse by other individual farmers, or to deliver water and maintain systems well enough to render his own overuse untempting. If land reform had been implemented, so that big landlords could not subvert new participatory authorities in traditional systems; or if maintenance and water-management had received more priority in modern systems; then a 'core' of farmers, sufficient to uphold the new means of water control, might have become effective. In practice, in an island-wide spate of gross water overuse – perfectly rational for each farmer, mistrustful of both his neighbours and the control and delivery capacity of the new water managers – tail-ender and second-season coverage of, and returns from, both old and new gravity-flow systems were extremely disappointing. Farmers increasingly sought, and after 1977 obtained, a return – at least nominally – to the *vel vidane* system. But irrigation in Sri Lanka remains a war of each against all.

The lessons for 'democracy' are two. First, both 'participation' and (unless costly and unacceptably Draconian) system-level centralisation are equally hopeless methods of moving from PD to CO in irrigation systems, unless either price-incentives or support – presumably State support – for physical controls exist as ultimate sanctions. Second, party-politicisation of managerial responsibility, while helpful to the poor in some other circumstances,[46] in the case of irrigation so damages confidence in water management – and therefore so stimulates defection from CO arrangements by farmers fearing that unless they overuse water now, they will be left high and dry by non-delivery later – as to be prohibitively costly.

Four approaches appear relevant. (1) Seek circumstances where the assumptions for CO are met, and try to re-create those circumstances elsewhere. (2) Use water pricing or (3) irrigation structures to create incentives for optimal use. (4) Reform the institutions of water management, at irrigation-bureaucracy and/or farm level.

(1) Apparently, in South Indian villages, voluntary and endogenous cooperative institutions for gravity-flow water management thrive if and only if such water is (a) scarce enough for the improved chance of a CO allocation to be worth the cost of such institutions, but (b) not so scarce as, once more, not to be worth that cost, and (c) supplied from the main system with sufficient reliability – given the scarcity – as to keep reasonably small the risk that the cost will be wasted.[47] Institutional costs of this sort here stand for the 'transaction costs', of resource transfer, which have for Coase to be 'sufficiently small' to produce his result, that externality assignments not affect optimal use of (irrigation) resources. Such conditions are rather rarely fulfilled – and do nothing to improve *inter*-village allocation (least of all if villages are far apart), or to improve on corrupt or inefficient main-system decisions made by irrigation bureaucracies, even if the costs to farmers of such improvement are far smaller than the benefits. Farmers are just too small and scattered to handle *distant* free-rider or cost-sharing problems – the leading problem being, not that some may overpay for costs of traditional-indigenous cooperative water control while others default (even then the net benefits to overpayers would be positive), but that insufficient resources may be collected to maintain control.[48] This underlines the great importance of defining the right sub-regions, if 'democracy' or 'participation' is to work as a remedy for PD. As with TC (p. 82), so with irrigation: it is too simple to say 'as population density grows, reduce the risk of PD by reducing the size of the area in which CO is sought'. Technical separability – here of common water, there of common grazing – is crucial too.

(2) Charges *per cusec* were once widely advocated by the World Bank, and have sometimes worked, but the approach has in many cases been abandoned. Metering offers technical difficulties, is usually infeasible at small-farm (and especially small-plot) level, and at outlet level

requires non-price allocations – with the attendant risk of PD – below the outlet. Also meters, like sluices, can be broken. *Per-acre* charges are more feasible. However, betterment levies on irrigated land do not provide incentives to reduce water use; and crop-specific per-acre levies, higher for thirsty crops, are seldom enforcible. Official water pricing does not transfer cash from gainers to losers (of less), or bribes from potential losers to potential gainers (of less), as would be required to move from PD conflicts to a Coasean negotiating process.[49] The central problem with price solutions is the combination of (differential) risk-aversion with institutional transition; cattle taxation provides a much better chance of overcoming this problem in the TC case than do attempts at irrigation pricing in this case.

(3) Proper choice of physical irrigation structures – notably cross-bunds – can greatly assist irrigation managers to reduce sub-optimality in gravity-flow systems. But this achieves COs via outside control, not via Coasean contracting among farmers. Even further from Coase's route is the (quite realistic) prospect of an inexpensive microchip-controlled system, steering water into secondaries, and adjusting depths, on the basis of instant information on crop-water conditions throughout the irrigable area, and of an optimisation model.

(4) Institutional reform, too, seems to achieve COs best by non-Coasean methods. (a) *Warabandi* – rotational irrigation – while probably applicable only to specific terrains and with good communications,[50] has been highly successful there. It depends upon outside bureaucratic enforcement, not on farmer agreement to exchanges that produce a social optimum. (b) Farmers below the outlet do sometimes reach agreements on water assignments, to reduce the output losses due to private maximisation despite external costs; but such agreements seem to apply only where delivery to the outlet is fairly reliable (note 47). (c) In groundwater systems, the conflict between medium-scale deep tubewells for bigger farmers and shallow tubewells for small farmers, both with land above the same water-table, is usually resolved to the detriment of the latter (and of net social product) as bigger farmers take what they want and the water-table falls.[51] The institutions by which smaller farmers could combine to pay the bigger farmers to restrain water use, and by which such agreements could be enforced, appear too costly to create; the institutions by which bigger farmers (if canal headenders) would be compelled by law towards restraint, or (if deep tubewell irrigators) charged for excess use to compensate for lost net output to handpumpers, are opposed effectively by bigger farmers (and townspeople dependent on their surpluses). Ownership and sale of

tubewell-water by *smaller* farmers or the landless – a counterpart of one Coasean *larger-farm* recipe for TC (note 41) – does seem feasible, if organised.[52] (d) The contact between tubewell management in the Pakistan and Indian Punjabs epitomises the failure of perfectly rational groundwater users to be, as it were, covered by the assumptions of Coase's Law. In the 1960s, Pakistan was commended by the World Bank and others for encouraging freely-spreading private tubewell ownership, while India was condemned for insisting on public ownership or at least control of private siting. On Coasean assumptions, Pakistan's farmers would have negotiated private deals to allow only the socially optimal rates of water depletion and land salinisation (which, of course, exceed the zero rates advocated by conservationists!). Those who accept these assumptions – not necessarily Coase – would also tend to argue that Indian irrigating, siting, and zoning bureaucracies would be over-cautious, less informed about optimal siting and depletion than farmers, and at worst tending – perhaps corruptly – to increase their own income or patronage by their decisions. Conclusion: Coasean Pakistani negotiation good, Indian Punjab 'managerialism' bad. The realities were different. By the mid-1970s, several parts of the Pakistan Punjab revealed fallen water-tables, and/or increased salinity from tubewell water overuse, much above what might be justified economically even at high rates of time-preference. In the Indian Punjab, where the authorities had until the 1970s relied on bureaucratic siting of tubewells rather than private dealing on Coasean assumptions, the result, appeared to come closer to social optima.

Why don't the various participants in irrigation allocations – head and tailenders, alone in farmer-owned systems, otherwise with controllers (a plus) who have self-interests not necessarily or solely maximised by optimal water allocation (a minus) – organise water to maximise net farm product from all participants, and bargain about distributing this (largest possible) net benefit? The obvious reason, absence of institutions – even if expressed more correctly, as *high cost* of new institutions able to command a 'core' of farmer support during transition from authoritative local institutions (like the *vel vidane*) to as yet less-accepted institutions, participatory-local (cultivation committees) or State-central – begs the key Coasean question. Why should not the existence of a Pareto-superior, attainable water outcome lead all farmers to bear the cost of, and/or accept and enforce the decisions of, appropriate institutions?

Underlying the 'absence of institutions' in irrigation management is the problem of risk. If a head-end farmer in a big gravity-flow system sees water in a canal near his field, and believes there is a risk that he won't see it again unless he takes it quickly, he will take what he can, and indeed leave himself a reserve (if feasible) against future emergency. Even in private, farmer-owned irrigation systems, the head-ender (and water-owner) will tend to take more water, and sell less to tail-enders, than would be the case if he were maximising expected net farm profit. He takes more water in order to reduce his risk of being left with inadequate water later. Sometimes risk is the end of the story: without adequate insurance arrangements, even if water markets are perfect, top-enders will use more, and tail-enders less, water than would maximise their *expected* joint net income. The less the risk in the top-ender's total activity set – that is, consumer as well as producer risk – the less his aversion from extra risk due to water delays later; also, less water-sensitive or water-timing-sensitive crops help.

In many cases, however, the 'risk' is not just of physical water failure – not enough rain, so that top-enders wish they had retained and stored more irrigation water – but of human failure. Tail-enders are reluctant to rely on water that head-enders, or water authorities, may either fail to deliver due to bad management, or choose not to deliver because – despite contracts to do so – they find more profitable opportunities. Institutions to enforce contracts, or to define liabilities precisely, are inadequate; once more, even if the CO can arise (p. 52) from *any* clear assignment of liability for external cost, where there is *no* clear assignment Coasean negotiations give way to PD, cheating, and non-CO. High risk of (and high risk-aversion from) non-enforcement, and absence of institutions to enforce contracts or clarify responsibilities for externalities, feed upon each other. And (as the Pakistan 'over-tubewelling' story shows) high risk, political and other, can lead even big farmers into very high time-preference and 'water mining' – alas, also salt mining – inconsistent with the good performance of Coasean institutions.

4. Townward migration: problems with Coasean interpretations

We consider four. (1) Is there significant overshooting, as migrants respond to the *probability* (< 1) of an urban job, so that some migrants for some of the time are involuntarily jobless in cities – and could Coasean contracts avoid the situation by which some of the migrants raise unemployment rates (risks) for all townspeople? (2) Why do not markets, or bargains, reduce townward migration until expected marginal private benefit falls to equal expected marginal [private *plus external*] (e.g. urban congestion) costs? (3) Should not these market-bargain reductions also allow for expected marginal costs, if any, borne by rural people who stay behind? (4) Can risk-averting motives for migration be accommodated by Coasean side-payments to COs? Of these four, only (1) – the most familiar – in fact presents no threat to Coase's assumptions.

(1) Like many arguments based on imperfect information or market failure, this usually turns out unimportant empirically, except in the very short run and/or in areas remote from the place where incentive structures have changed. Such exceptions can have major income-distribution effects (*nearby* villages migrate to, seize, and protect against later competing remote migrants, scarce urban jobs), but few allocative effects of the type that Coase's Law seeks to deny. More fundamentally (1) claims an inefficiency simply because – in order to maximise discounted value of lifetime *expected* income streams – working migrants knowingly move from lower rural unemployment rates (given age, sex and skill) to higher urban rates. Migrants do this because the discounted present value to them of (higher) expected income, multiplied by lower expected employment, is for all lifetime streams higher in rural than in urban places.[53] But is this inefficient? (a) First, is it proven? Undoubtedly, urban unemployment rates exceed rural rates, even holding income constant.[54] But this does not prove that a marginal worker raises his unemployment risk by migrating. (b) Assume he does. This could be because the proportion of workers not self-employed, and especially of casuals, is higher in towns. Many migrants would be in such groups even had they stayed in the villages. By migrating, they merely 'urbanise' an unemployment-prone workforce structure that would otherwise be rural. (c) Apart from this, migrants are probably more 'unemployment-prone' than others within their parts of the age, sex and workforce structures – this may be one reason why they move – and, once more, their urbanisation merely transfers unemployment townwards, rather than increasing it. (d) If the migrants had stayed behind and found rural work, with the same rural land and capital, they would have cut rural average product – and (given urban land and capital) raised urban average product. By urbanising, the migrants implicitly judged the former effect greater.[55] To prove inefficiency, we must prove that judgement wrong; why

should it be? Migrants soon tell their fellow-villagers whether the city streets are paved with job prospects at good incomes or not.

(2) So Todaro-style overshooting probably seldom constitutes a non-Coasean effect of urbanisation (because, apart from raising urban unemployment it cuts rural unemployment, especially in slack seasons; because of the productivity effect (1d) above; and, therefore, because external costs to urban workers are offset by external benefits, both via lower unemployment rates and via productivity rises, to rural workers). However, Coasean bargains fail to prevent excessive, non-Coasean congestion-cost outcomes of urbanisation. Housing and transport congestion and deterioration, even if fully anticipated by *migrants*, are imposed on *settled* townspeople. The offsetting rural decongestion can reasonably be assumed to have insufficient benefits to outweigh the extra urban congestion costs, especially since townward migrants most often move to the parts of towns already most congested. There are no obvious ways in which bargains or contracts, among the huge populations affected (townspeople in congested areas, plus *all* potential migrants to such areas), are feasible. Governmental attempts to restrict or control townward migration (Djakarta, China, S Africa) are apparently based entirely on urban welfare and pressures, and cannot reasonably be seen as an implicit contract or bargain involving all potentially affected persons. This is no negotiable CO, but an odd sort of PD; *all* migrants and townspeople would be better off, as at [2, 2] in Table 3.2, if *all* migrants could be offered, and persuaded to adopt, the following strategy: 'Throw a die once a year if you intend to migrate. Migrate if it comes up 1 or 2. Otherwise obtain a Concessional Rural Development Loan, to improve your rural income expectations, financed by townspeople.' (More scientific ways of locating recipients could be devised!) But such a strategy is not on the menu. In choosing to migrate or to stay, even if such a strategy were available, the potential migrant would need to rely on trust or enforcement, in a world made, familiarly, more difficult by the increasing numbers of transactors to the PD game.

(3) In rejecting the Todaro outcomes as examples of non-CO impacts of urbanisation under (1), we stressed the *positive* rural externalities from 'urbanising' some unemployment. However, *negative* external effects of urbanisation on rural people can also exist, and can cause non-COs, even if (as is usually the case) each migrant, or originating household, correctly foresees net private gain. Many of the migrants are skilled, educated, potential rural leaders or entrepreneurs (even if currently at high risk of unemployment); they are drawn by expected

private gains into urban life. Yet the marginal *social* return, say, to a doctor almost anywhere in Asia or Africa is higher in rural areas.[56] This disparity between private and social return comes about in several ways, none of them captured by the term 'market failure'. First, the power-structure may be skewing urban rewards up, relative to rural rewards, both for doctors practising publicly and for patients able to pay them privately. Second, society may value life in itself, rural or urban, not expected lifetime income. In either case, it could be argued that nothing has gone wrong with Coase's Law – it is merely that somebody does not like the prices to which migrant medical trainees respond. But this cannot be quite right, (a) because, as relatively abler rural people go to live in cities, the political process enables them further to skew prices to favour the cities, (b) because there *is* some social product lost if relative prices induce doctors to migrate to lower-yielding work, (c) perhaps above all, because there is no clear *signalling mechanism* by which rural (or urban) externalities can be reflected, via offers of bargains, in incentives to potential migrants. Unlike (1), something is going wrong via (3) with COs for urbanisation. Unlike (2), that something is not usefully captured in a PD model.

(4) Externalities not susceptible to Coasean bargains may also be introduced into migration (as into irrigation) by risk. A major motive for migration may be to diversify a family portfolio, for instance to provide a bedrock income when *either* village *or* town faces severe income falls.[57] If so – and even if a migrant reduces expected non-migrant village income by a little more than he raises his own expected income – non-migrants may be unable to bribe the migrant to stay put, because they can transfer only sufficient to meet his expected (mean) rural–urban income gap. They cannot guarantee to make that income available in years of village harvest failure – indeed, are very unlikely to be able to do so. (Better credit or insurance markets might help, but at high transaction costs.)

5. Population and isolation: CO v PD

Cassen has applied, to population decisions, a version of Sen's 'isolation paradox'.[58] Suppose that each couple relies, for security in old age, upon remittance income, out of a job obtained by a son who survives to adulthood. Suppose, further, that the rate of investment does not suffice to build up enough capital stock to employ all 'sons', at wage-rates sufficient to permit such remittances and equal to the full-employment supply price of their labour. Now, the more children couples produce, the more workers will compete for jobs *14–55 years hence*; therefore, the lower will be the proportion of their time spent in employment, their wage-rate, the proportion of such workers who remit to support their aged parents, and the average remittance by each remitting worker.

Each couple *now*, therefore, would gain doubly by entering into an enforcible contract with all other couples to restrict family size. There is a short-run gain to couples, because costs of child care (and infant and child mortality rates) fall. There is a long-run gain – both to couples in old age via expected value of remittance income per couple, and to society via GNP per person – because (say) all 1000 couples produce 2 children each, to compete for 2500 jobs, whereas in the absence of such a contract all 1000 would produce 3 children each, to compete for a not-much-larger number of jobs – perhaps a smaller number, if higher child–adult ratios bring lower savings/income and 'hence' investment/ income ratios – at a lower real wage rate. Both GNP per person and expected income for each couple are raised by a 'family planning contract'.

However, the couples are *isolated*, and cannot make, nor if they did could they enforce, contracts for lower completed family size. If all other families are conceiving as many human tickets to the job queue as they can, then so must you and your wife, even if each decision lengthens the queue. (Incidentally, you, or such children as did get jobs, must later support your queueing children.)

This 'population-contract isolation paradox' (PCIP) has some similarities to PD, especially TC. But a crucial difference, in respect of the consequences for COs, is in the time-sequence. We have seen (pp. 71–2) that Coase – because concerned mainly to show that liability rules for negative externalities do not affect allocative efficiency (assuming zero transactions costs) – does not discuss the rule that prior claim entitles to compensation for subsequent damage; such a rule affects distribution, but not allocation, if Coase is right (and if the two are separable[59]); and we have objected that general faith in the fairness of liability rules affects the enforcibility of *any* rule. If people believe that prior claim, or vested interest, is naturally just, the cost of enforcing rules or contracts that ignore priority will tend to be very high, perhaps prohibitive. Such priority will be needed to get a transition from PD conflict to CO negotiation accepted.

However, the time-sequence of PCIP prevents its resolution via a prior-claim liability rule. Very large numbers of parents are procreating more or less at once, in ignorance of each other's decisions. In an endless chain, each cohort of parents is victim of the 'prior claim' of earlier cohorts, and impose of its own prior claim on later cohorts. No just break-point in the chain can be established by imposing a liability rule. It makes no sense to break the chain, to define some latecomers who must have few children or compensate 'earlier' procreating couples for damaging their children's job prospects. For, even with perfect knowledge, it is precisely the early-comers' many children that compel each late-comer couple to have many children too, to ensure a given probability of jobs for them and hence of remittance income for the couple when old. There is no analogy to the doctor–confectioner case; the late-comer there (confectioner) can choose other locations, quieter machines, etc. (The herd-size case is more like the doctor–confectioner case.)

In the case of PCIP, therefore, we seem to have – as with some irrigation examples – a situation which cannot be moved out of PD via agreement to negotiate with prior-claim rules to assign liability for external costs, yet which is plainly sub-optimal: all couples could gain by enforcing a contract to reduce the family size norms of each. Even some evasion, some free-riding, could take place and still leave all couples gainers, and all children of non-evading couples facing better survival-chances as well as higher rates of employment and real wages. Yet, of course, no such family size contract has been devised. There is ample evidence that family size norms, rather than family planning methods, are the main determinant of live-births per couple. These norms are kept high by aversion from risk, notably the risks of insufficient children surviving to adulthood, or of insufficient survivors being employed, or earning enough, in adulthood to remit to their parents. Yet each couple's high family size norms, by raising actual family size, increase for all couples those very risks – pre-adult death, adult unemployment – against which the norms were selected to insure. Old-age pensions for couples without adult children, by inducing lower family size norms, could well raise GNP per head – directly by reducing population growth, and thus indirectly via switches of investment from capital widening to capital deepening – enough to justify such pensions *as investments*. But neither such pensions, nor other disincentives to large family size, constitute, however implicitly, the sorts of bargain or contract, envisaged by Coase as likely to exhaust all possibilities of moving nearer the Pareto frontier if potential GNP gain is large relative to transactions cost. Coase envisages negotiations, free contracts, or mergers to internalise externalities. We are talking about State or group

6. Beverage crops: a layered PD?

Tea, coffee and cocoa are each in very price-inelastic world demand. Each Third World producer country gains most if others restrict output and it does not; least if it restricts and others do not; much if all restrict, but little if none restrict. Such a 'country-player PD' already raises two new problems for Coasean optimisation: the great distance among transactors, and the higher time-preference of the poorest among them. But worse is to come. The PD has a second layer. Some LDCs, for example Sri Lanka (tea, 1955–65), at times produce shares of world output well in excess of price-elasticity of demand. It would thus pay even such *single countries*, in the short term, to restrict output. Within such countries, there is a second-layer PD among tea growers: each wants the others to restrict output, wants to expand his own, and dreads that all may.

For LDC tea producers *as a whole*, a 10 per cent cut in tea output and exports would lead to a rise in prices of about 30 per cent in the short term, and almost certainly over 20 per cent even in the long term. Yet such cartels do not last; and the reason is not, *à la* Calabresi (note 10(c)), that consumers, seeing a net gain if they can bribe producers to refrain from restricting tea or coffee output, offer such bribes.

Consider the position from the viewpoint of the individual grower of, say, tea. Any land that he takes out of tea is useless for 2–3 years of clearance and rehabilitation, followed by 5–7 years of early bush growth if he replants a tree crop. Other crops than tea – especially non-bush crops – as compared with tea usually yield far less net value-added per acre. If other growers, around the world, similarly restrict output, the grower will gain net income; but, first, he has no guarantee that other growers *will* restrict; and, second, if they do, why should he not maintain his own tea acreage and free-ride on the price rise secured by the output restrictions of others? Small growers, often the most efficient tea growers, are both more risk-averse than other growers, and have higher time-preference: will they abide by acreage or yield controls, especially since enforcement costs are greater than for big estates? In tea (and to a lesser extent in coffee), producer action to secure joint maximum income – by some 'fair' agreement to share cuts in world tea output, until price-elasticity of demand for it is unitary is further impeded by the dynamics. Old, seed yields eventually decline; new, clonal yields start much higher (and costs per acre only somewhat higher). Shifts in market share to new producers, and new producing nations, tend to happen for that reason, especially because planting new tea bushes has much lower opportunity cost than replanting old tea areas.

World agreement among tea-producing nations to restrict output thus seems unlikely, because these nations face quite distinct incentives. With price-elasticity of demand for world tea exports around -0.3, it is hard to see why a country exporting 1 per cent should be keen on restriction, while one with 35 per cent clearly would. Yet side-payments from 35 per cent to 1 per cent nations would set precedents for blackmail by 1 per cent, $\frac{1}{2}$ per cent and even 0 per cent nations, threatening to *start* growing tea. It is not transactions-costs, or limitations on bargains, or 'market failure', in any of the usual senses, that prevents producers from controlling the external cost to each of expansion by each (of course this is a *pecuniary* external cost in Scitovsky's sense: see note 5). It is differences in interests, plus risk-aversion, and high preference by some for present over future returns. These differences are compounded by international and intra-national transactors in large numbers, at great distances, and not readily controllable, even by sanctions to which all have agreed.

7. Contributor's Dilemma (CD)

Suppose that each of two or more villagers would benefit from a *public good* (PG) – a well, a fence, the services of a *vel vidane* or a guard to keep animals off standing crops, or a guild or trade union to affect the price or quantity of marketed output or labour.

> It can be true of each person that if he helps [to build or finance the public good], he will add to the sum of benefits, or expected benefits. But only a very small portion of the benefits he adds will come back to *him* [and this may be less than the value of] his contribution. It may thus be better for each if he does not contribute. This can be so whatever others do. But it would be worse for each if fewer others contribute. And if none contribute this would be worse for each than if all do.[60]

In terms of Table 3.3, the CD is a true PD. For *I*, it is best if *II* alone pays (Strategy 2), the public good is provided, and *I*, by paying nothing (his Strategy 2), free-rides; worst if *I* alone pays (his Strategy 1), the public good is provided, and *II* does not pay (Strategy 1) and thus free-rides; second-best, that both pay the subscription (Strategy 2) so that neither free-rides, and each gets a 50 per cent refund or a higher-grade PG (fencing, field-guarding, etc. is done to a higher standard); and third-best if neither pays and the PG is not provided at all. For *II*, these respective options are, in order of preference, ranked 4–1–2–3. As in Table 3.3, self-interest suggests that *I* and *II* each adopt the dominant 'don't pay' strategy. Both *I* and *II* seek to free-ride, and thereby ensure there is no horse.

Note how artificial is my presentation of CD as a *two-person* PD. Any of three other assumptions, each at least as likely as mine, if there are two (or few) 'players' destroys the PD framework. (a) For each villager, 'I pay and he doesn't' could well be better than 'I don't pay, he doesn't, and there's no PG'; it pays the two villagers to negotiate, because each knows that – unlike the PD case – he loses by cheating subsequently, since the PG depends on payment by both. (b) The Table 3.3 structure is correct – i.e. (a) is wrong – but the flow of benefits to all users from the desired PG might well increase smoothly, as outlay or work-input increases, without sharp thresholds or very drastically diminishing returns. (c) The PG may well be price-excludable.[61] (d) Even if none of the above applies – so that the pay-off table is a true PD, like Table 3.3 – the two villagers might well know each other (especially if they stand to gain from a PG common to them only) and hence would probably negotiate to share the cost of providing and maintaining the PG. Coasean arguments apply.

In three senses (d) is not a 'market solution'. First, it is not impersonal, but depends on personal knowledge and face-to-face dealing. Second, it is closer to bilateral monopoly than to perfect competition. Third, if each party prices a unit of services from the PG at its marginal utility to him, or such a unit at the marginal cost of supplying it, there is no guarantee that the two valuations coincide, or – more significantly – that either provides an acceptable procedure for sharing the cost of provision. A sense of fairness might suggest that villagers share costs of the PG in proportion to their share in its benefits.[62] This 'average not marginal' approach, probably implying price discrimination, is neither a market solution nor even one that has much to do with the price mechanism. Yet such an approach may be essential to ensure the sense of fairness needed, if each party is to rely on negotiated outcomes being adhered to by others.

Accepted fair agreements – or agreements imposed by one strong party and one weak party – as in (d) are nevertheless likely in two-person CDs. Hence PG provision seldom generates free-rider problems and CDs – and hence problems of authority, democracy, or 'Oriental despotism'[63] in the control of irrigation systems – in very small communities. It may be one reason why the rare surviving cases of apparently non-hierarchical societies occur in very small clan-like groups, such as those of the Kung.[64] But very small communities get bigger, not only when population grows, but when the requirements of economic specialisation, central (e.g. village) services with scale economies, or military defence so indicate. Hence the causes or origins of feudal hierarchies, often interpreted as direct responses to the changing technology of farming,[65] can also be seen as requirements of public-good management, when changing technology – military or productive – makes for bigger communities. These imply less face-to-face negotiation (weakening objection (d) above); a smaller share of benefit by each in a public good enjoyed by all (weakening (a)); and a search for economies of scale in construction and use of the public good, is constructed, weakening (b) above. So, in a many-person community, and with price-excludability for the PG infeasible or very costly, can a tolerated coercion simulate (d)-type agreements such as prevail in very small communities? One of the many senses of *noblesse oblige* may have been the feudal lord's obligation to see that adequate military defence – from which all in a baronial system derived a small net benefit even if all served in the army; but which each would rather see provided by armed service from others – was made available on a basis of 'fair shares for all', and not frustrated by PDs with non-CO outcomes as communities grew in numbers.[66]

But centralised modern states are inconsistent with, and come to dominate and displace, feudal communities. If specialisation and public services – and in LDCs also rapid population growth – increase the number of CDs that are true PDs, what is to replace the sense of fairness and/or authority structure in the newer societies? Some form of participation or democracy is one possible answer.

This may also be necessary as increases in community size generate, out of a series of CDs, Olson's problem.[67] This stems from the fact that free-riding is much easier to detect, penalise, and create hostile valuations toward, in a small than in a large community. The temptation to avoid paying one's subscription to a PG (and the likelihood that (a) on p. 96 is wrong) also increases as community size rises because, as the community grows, further increases in the cash or labour 'subscription income' of organisations supplying PGs are increasingly likely to show diminishing marginal returns in general, and a rising proportion of bureaucratic expenses in particular. Olson's problem is that interest-groups seeking to create PGs for large communities are, or become, weak; whereas those creating PGs for small sub-groups – often, as with cartels, PGs that harm other members of the larger community – are strong, because better able to enforce subscription and avoid free-riding. Olson stresses the need for rapid change in societies, to avoid the entrenchment of interest groups representing small – perhaps because obsolescent – groups of professionals, businesses or workers, yet able to maintain coherence because their very smallness avoids PD and permits subscriptions to be collected. Such rapid change is essential in very poor societies to overcome mass poverty, but is it likely to overcome Olson's problem? Its effect in reducing the similarities of successive experiences – and hence in reducing one's chance to apply lessons from other players' responses to one's own non-CO plays of a single PD, and thus to turn non-CO dominance there into a CO solution to a repeated PD – militates against this hope: Olson's solution may help *create* single-play PDs (see p. 63, Argument 4a). With Olson's problem also, some form of participatory democracy, in which cost and benefit sharing by all participants is obtained by voting, or meeting to decide, on both the PG itself and on the general financing principle,[68] may be a more hopeful approach.

Population growth, specialisation, provision of public services such as schools, and incorporation of remote persons (and subsistence systems) into general policies (and exchange economies), all tend to raise the size of physical communities,[69] such as villages, users of a fence or canal, etc. This raises the likelihood both of true 'PD-shaped' Contributors' Dilemmas and, therefore, of Olson problems – in small groups within physical communities that cannot enforce sufficient 'contributions'. Feudal hierarchies and Oriental despotisms may replace a sense of 'fairness' as a way for a moderately-enlarged community to obtain corvee labour, tithes, or other subscriptions; but, in much enlarged societies with less hierarchical values, an illusion or reality of democracy or participation may be indispensable.

VI

The CD/free-rider case was left until the end of the last section, because it both introduces and summarises the case for democracy in LDCs, made out by the need – in the cause of economic *efficiency* (not 'merely' equity, which generates a case for democratically equal voting rights directly) – to fight against the tendency to move from COs to PDs during modern development. This tendency is due to the combination of features of traditional poverty (risk-aversion), development (rapid change), population growth, and transition of trust.

It is not argued here that all good things go together. Any political arrangements that 'hold the ring' – including highly authoritative ones – can control, and often have controlled, non-CO tendencies effectively, most often by severely penalising them. A rational oppressor – if it pays him to leave some common grazing or water rights – has every reason to see the commons preserved, not destroyed by PDs (see p. 70, condition (4) for the move into Phase 3 of TC) – though, unfortunately, also both reason and power to see those others pay for it, and to expropriate a large share of common product for itself. However, these forms of control-without-consensus involve very expensive policing – at the cost mainly of investment, if societies are too poor to cut consumption much (given the leakage of surplus into rulers' luxury consumption). In the rest of this paper, we summarise the ways in which a PC–CO transition might be eased or encouraged by 'democracy' or 'participation'. We close by asking whether their other efficiency and equity impacts might outweigh any possible benefits from more COs and fewer PDs.

We observed (p. 50) that an all-PD society would be ungovernable, asking whether their other efficiency and equity impacts might outweigh any possible benefits from more COs and fewer PDs.

We observed (p. 0) that an all-PD society would be ungovernable, while an all-CO society would require government only to 'improve' distribution – which might be necessary to create the sense of fairness that persuades potential defaulters to observe COs without (unacceptably costly) enforcement. Yet PDs are, for reasons discussed, 'taking over' from COs in many areas of Third World life. There is a transition of trust, from powerful authorities that enforced COs because they too gained from PGs and the protection of the commons, to States often lacking local knowledge or power, and sometimes served by underpaid, weak, inexperienced or corrupt officials (p. 51). Can or should such societies adopt democratic and participatory approaches, regaining the capacity formerly found through older hierarchies to secure some agreement on relative values of incomes for different persons, but avoiding the abuse of surpluses and the restriction of others' actions associated with those declining hierarchies (pp. 81–2)?

If democracy really distributes power over grazing or irrigation policy fairly equally in some respects, might otherwise poor and weak graziers or irrigators be more willing to accept control or incentives favouring COs, without the need for infeasibly costly controls? Certainly the assumptions on which any of the three routes to a CO – Coasean negotiations, markets, or mergers to internalise externalities – can get rid of PD behaviour without State action are very strong (p. 55). Democratic or participatory controls over such action would seem required if the State is not to become overweening through its role in such necessary action.

Simplistic optimism about such controls is silly. Irrigators in many places appear to be saying: participation doesn't work, can we please have our *vel vidane* back (p. 34). Some of the structural causes of PD outcomes – one-off plays, rapid changes that invalidate repeated-PD assumptions – are not relevant in any obvious way to the presence or absence of democracy. But other arguments against adopting non-CO strategies in PD – altruism; internalised acceptable (i.e. for most, more egalitarian) rankings of persons and their extra incomes; acceptance of costs of joint enforcement of agreements (pp. 67–7) – appear likelier to lead to COs in democratic environments. Some way to reduce the massive PD wastes during transitions – from hierarchical, local to modern, State systems; from circumstances of ample commons to circumstances where the negative externalities from private maximising suffice to finance social controls against such externalities (p. 69) – is required. Traditional and local means of participatory control (irrigator groups, rotating credit-savings associations) are well worth trying, and have some recorded successes. So do devices to get assets to poor cooperators (note 52).

If the TCs and other PDs discussed in this paper are local, it is unlikely that central, formal, multi-issue, electoral democracy is of the essence in converting the outcomes to COs. Such formal democracy is in some ways an extremely important protective device for the poor and weak, and is much likelier than undemocratic central systems to create institutions for local, issue-specific, participatory democracy. However, it is these latter institutions that count most in the battle against PD waste.

'Participation' is one of the most abused OK-words in the literature. It cannot usefully mean that non-specialists take complex technical decisions about channel layout. Much too often, it means undue influence by local notables on central sources of public money (Bierce, one feels, would have so defined it). Often, too, it has been a pseudonym for (a) harmful party-politicisation or (b) blaming the victims – for example when the irrigation bureaucracy fails to deliver water through incompetence or corruption, it attacks the farmers for failing, through participatory water-users' groups, to ration the water that the bureaucracy has made suddenly scarce. Yet, if a 'commons' has to be controlled or a PD avoided, it is fairly evident that control by all gainers from [2, 2, ...] outcomes represents the best hope of getting CO solutions at acceptable enforcement cost: of increasing altruism and internalisation of CO-values.

Moreover, we have at several points stressed that larger groups are more prone to PDs, and to high control costs to ensure COs[69]. Yet it is over-simple to conclude that 'smallest is beautiful' in designing democratic institutions to manage a PG or to avoid a TC. Whether a water source or a common grazing is separable is in part a technical matter (pp. 82,85). Decentralised or federal forms of control carry their own costs.

The naïveté of the views that either 'getting the prices right' or State controls, *as such*, can solve major development problems is clearly brought out by the CO–PD alternative. Coase's own procedures sharply depart from either of these naïve views, stressing instead negotiation (though with market or merger alternatives) under law. But how is such law to be enforced at acceptable cost? The old hierarchies are decreasingly trusted. Populations, and (even more) dyadic relations, are increasing rapidly, raising the costs of authoritarian control (p. 71). Developmental change reduces the prospect that repetition of PD can induce COs (p. 73). Yet poverty maintains high individual aversion from experimenting with 'dominated' CO strategies in single PDs. Centralised policies to upgrade common irrigation or grazing are in these circumstances often counterproductive (sec. V(2)). Localised decisions about, and shared responsibility for, public goods may in these circumstances be the only cost-effective solution for a poor country to the proliferation of PDs.

NOTES

1. The need for foreign policy towards, or collective defence against, non-members of the society does not constitute an exception, even if such a need can be discharged only by a single authority (an extreme case of scale economies). All CO agents would pay for that authority voluntarily.
2. D. Parfit, *Reasons and Persons* (Oxford, 1984) p. 58. He adds (p. 59) that

so-called 'repeated PD', where two-person cases *are* common, is not really PD at all, because the pay-off on each play includes not only the entry in the box for that play, but also, implicitly, the expected value of the effect, on one's net gain from all future plays, of adopting the strategy next time. That is why the cooperative solution is quite common in 'repeated PD' (A. Rapoport and A. Chammah, *Prisoner's Dilemma*, Michigan UP, 1965) although strictly dominated, in a single-play two-person game with complete isolation between the players, by the non-cooperative solution.

3. This will surprise believers in perfect competition. But this ideal type is entirely different from Coase's. Almost all Coase's examples (R. H. Coase, 'The Problem of Social Cost', *Journal of Law and Economics*, 1960, 3 (Oct)) are of *two-person* situations, in which juridical decisions on compensation rules are shown not to affect the subsequent activity levels of *interacting* pairs of self-interested negotiators (with zero costs of negotiation and of contract enforcement). Perfect competition secures *many-person* optimisation on very strong assumptions, one of which is *negligible interaction* between, or impact of action by, any one person on any one other person. The model can be extended to handle Coasean problems by assuming perfect markets in externalities, but (like, in another context, the Arrow–Debreu assumption of perfect conditional forward markets) this piles Pelion on Ossa of implausible assumption.

4. 'As societies evolve, land-use patterns change, and populations grow, the regulatory mechanisms that earlier maintained balance between men and the environment often break down, and the prudent use of renewable resources can no longer be effectively asserted' (circular letter from National Research Council, Office of International Affairs, Board on Science and Technology for International Development, Washington, DC, 11 May 1984, received after writing this section).

5. In a *global* sense – i.e. transcending the society producing the product – this last is a 'pecuniary externality', corresponding to a benefit for non-members of the society, and thus not leading to resource misallocation (as does a technological externality, unless negotiated between the parties to a CO: see W. Baumol, 'On taxation and the control of externalities', *AER*, 62, June 1972, for the application of Scitovsky's distinction to COs). However, if 'the society' comprises only the producing and marketing community, then *local* optimisation, by cartel action to reduce sales, raises 'the society's' benefit and *should* – on Coasean assumptions – be reached by Coasean negotiations, although (a) each producer within 'the society' must restrict production, yet gains from so doing only if others also restrict, and (b) consumers outside 'the society' lose all, or more than all, that the producers inside it gain. See the discussion of tea and coffee production in Section V, and also note 1 above.

6. In the sense of the peasant-studies literature: a small group of people with common customs (*mores*), adherence to which is 'morally' approved. See S. Popkin, *The Rational Peasant* (University of California Press, 1979). The transition described here is between 'societies' with distinct modes of reaching social decisions. It is not a transition – of the type deplored by Toennies – from an 'organic community' (based on solidarity rather than

on transactions and the exchange of benefits) to a 'society' of reflectively willed individual maximisation in a framework of economic relationships governed by impersonal laws (J. Freund, 'German sociology in the time of Max Weber', in T. Bottomore and R. Nisbet, *A History of Sociological Analysis* (New York: Basic Books, 1978) especially pp. 153–7). Certainly an organic 'community' – where members do not, as in a 'society', each 'seek ... his own advantage ... setting aside agreements of wills', in Toennies's words (ibid., p. 157) – would generate COs, not PDs. Unfortunately, outside the cave, such pervasive community is not an ideal type but a myth!

7. If a common good – such as field-guards to prevent straying animals (R. Wade, 'The social response to irrigation: an Indian case study', JDS, 5, 16, 1, October 1979) – is sufficiently beneficial for an individual to make it worth his while to pay his share (however determined) of the cost, he does not need to know that *all* other members of society will pay their share. He needs only to expect that *sufficient* members will do so to finance *enough* of the common good – e.g. enough guard-hours – to provide that individual with *sufficient* benefit (in this example, grain saved from animal depredation) to exceed the value of his share of the cost. Expected value of net benefit has to be positive. For the relevance to 'probabilistic v game-theoretic' formulations, see p. 00, Argument 2.

8. Subject to absence of Bickerdike effect (see below, note 10) and also to the assumption that changes in income-distribution within a society do not affect relative prices of commodities – assumptions plausible only if the society is very small compared to, and trades freely with, some total population.

9. A special problem, not considered here, arises in very affluent societies where, say, 80 per cent are comfortably off while 20 per cent remain extremely poor.

10. M. Reder, 'Chicago economics: permanence and change', *J. Econ. Lit.*, XX, 1, March 1982, p. 22. If sound, this normally works even in the long run, notwithstanding three apparent objections. (a) 'Varying the quantity of the externality' (or the cost of bearing it to any parties) may 'drastically alter the distribution of wealth by changing relative prices (including shadow prices)' (ibid., p. 22) – but this invalidation of CO, like the analogous Bickerdike exception to Ricardian trade theory (C. F. Bickerdike, 'The theory of incipient taxes', *EJ*, XVI, 4, December 1906), is probably very rare. All the discussions of CO appear to ignore the fact that (b) *incidence* of external cost differs from *impact*, due to elasticity-dependent backward and forward shifting in standard tax-theoretic ways – but only distribution of gains, not existence of CO, is affected. (c) 'Liability rules affect the relative wealth', say, of F and L, even without changing relative prices; this can affect *future* ratios of F to L outputs, and hence consumer benefits, but with no harm to CO. Suppose F-output rises, but smoke emissions cut L-outputs. On Coasean assumptions of 'rationality, no transactions costs, and no legal impediments to bargaining [, because consumers] who lose from this "misallocation" would ... bribe' F to produce less (or to install smoke filters), or L to launder less (or to

protect laundry from smoke): G. Calabresi, 'Transaction costs, resource allocation and liability rules', *J. of Law and Economics*, 11, April 1968, pp. 67–8.

11. For example, much theoretical and empirical work suggests that, in a (village) society with both sharecropping and owner-farming, resource-use levels and efficiency probably do not differ between the two types of farms, *ceteris paribus*. But a society in which 80 per cent of farms are sharecropped may well, nevertheless, differ in resource-use and efficiency from a society where 80 per cent are owner-formed, again *ceteris paribus*. In developing countries, especially during rapid change, both sorts of (village) society often coexist.

12. For a summary, see M. Lipton, 'Agricultural finance and rural credit in developing countries', *World Development*, 4(7), July 1976. For a subsequent discussion of a well-functioning market with bad results, see A. Berry and R. Sabot, 'Labour market performance in developing countries', in P. Streeten and A. Jolly (eds), *Recent Issues in World Development* (Oxford: Pergamon, 1981).

13. The entries in Tables 3.2 and 3.3, and the argument that the many-person analogy is much likelier than the two-person, are from Parfit, *Reasons and Persons*, pp. 57–8.

14. We may read II's strategies as those of a 'representative' irrigator, or of a 'core' (minus one member) acting jointly.

15. We do not need to assume that the two caches are the same size; or that the prisoners have identical income–utility functions or comparable utilities; or that survival long beyond twelve years is certain for both – but these assumptions help!

16. Because that reward would then have to be added to both a and a_1, in box [1, 1], making it bigger than $(b+b_1)$ and destroying the PD general form of Table 3.3. However, it *is* perfectly feasible for both players to be offered this huge reward for sole confession, making *both* c and c_1 sufficient to exceed $(b+b_1)$.

17. For examples, Table 3.7 might be amended to Table 3.7A by changing the entries for the strategy [2, 1] only from (0, 25) to (0, 15). The box sum at [1, 2] is preferable socially to [2, 2] in Table 3.7A as in 3.7; but [2, 1] is preferable to [2, 2] in Table 3.7 only, *vice versa* in Table 3.7A.

18. Usually the problem is defined as that of reaching [2, 2]. However, as Table 3.7 shows, [1, 2] or [2, 1] might produce a larger 'social product' than [2, 2].

19. A. Sen, 'Isolation, assurance and the social rate of discount', *QJE*, LXXXI, 1, Feb 1967; R. Cassen, *India: Population, Economy, Society* (London: Macmillan, 1978) pp. 74–5; P. Warr and B. Wright, 'The isolation paradox and the discount rate for benefit-cost analysis', *QJE*, XCVI, Feb 1981.

20. A subtler probability issue was raised in discussion. Suppose each entry in Table 3.5 is not certain, but is an *expected value*, or long-run average outcome, 'disturbable' by Nature. For instance, if [2, 1], a 1 in 5 chance of heavy rain gives pay-offs $(-1, 11.5)$; a 3 in 5 chance of normal rain (.25, 9.5); and a 1 in 5 chance of light rain (.25, 9.5). Multiplying pay-offs by probabilities and adding for each player, we get (0, 12) as in Table 3.5. If variability – riskiness – is more for some Table 3.5 outcomes than for others, then risk-aversion by one or both players *might* make a CO likelier.

Could 'policy' exploit this to approach COs, e.g. by insurance conditional on CO irrigation strategies (see V(3) below)?
21. For an outstanding popular exposition, and an account of empirical demonstrations that tit-for-tat does best in multiply-repeated PDs, see I. Hacking, *New York Review of Books*, 28 June 1984, reviewing R. Axelrod, *The Evolution of Cooperation* (New York: Basic Books, 1984). For Axelrod's original work, see R. Axelrod, 'Effective choice in the PD', *Journal of Conflict Resolution*, 24, 1, March 1980, and 'More effective choice in the PD', *JCR*, 24, 3, Sept 1980. Tit-for-tat might seem to yield a dreary sequence of [1, 1] – until somebody tries [2] once. ...
22. Parfit, p. 59. Parfit claims a repeated PD *cannot* be 'even a single true PD', but: (a) This is not true on the last play of a repeated PD. (b) Theoretically, this fact creates a reciprocal version of the so-called 'unexpected examination paradox' – *I* knows *II* will act selfishly on the last play; therefore the *threat* that *II* may do so does not deter *I* from selfish action on the penultimate play; thus *II* knows *I* will act selfishly then; therefore the threat of such selfishness does not deter *II* from selfishness on the antepenultimate play ... etc. (Axelrod, *Evolution of Cooperation*). (c) Leaving aside this argument – irrefutable, but in many-repeat PDs implausible, because it is to each player's advantage *ex ante* to adopt tit-for-tat even though in the above sequence it seems pointless *ex post* – *I*'s *gains*, in the future PD plays, from a [2, 2] solution in structures like Table 5 need not exceed *I*'s *losses* from cheating his way into [2, 1] this time. (d) In this case, some degree of altruism, or societal sanctions, can transform true single PDs, within a repeated PD, into COs.
23. Those familiar with two-person zero-sum game theory (see, for instance, J. Williams, *The Compleat Strategyst*, RAND, 1954) may wonder if 'mixed strategies' might convert a single PD into a surrogate repeated PD and hence raise the change of a CO. Unfortunately not: if [1] is dominant, why should either player adopt a mixed strategy implying a non-zero probability that he will adopt [2], *unless he trusts the other player to do so?* If he does – which can be so only if the other also trusts him – why not go for a *certain* [2, 2]?
24. For evidence, see J. Murningham and A. Roth, 'Experimenting with continued play in PD games', *JCR*, 27, 2, June 1983. This could apply also in Table 3.7, with respect to the likelihood of homing in on a sub-optimum [2, 2] rather than on the social pessimum [1, 1] – let alone the optima [1, 2] or [2, 1].
25. 'Terrible is the temptation of goodness': Bertholt Brecht, *The Caucasian Chalk Circle*.
26. The outcomes in Table 3.8 are especially likely to get to [2, 2] in a repeated game, even if each unit is quite large, owing to the regret inflicted by a tit-for-tat strategy; see note 21 above.
27. 'Conspiracy to pervert the course of justice.' 'Normally', because – for example – a British motorist can legally insure against disqualification for drunk driving, and presumably could do so even if the insurer happened to be his publican!
28. This is a major argument of Parfit, pp. 64–6. As an economist, I see two problems. First, altruism is a respecter of persons; if I play Tables 3.5–3.7

against a pauper, I feel far more altruistic than against Sheikh Yamani. Second, my altruism may well depend on my feelings about (a) whether other people are altruistic, (b) whether my altruism benefits the apparent gainers, or some other persons, perhaps wealthier than me, who are enabled by it to be less altruistic – or to advocate low taxation and low social-security benefits with a better conscience. Moreover, one requires sufficient, not too much, altruism; 'pure altruists, who give no weight to their own interests, may' – indeed in situations where there is a plain, non-altruistic PD must, as a little thought about Tables 3.5–3.7 will prove – 'face analogues of' PD (ibid., p. 66).

29. Rapoport and Chammah, *Prisoner's Dilemma*.
30. 'Ensure' and 'all' can easily be put into the language of deterrence, and elasticities, and *probable* detection of overgrazers. 'All' can also easily be translated into the 'sufficient core' or implicit coalition of (vii) in para. 1 of sec. V(1).
31. E. Boserup, *Conditions of Agricultural Progress* (Asia, 1960).
32. A true public good – a concert, a park, 'knowledge' – does not lose value to X because it is also consumed by Y. Once congestion or other negative externalities appear, a good is no longer truly public.
33. A public good (or any other common good or resource) may under certain circumstances be 'price-excludable'. Entry charges are usually levied for concerts. Many authorities have successfully taxed cattle, or even charged for entry to common grazing.
34. L. Hardin, 'The tragedy of the commons', *Science*, 162, 13 Dec 1968, and R. Kimber, *The Tragedy of the Commons Reappraised*, Keele Research Papers, Dept. of Politics, Keele University, 1983, agree on this, though on little else.
35. Nor is it at all likely at normal stocking rates. These could rise gently for many years – with steadily increased outlay on improved grasses, on costs of herd management, etc. – without any sudden decay of rangelands. But the need for such 'steadily increased outlay' would ensure an even larger negative social return from private herd expansion.
36. Coase does not explicitly so assert, but he does implicitly: 'With costless market transactions, the decision of the courts concerning liability for damage will be without effect on the allocation of resources'. Yet the decision must affect both the cost of transactions and the extent of a 'moral community' that allows them to be enforced.
37. 'Commonsense morality' is reinforced by the fact that, if latecomers have the same rights as incumbents, any one *potential* latecomer (confectioner?) could charge protection money to incumbents (doctors?) in *every* accessible area to keep out – and thus 'earn' large rent for threats devoid of output!
38. Also, each community (e.g. tribe) becomes much more resistant to the settlement of *other* communities' herds upon its lands.
39. Announcing the period might seem counter-productive, as all other graziers would delay cooperation until the last moment. But non-announcement could be worse.
40. Kimber, pp. 3–4.
41. This is precisely analogous to the argument about 'the importance of being

unimportant' (H. Henderson, *Supply and Demand*, Cambridge, 1928), and to the proposition that the gains from trade are greatest for the smallest countries (because these have the highest costs from seeking to produce a large number of goods with diverse input-mixes). The analogies – by making monopolies, monopsonies and cartels harder to attain – are welcome. The situation here is a mixed blessing; it is good to weaken hierarchies, less good to weaken the prospect of breaking down a non-cooperative PD outcome.

42. Notably, animal ownership and care are often private even in countries where land ownership, and much crop farming, is in State or collective hands.
43. 'A landowner who has control of a large tract of land may devote his land to various uses taking into account the effect that the interactions ... have on the net return on the land, thus rendering unnecessary bargains between those undertaking the various activities' (Coase, p. 16).
44. Measured as *you* choose (downward semi-variance as proportion of mean, safety-first rules, etc.).
45. Or, in a bad year, even for a first crop. Complicating factors are (a) that head-ender paddy farming may require so much water that there is none left for tail-enders to grow anything, though social product would be higher if all grew less thirsty crops, and *all* would benefit if side-payments to non-paddy head-enders were reliable; (b) that head-enders *alone* are in a PD in low-rainfall years, but in high-rainfall years the PD is likely to exist only for head-enders and tail-enders taken together.
46. B. Baviskar, *The Politics of Development: Sugar Co-operatives in Rural Maharashtra*, Oxford UP, Delhi, 1980.
47. Wade, 'Social Response to Irrigation'. This corresponds to 'Phase III' of our evolving PD (p. 69), in which the difference between [1, 1] and [2, 2] box sums has become so large as to cover the costs of setting up and running systems for joint control.
48. This is the problem about R. Kimber's objection – in 'Collective action and the fallacy of the liberal fallacy', *World Politics*, 33, 2, June 1981. PD exists in respect of the financing of collective goods – viz. the 'contributor's dilemma' (Parfit, p. 61). The loss to a contributor if non-contributors prevent the provision of a public good on which he relied because he subscribed, is far greater than the trivial sum of his subscription, which might well, as Kimber asserts, be returned. See below, sec. V(7).
49. Such objections apply only to pricing officially imposed, especially on big schemes. Tubewell water, owned by one farmer (or a cooperative of farmer-purchasers), is often sold to many smallholders, and the price can well include elements of PD side-payment. Here, too, however, patchwork-quilt plots – and channel design to help bigger users, or coop managers, near the water source – produce results far from CO.
50. R. Wade, 'The World Bank and India's irrigation reform', *JDS*, 18, 2, 1982.
51. M. Howes, 'The creation and appropriation of value in irrigated agriculture', in M. Greeley and M. Howes (eds), *Rural Technology, Rural Institutions and the Rural Poorest* (CIRDAP/IDS, Comilla, 1982).

52. G. Wood, 'Provision of irrigation services by the landless – an approach to agrarian reform in Bangladesh', *Agricultural Administration*, Vol. 17, no. 2, 1984.
53. M. Todaro, 'Income expectations, rural–urban migration and employment in Africa', *ILR*, 104, 5, November 1971.
54. M. Lipton, *Labour and Poverty*, World Bank Staff Working Paper no. 616, Washington, DC, October 1983, pp. 49–50.
55. If labour markets are well informed, and if ratios between wages roughly equal ratios between marginal products – much weaker assumptions than are needed for the full neo-classical model – then Todaro-style labour migration occurs if, and only if, the discounted present value of expected urban marginal labour-productivities exceeds that for rural productivities. That is, the migrant worker acts as if he expects that he will contribute more to urban than to rural output, and will be paid according to his contribution; so he migrates. Implicitly, he therefore expects that by staying behind he would have raised rural product less, in value, than he would have reduced urban product. But he would, by staying behind, have raised rural workforce by one, and cut urban workforce by the same amount. That proves the statement in the text.
56. In India, where the rural–urban disparity in doctor/patient ratios is far lower than in most LDCs, rural age- and sex-specific death-rates remain far above urban levels, yet urbanisation of trainee – and trained – rural-born doctors continues. See A. Mitra, *India's Population: Aspects of Quality and Control* (New Delhi: ICSSR/Abhinav) vol. 1, p. 223; and M. Lipton, *Why Poor People Stay Poor* (London: Temple Smith, 1977) p. 458, and 'Urban Bias Revisited', *JDS*, 20, 3, April 1984.
57. O. Stark has developed this idea in many papers. Its original exposition is O. Stark, 'Utility, Technological change, surplus and risk: The microeconomics of rural-to-urban migration of labour in less developed economies', D. Phil thesis, University of Sussex, 1975.
58. R. Cassen, *India: Population, Economy, Society* (London: Macmillan, 1978), pp. 74–5.
59. If distribution (via demand patterns, mainly) drastically affects relative prices – i.e. in a big, closed, or high-transport-cost economy – the separation is very dubious.
60. Parfit, p. 61.
61. M. Burns and C. Walsh, 'Market provision of price-excludable public goods: a general analysis', *JPE*, 89, 1, 1981.
62. Or in proportion to ability to pay ('taxable capacity'); this solution, *acceptably* equitable (and hence with *reasonably small* costs in keeping 'tax' evasion *tolerably* low) – weasel words all! – is of course just as inconsistent with market-price paths to COs, and also with negotiation in its usual sense.
63. K. Wittvogel, *Oriental Despotism* (Yale UP, 1957).
64. R. Lee and I. DeVore (eds), *Kalahari Hunter-Gatherers: studies of the !Kung San and their neighbors* (Harvard University Press, 1976).
65. Of course, feudal authorities did a good deal of surplus extraction to support their own status, temples, luxuries, etc. as well as to finance PGs.

66. L. White, *Mediaeval Technology and Social Change* (Oxford: Clarendon, 1962).
67. M. Olsen, *The Rise and Decline of Nations* (Yale UP, 1982).
68. It is possible even for voting to produce odd outcomes, sometimes (via strategic voting) of a PD type, sometimes along the lines of Arrow's Paradox of Voting (K. Arrow, *Social Choice and Individual Values* (Yale UP (for Cowles Foundation), 1963). But 'an election is seldom a true PD' (Parfit, p. 61) and Arrow's cyclicity problem, though conceptually of the first importance, arises only when preferences of three (or more) equal groups are ordered in three (or more) distinct and inconsistent cycles – i.e. very 'seldom' once more!
69. The list of causes deliberately excludes urbanisation. It is not clear that urbanisation much increases the number of people with whom a migrant, at an average moment of life, shares the benefits of the average £'s worth of services from PGs that he consumes. It may do, but it needn't.

4 The Political Process: Market Place or Battleground?

WILLIAM RODGERS

On holiday in a far-away country, I found amongst disintegrating books a copy of *Encounter* for December 1964. A series of articles under the general heading 'The New Britain' dealt with prospects following the election a couple of months earlier of a Labour government. The first of these was by Andrew Shonfield. 'The distinctive thing' the new government had to offer, he wrote, was 'a different way of doing business'.[1] That way 'should in the end produce more wealth more consistently' than previous governments had succeeded in doing. He went on to refer to the possibility of Labour's eventually losing office having laid 'the foundations for a more rapid rate of economic growth'. Making 'the nation's productive apparatus yield more' was the government's task, with 'raising the volume of productive investment' and 'using our resources in manpower, technology and capital more effectively' the twin instruments of policy.

Andrew Shonfield was stating the conventional wisdom of moderate centre-left opinion of the time. In part, he was making the point that economic growth should come before re-distribution and re-distribution mainly apply to the resultant increase in national wealth. But he was assuming – he barely argued the case – that the pursuit of economic growth was a primary objective for government and one well within its grasp. Raising investment, utilising resources better – this was what the new government should do.

The word 'growth', meaning an incremental increase in GNP, probably first entered the vocabulary of politics about 1947 when Sir Edwin Plowden headed the economic planning staff under the Labour government and submissions were being made in relation to the Marshall Plan. But the thought behind the word – and, much more important, the expectation – was given political flesh in Harold Macmillan's famous declaration 'You've never had it so good' on which he rode to victory in the 1959 General Election.[3] Standards of living had risen as much between 1951 and mid-1958 as between 1913 (the eve of World War I) and 1939 (the eve of World War II). Macmillan successfully reminded the voters of how much better-off they had become with the implication that prosperity stretched to the far horizon.

From then on, for six or seven years, the promise of growth was part of the politician's armoury in the battle for votes. Within two years of the 1959 General Election, the prosperity of the 1950s had begun to tarnish, both with rising unemployment in Scotland and the North and anxiety about the comparative neglect of community and welfare services, 'private affluence and public squalor' in J. K. Galbraith's resonant phrase.[3] But the public appetite for growth was taken for granted and encouraged. If the Conservatives had failed, then Labour would have – to return to Andrew Shonfield – 'a different way of doing business'. The glad confident morning of October 1964 when Labour came into office heralded a government whose policies of planning and intervention would restore prosperity, giving us more money in our pockets and a better Welfare State.

The new government created the Department of Economic Affairs as the Department of 'growth', the institutional embodiment of Andrew Shonfield's hopes. To the DEA, 'growth' meant the planned growth of incomes in a non-inflationary way; the growth of the stagnant regions of Britain characterised by high and persistent unemployment (high, that is, by the standards of that time, usually 3–4 per cent) and low social investment; and the growth of new industries encouraged by government intervention, for example, through the Industrial Reorganisation Corporation. But the apotheosis of the DEA was the National Plan.[4] It announced the growth target as a 25 per cent increase in national output between 1964 and 1970, based on an annual rise in industrial productivity of 3.4 per cent.

The National Plan was published in September 1965, within less than a year of its conception; it was quietly put to death in July 1966 after an even shorter period of uncertain life. It perished – as all the bold vision of that government perished – in a sterling crisis and a tough set of deflationary measures. Far from being the beginning of new things, it was the end of an era. That twenty-one months of Harold Wilson's first government had more in common with the optimism of the 1950s than with what has followed.[5]

Did Harold Macmillan in 1959 and Harold Wilson in 1964 wantonly deceive the electorate with promises they knew they could not honour? I think not. They judged – quite rightly, in my opinion – that the voters *wanted* to maintain the momentum to higher living standards and that this was a proper ambition – quite rightly, too. They may have glossed over problems and hidden their doubts. But in the necessary shorthand of political Manifestos, they were not dishonest. Politicians must believe in their ability to succeed when others fail.

Nor were the voters neutral. They had enjoyed a decade of unprecedented prosperity. They had bought cars and television sets and refrigerators and washing machines. They had started going abroad for their holidays. Unemployment was negligible and inflation below 2 per cent. It would have been very difficult initially to persuade them that the bubble had burst and that the next twenty years was to be a great deal tougher.

Perceptions have since changed in a remarkable way. There have been periods of apparent remission when Conservative and Labour governments have temporarily reverted to optimism. But for the most part, since about 1966, politicians have stressed not the comfortable prospects of economic life but the harsh realities. They have done so as they have realised the limitations of their ability, the depth of Britain's industrial decline and the long time-scale for change. But they have also known that their previous failures have induced scepticism in the voters who no longer believe that previous levels of prosperity are readily attainable. At the General Election of 1983, claims that unemployment could be made to disappear overnight fell on stony ground. Two-out-of-five voters chose to support a government under which unemployment had risen to well over 3 million, a quite inconceivable prospect a few years ago. Every promise to reduce unemployment had to be accompanied by a warning about how long it would take and the limits of probable success – a million fewer over two years perhaps, but the other two million were a different proposition.

Voters are not indifferent to prosperity. A government which presides over rising living standards – more in the pocket to spend matters most of all, the rate at which inflation and unemployment are falling, rather less – has a much better chance of being re-elected than one that doesn't. But when it comes to expectations and promises, for the time being the voters take a sober view.

Whether this pessimism is justified and whether it is a comment on the failure of our democratic system of government or on the parties that have dominated it for half-a-century is a separate matter. But it diminishes the voters to deny them any capacity for assessing what are credible promises. In the 1980s every party ensures that its programme has been 'carefully costed': it does its sums, even if somewhat imaginatively. It talks about priorities for spending; some increase now, some later. The idea of the opportunity cost of new proposals is not too far away. But, even in 1959, Hugh Gaitskell, then the leader of the Labour party, made what was seen to be a major error by suggesting that Labour's programme could be paid for without any increase in taxation.[6] The voters could add-up. They were not convinced.

Does this mean that the political arena is not a battleground but a market-place with the voters shopping around for the best buy and the parties designing, producing and packaging their wares in the way most likely to beat the competition? Is it primarily a contest of wits between groups of men and women seeking the fruits of office and to persuade the voters, who range from the plainly gullible only as far as the moderately discerning? And if it is not these things – or not *wholly* or not *quite* these things – should our democratic system be moved in that direction, if it can be moved? It is nearly thirty years since Anthony Downs produced his economic model of how democracy is supposed to function and there have been other, similar, attempts to explain the political process.[7] I want to consider these matters as a practising politician who has taken part for most of his life in competition-for-authority, as Professor R. C. O. Matthews calls it, both within political parties and between them.[8]

First, as to the political parties, it is important to recognise that in Britain they have a continuing life of their own with many of the features of a club or voluntary association outside politics. They represent a point of view and are not simply support-teams for office-seekers. This point of view may be called an ideology or a tradition. In either event, it is an overall assessment of society – more or less internally consistent – what it is like, what is wrong with it, what it might become and how to get there. Parties of the left tend to be more explicitly ideological, strong on analysis and confident about change. Parties of the right rely more on continuity, bringing the past into the present. In practice, the Labour party is quite prepared to call Robert Owen, the Tolpuddle Martyrs and the Chartists as witnesses on what to do today;[9] while Mrs Thatcher has no hesitation in claiming the Conservative party to be the party of 'continuity *and* change'.[10]

That position broadly represents Conservative policy throughout the post-war years. Conservative governments have tended to conserve the new *status quo* they have inherited, having previously opposed it. Conservatives prefer to claim that they are centrist rather than right-of-centre and have shown a nimbleness in adapting to electoral moods, courting the floating voter and moving to the middle ground. But despite this and even before the advent of Mrs Thatcher as a 'conviction politician', the views of 'the party' had coherence and importance.

The Labour party is ambivalent about claiming to be ideological. But there is no doubt that it has more ideological baggage than the Conservatives, that this has inhibited vote-getting and proved difficult to get rid of, due to internal resistance. At one stage, some years ago, it was unwilling to commission private opinion polls, fearing that they would reveal unpalatable truths about the extent to which the voters rejected some of its more cherished axioms; and even in 1950, only 39 per cent of voters supported more nationalisation which was then, as it has remained, a major Labour commitment. I am not passing judgment. I am simply noting that Labour more than the Conservatives has tended for ideological reasons to persist in policies to its electoral disadvantage.

This is largely because political parties in Britain are run by activists who give a large part of their time to organising and campaigning on a voluntary basis. For the most part, these are not men and women moved by a personal desire for wealth, prestige or power. The financial rewards of politics are slight, only a limited proportion of activists ever hold paid office and the patronage system is limited (although it has grown rapidly in recent years around some local authorities, especially in London during Labour's leadership of the GLC). On the left, there is even some ambivalence about power: whether it carries a degree of moral opprobrium, can be bought at too high a price in terms of principle and corrupts through compromise. There are certainly some who over the years have preferred Labour to be a party of protest.

In 1974 there were, exceptionally, Members of Parliament and activists on the right of the Labour party – normally strong for winning power – who doubted whether Labour deserved to win because of its behaviour in Opposition; and half-hoped that it would not. This was the legacy of the decision of the Labour party, led by Harold Wilson, to oppose Britain's entry to the Common Market despite having been in favour of it when in government less than eighteen months before.

But the reluctance of activists to seek office at any price is not limited to Britain. In 1968, many registered Democrats failed to vote for Hubert Humphrey because of his support for the Vietnam War even although this meant a Republican administration led by Richard Nixon. The activists recruit members, appear at meetings, campaign at election time, attend party Conferences and discuss policy. They are articulate and forceful. Although party leaders can override them, this can be a painful, even a bloody, process. There is a degree of dependence – without the activists there would be no party; there is a degree of guilt – 'I enjoy office and they put me there'; and a loyalty, perhaps affection, based on long association and shared experience. The activist is a formidable factor in the equation of politics: he certainly distorts the market. By definition *un*representative, his views influence what the parties offer to the representative voter.

Again it should be said that the activist, so defined, is more characteristic of the Labour than the Conservative party and more influential in it.[11] This follows from the greater weight given to ideology on the left and it leads to greater competition-for-authority between factions in the Labour party than between factions in the Conservative party. The One Nation group of Tories was an important influence within the Conservative party in the immediate post-war period, although pushing in the same direction as R. A. Butler when he founded the Conservative Political Centre and launched the Industrial Charter.[12] The Bow Group and various associations of younger Conservatives have lobbied for particular views, and the Monday Club has been an influence on the Conservative right. But argument has been subdued and gentlemanly compared with upheavals in the Labour party and it is doubtful whether it has ever done much electoral damage.

Factionalism in the Labour party has been endemic since its earliest days. Members of the ILP saw themselves as political guerrillas before 1914; Lansbury was trounced by Bevin at the 1935 Labour Conference and Stafford Cripps was expelled two years later for supporting a Popular Front with the Communist party. In more recent times, Hugh Gaitskell, as leader, asserted his authority to reverse the decision made at Scarborough in 1960 in favour of unilateral disarmament but failed to carry the party in his attempt to revise Clause 4 of Labour's Constitution.[13] There has been a continuing struggle over eighty years between the right of the Labour party and the left, often savagely fought with little thought to its consequences for public opinion. The emergence of the Militant Tendency in the 1970s is another measure of internal factionalism. Sometimes there has been a plainly stated indifference to political power short of the millenium; sometimes a rejection of electoral victory 'bought at any price'; and sometimes an argument about what the voters will or will not accept if persuasion is thorough and persistent. But the competition-for-authority within the party has been vigorous.

I make a distinction – for convenience because it is only half valid – between factions who argue about ideas and pressure groups who lobby to their own direct advantage. These are to be found within political parties as well as in the political process outside. For half a century, the two major parties in Britain have been class parties. Within the Conservative party there has been a predominance of the better-off; the owners of capital, the senior managers, the major professions, the upwardly mobile. The General Election of 1979, for example, produced 82 company directors, 52 managers and executives and 54 barristers amongst Conservative MPs, over three times as many in these categories as Labour: a large part of the income of the Conservative party comes in company donations. The Conservative party could never win an election without very many working-class votes. But the voice of what used to be called 'private enterprise' is loud within it.

But the internal pressure group is best seen in the case of the trade unions and the Labour party. The trade unions have a defined constitutional role and a major say in policy-making. In the 1980s they acquired the right to help choose the leader of the Labour party through an electoral college. As a result of affiliation fees, they provide the Labour party with 90 per cent of its income. They cannot be said to represent the working-class when only a proportion of working-class voters belong to trade unions; they cannot be said to represent the political opinions of their own members when, at the 1983 General Election, only 39 per cent of trade unionists voted for Labour candidates. They are essentially interest groups that, over many years, ensured that the transport policy of the Labour party was the NUR's, the energy policy the NUM's and policy towards the public service NUPE's and the General and Municipal Workers'. Labour governments, particularly in the 1970s, deferred disproportionately to their wishes. Despite intense public concern, Mr Callaghan's government was paralysed in the Winter of Discontent of 1978–79 because of its unwillingness to confront those trade unions responsible for a devastating series of strikes. It was plain what the great majority of voters expected of the Government, but the trade union pressure group was the decisive factor. In the General Election, Labour went down to its worse defeat in fifty years.[14]

Let me add a further word about Members of Parliament. Strictly speaking they might be seen as activists in their finest flower. This has certainly been the route most of them have taken to elected office. But I doubt whether they can be easily classified as selfish careerists – interested only in office; or as ideological zealots – interested only in the rightness of their cause.[15] I am not aware of any study that adequately considers the factors – psychological, environmental – that make some men and women politically active.[16] Obviously there are affinities in every direction with other careers and occupations: most Members of Parliament have a capacity to be successful at something else. It is not only a first class combination of second class abilities, as someone, half-kindly, half-unkindly put it.

I am not competent to explore this question of internal motivation. But I *am* clear that the idea of public service, old-fashioned although it may sound, has a role alongside ambition and ideology. There is genuine competition 'to do good', and not only on the scale of constituency matters where the MP is more and more a cross between priest and social worker.

During the past quarter-century the composition of the House of Commons has changed. In the 1950s, there was a significant number of Conservative MPs who knew more about winter wheat and Jersey cattle than about Order Papers and Early Day Motions. They were matched by Labour Members with parchment skin and worn hands to whom formal speeches came less easily than reminiscences about the pit, the blast furnace and the signal box. They were content to be the ballast in the ship of state, bringing wisdom and plain speaking to the counsels of their parties. Unlike many of their colleagues, they did not believe that they carried a Field-Marshall's baton in their knapsack. Today the House of Commons on all sides is more meritocratic and fewer Members are content to have merely a walk-on part.[17] But although three out of four of them will never serve in Government, only a small proportion will retire early through thwarted ambition. I make this point because I believe that 'public service' remains a real factor in political behaviour. I am not sure how the market would account for that.

I turn to the voters. What do they want, and how capable are they of judging whether they can get it from one political party rather than another? The simplest assumption is that the voters ask, 'What's in it for me?' and make a rational choice. Thus they take a narrow, self-interested and short-term view, taking for granted that the goods on offer are genuine and properly labelled. This is the voter as consumer.

But, here again, this grossly simplifies a complex process of choice, even if the initial, perhaps major, characteristic of voter behaviour is close to this.[18]

In the first place, interest goes beyond self. It extends to members of the voter's family: to his children who he believes deserve a better education than he had; to his parents who ought to enjoy a decent pension. It extends to others outside his family circle: to sufferers from cancer for whom there ought to be a cure, to the victims of criminal violence for whom there ought to be compensation. It extends not only to individuals but towards conditions in society: the homeless, the mentally ill.

Take aid to the Third World. In 1983, a specific commitment to this was found not only in the Manifestos of the Labour party and the SDP/Liberal Alliance, but of the Conservative party too. But the great majority of voters would not have noticed the omission of overseas aid from the Manifestos and most of them would be neutral if not hostile to the idea. Commitments were included partly because the minority positively in favour of aid to the Third World is articulate and sympathetic, including the Churches; partly because on the left this minority includes many activists; and partly because of Britain's international reputation. But in addition there is the moral imperative felt by many Members of Parliament and senior politicians. It is simply *right* to help relieve the most intolerable of world poverty.

I am not saying that these are decisive factors that determine voting; or that all voters take account of all or any one of them; or that voters believe that Governments have a capacity to change them. I am simply saying that the selfish voter is not *all* selfish.

Secondly, there is the question of the short-term view. Of course this is important. Most people's lives are full of short-term decisions. Tomorrow we might be dead. The nature of our political system, with Parliaments that tend to last $3\frac{1}{2}$ years in peacetime encourages the short-term view. But making sacrifices today in order to win at least a medium-term benefit is common. The disruption of wartime and the austerity of the late-1940s was a price paid for a better world to come, freer and more secure. The 2 to 1 vote in the Referendum of 1975 in favour of Britain's continued membership of the European Community had much to do with long-term advantages, despite immediate dissatisfaction. It was certainly possible for politicians to argue in 1975 that the benefits of membership would be postponed for a generation: 'I do not promise that it will make our lives easier ... but think of our children ... think how it will be for them'.

The history of pay policy carries a similar message. The surprise is not that over the post-war period a series of expedients have succeeded only for a short time but that they have succeeded at all. Voters (as wage earners) have been persuaded to accept voluntary wage restraint because they have been persuaded of its longer-term benefits. In the two and a half years that followed the Stafford Cripps White Paper of February 1948,[19] wage rates rose by only 5 per cent although retail prices rose by 8 per cent. In the second half of 1966, there was an effective six-month wage freeze. Even in the sceptical 1970s, Mr Callaghan had three successful phases of wage restraint, even if the fourth ended in disaster. Incidentally, politicians found that the most important factor in winning support for pay restraint was a sense of fairness. Voters (as wage earners) were willing to suspend their selfish pursuit of 'more' in a free-for-all provided that others suspended *their* pursuit – and market prices did not rise while their demand was withheld. I believe that a party offering a pay policy in its Manifesto is not disadvantaged politically thereby.

Third, what about the produt itself? Are the voters capable of judging it? I have already said that I believe they are. I have referred to Gaitskell's tax promise in 1959; and to the scepticism of voters about sudden cures for unemployment in 1983. Even ten years earlier, in the General Election of 1974, the voters had been sceptical about the claims of the parties to solve the problems of inflation and unemployment. I do not call this cynicism. Nor do I think it is mainly induced by the parties saying 'Its not our fault ... nothing can be done'. Since 1979, the present Government has certainly suggested that unemployment (although not inflation) is God-given and part of the natural order of things. But the perception of the voters pre-dates Mrs Thatcher. It does not block-off the initiatives of politicians but requires politics to be increasingly honest. Even without a Consumer Council or a *Which?* magazine, voters look beyond the packaging and have a shrewd sense of what lies within.

There is another way in which the understanding of the electorate has grown, following the disappointments experienced by governments. It is doubtful whether many voters recognise that industrial primacy passed from Britain at the turn of the century, that our visible trade was heavily in deficit in the 1930s, and that the loss of overseas earnings during wartime together with the end of Empire had put Britain in a critical position even by the prosperous 1950s. But in the last 20 years awareness of the external factor has grown both as the context within which Governments are obliged to operate; and as the sudden squall, impossible to forecast and difficult to ride-out, that leaves behind a trail of devastation. The sterling crisis that ditched the DEA and the expansionist plans the 1964–66 Labour government may have made some impact on public opinion. But the arguments over Britain's membership of the European Community, both the first Macmillan application and the second Wilson try, focussed attention on Britain's isolation and dependence. The oil crisis of 1973, affecting the Heath Government, was another consideration. Overall, partly stemming from undoubted military strength, and partly from her obvious industrial and technological capacity (for example, in space research and travel), awareness grew of the critical importance of the United States. It is not mainly anti-Americanism or a false emphasis on sovereignty that makes it easy for any British government to point to American interest rates and American budget deficits in explanation of its own limited room for manoeuvre. Britain is seen to be in the Second Division. We should be able to do better than France and Italy, and Germany too. But the United States is in a different league. We are dependent on how they play the game.[20]

I have referred to interest groups within parties. What about pressure groups outside? The pressure group is the voice of a minority. But the pressure group seeks either to persuade public opinion of the rightness of its cause – creating sympathy even when there is no outright conversion – or to convince the political parties that its own support, although limited, is floating and might be the margin between winning and losing an election. 'Putting together the coalition' is seen to be the key to success in American Presidential elections. Walter Mondale was much criticised during the primaries of 1983 by the purist supporters of Gary Hart for doing precisely that. But this often appears to be a ritual of public appearances and soothing words rather than a basket of policy concessions. The Presidential candidate wears a cowboy hat, addresses a convention of Veterans, appears in the Bronx and joins a St Patrick's Day parade. The platform approved at Dallas or San Francisco bears little relation to these activities. Pressure groups in Britain (rarely ethnic, although the importance of the non-white vote is growing steadily) expect more and achieve more in policy terms. For many years, lobbyists worked for trade associations and professional bodies broadly on the business right of the political spectrum – the National Union of Manufacturers, the NFU and British Medical Association. The most identifiable – some would say the most successful, others the most notorious – was the 'Road Lobby' inspired in the 1950s by the

Road Haulage Association and, through the Roads Campaign Council, civil engineering and contracting firms.

In the last two decades a new generation of pressure groups has emerged on the welfare left of the political spectrum such as Shelter, MIND, the Disablement Income Group and the Child Poverty Action Group. There is no doubt that they have made a major impact through a combination of moral appeal and detailed research and investigation. The success of some of this may be attributable to their symbolic importance with women who are a majority of the electorate. More often than not, the one parent in a one-parent family is a woman. More often than not, it is a woman who looks after aged parents day-to-day or ministers to the mentally and physically disabled. These particular women are a minority but many women can identify with their role and problems.

I have described the factors that in my experience help to determine the course pursued by political parties in Britain and concluded that they are not the result of a simple calculation designed to give the voters what they want. I have also suggested that the voters take more than a short-term and selfish view of the choice they are called upon to make. They are increasingly sophisticated and informed; and sceptical about what political parties can achieve. I want to draw some conclusions about this but first must enter a caveat.

I am not suggesting that there are no policies which the parties and voters approach in a simple market way, or no occasions when the market is dominant. My aim has been to redress the balance against an economic theory of democracy of the kind that Anthony Downs espoused and some economists today might like to follow. I will give an example of my own to concede that the market sometimes works perfectly in politics. Consider the subsidy for house purchase through tax concessions and mortgage borrowing. It is extremely difficult to claim that this fulfils any economic or social purpose. It diverts savings from industry and entrepreneurial investment; raises house prices; reduces geographical mobility and makes it difficult to have a rational policy towards subsidies in the public sector. The continuation of such tax concessions is incompatible with the logic of a strongly market-orientated Conservative government; it hardly matches the declared egalitarianism of successive Labour governments. But neither party has been prepared to face the change. Each party counts the votes it believes it would lose and decides that the price is too high. Such straight issues involving taxation are probably most subject to the market. It is not easy for the house buyer to see what benefit he or anyone else will receive as a result of his loss of mortgage relief.

It is also plainly the case that political parties become more market-orientated as a General Election approaches. In the 1950s, governments in power were particularly sensitive to increases in the retail price level and hoped to combine pre-election tax cuts with inflation rates as low as 2 per cent. In the 1980s, concern about unemployment is offset at least in part by facilitating the growth of real incomes for those still in work. Each of the old major parties has an eye to cossetting its own, traditional voters by the incidence of taxation and the distribution of public expenditure it chooses. It would be naïve to suppose that shrewd calculation – cynical calculation as some might prefer to call it – does not play the largest part in the preparation of a Party Manifesto, granted only greater room for manoeuvre in the Conservative party. My argument is that the Downsian model highly simplifies a complex process, particularly if it is seen over a period of many years.

But would we maximise total satisfaction in our nation and bring to our people in abundance the material rewards of democracy if the market for politics as a whole conformed more closely to attitudes to home ownership and party behaviour in pre-election periods? I hope that I have shown that to be an unreal question, given the way our political system has developed. With a strict two-party system, a high degree of consensus and steady economic growth, the market analogy might have greater justification. But even in the optimistic 1950s, the age of Butskellism, when 95 per cent of the electorate voted either Conservative or Labour, I doubt whether such a model fitted the British experience. It is even less appropriate today when the two old major parties have polarised their positions; their aggregate vote has dropped to 70 per cent and a new party – or Alliance of parties – occupies the middle ground, towards the centre-left. On all the evidence, the voters are more politically footloose than ever before, as partisan de-alignment proceeds.[21]

A change in our voting systems would of course have radical consequences. The effect of Proportional Representation would be to enhance the voters' choice. There might be more parties in the market for their votes. More important, voters would be able to indicate their scale of preferences. As a result, no vote would be a wasted vote because every preference would be reflected in the distribution of seats in the final outcome. There would be no need for tactical voting whereby the choice of second-best provides a means of avoiding the election of the candidate the voter likes least. A one-party state confronts the voter with monopoly. The first-past-the-post system tends towards a duopoly and a very small share of seats for other parties in the market. PR would create the most open market conditions.

Short of Proportional Representation, which will certainly not govern voting in the General Election of 1987–88, what is the likely response of the political parties, given the nature of the competition and the market as I have described it? I have suggested that the age of optimism for governments – voters abandoned it rather later – ended in the mid-1960s. Since then, and more particularly in the last ten years, the two old, major parties have made a virtue of turning their backs on the Keynsian consensus of the post-war years, claiming that it was no longer capable of achieving adequate growth and thus satisfying voter expectations (lower although these now are). This is not the sole cause of the polarisation of politics between them, but it is the occasion and – when justification is needed – the excuse. Labour began noticeably to move away from the middle ground in the early 1970s. This made it much less dangerous for Mrs Thatcher to abandon it herself from 1979. As Labour was less attractive to the floating voter, she had no need to worry about losing him. In turn, the more extreme Mrs Thatcher was seen to be, the more Labour was pushed by internal factions to the ideological left in reaction and anger.

The arrival of the Alliance makes polarisation no longer a safe electoral option. The middle ground has been occupied. Whatever the short-term prospects – given the electoral system and the heavy concentration of Labour and Conservative votes in the North and South of Britain respectively – neither of the old parties can be indifferent to their vulnerability as long as they remain in extreme positions. Initially, both will seek to discredit the Alliance on the same grounds: that the Keynsian consensus failed and therefore the Alliance offers shop-soiled and damaged goods which the voter should not be tempted to buy. But the Conservative party either under Mrs Thatcher or a successor will begin to move back towards the centre, putting itself in a position to compete for middle opinion.

For reasons I have tried to explain, it will be much more difficult for Labour to make this adjustment. The leadership of the trade unions, if by then they have taken cognizance of the views and voting habits of their members while remaining committed to a political role, may bring internal pressure to bear for a move back towards the centre. They will have to overcome the resistance of the activists and the force of ideology: and they will find that for the Alliance the middle ground extends left-of-centre. A substantial part of Labour's former market share will have been appropriated.

This raises further questions upon which Anthony Downs reflected.[22] Will the voters judge by the record of the parties or by policies, which in effect means Manifesto promises? In normal circumstances, voters are more influenced by the record. Thus, if the record of Conservative governments between, say, 1979 and 1988 was judged to be relatively better than the record of Labour governments before 1979, then in a two-party system, the absolute performance of the Conservatives would not matter too much. The existence of the Alliance as the third choice in the market changes this.

It may be that the absence of any record in government, despite the Ministerial experience of several of its leaders, will be a disadvantage. But the likelihood is that the existence of the Alliance will mean that policies – promises – will matter more than the record. At the very least, Mrs Thatcher cannot take the risk that this will not be the case. She cannot rely on her record alone, least of all any claim that it is better than Labour's. Here again, in performance as well as policies, the safe course is to move towards the middle ground.

As for the voters, a majority will clearly shop-around at Election time as never before. But I doubt whether they will take a more short-term and selfish view of what they find on offer. They are better informed than ever before; they are mature about politics; and more than 7-out-of-10 of them go to the polls.

It is an opportunity that politicians ought not to miss. Twenty years ago I shared Andrew Shonfield's view about the priority for economic growth and the scope for government intervention. I believed in the National Plan and served as a Minister in the DEA. I am now less sure about the scope for governments in industrial policy; and about the merits of the public sector. Much attention has been given to economic and industrial policy but governments have thought too little about priorities for *social* policy. They have not said often enough, 'What is the quality of life which we would wish to characterise our country?' They have not discussed a formula for social harmony that would most command support.

But I am not recommending a retreat from government. I have spoken of ideology in mainly pejorative terms. I am not sure I should have done. Downs defines ideology as 'a verbal image of the good society and of the chief means of constructing such a society'.[23] If that definition stands, then I would wish to be an ideologue. I believe that politicians should offer some vision and should raise the sights of voters beyond their immediate objectives and expectations. This is not a matter of offering more than they can deliver – 3, 4, 5 per cent growth, for example, for the rest of this decade – but of discouraging the view that what is generally regarded as bad about Britain or the world cannot be made better. It is one thing to point to the factors that have led to over three million men and women being out of work and not to blame it wholly on this government; quite another to abdicate all responsibility for seeking to bring unemployment down. In Britain today, too many people are poor: that is a value judgment but one which most would share. I do not think it acceptable to be indifferent to those reforms in taxation and social security that might provide a remedy.

Mrs Thatcher is said to be a conviction politician. There is no fault in that. But there is not only one conviction or, I hope, only one politician with the capacity for leadership.

NOTES

1. Andrew Shonfield, 'The Economic Issue', in 'Spectrum', *Encounter* vol. XXII, no. 6, December 1964.
2. Macmillan first used the phrase in a speech at Bedford in the summer of 1957 and repeated it in the House of Commons shortly afterwards. It did not feature in the Conservative Manifesto of 1959 but came to encapsulate the spirit of the age.
3. Galbraith precedes his chapter on 'The Theory of Social Balance' in *The Affluent Society* (London: Hamish Hamilton, 1958) with a quotation from R. H. Tawney. Galbraith's proposition was not original but its restatement was prescient, particularly when juxtaposed with Macmillan's apparent complacency.
4. The National Plan, a White Paper of nearly 500 pages, was endorsed by both sides of industry in the National Economic Development Council as 'within the nation's capacity'. Its preparation was a remarkable achievement and a measure of the irresistible energy and considerable powers of persuasion of George Brown, the First Secretary of State.
5. The continuity of Harold Wilson's period in office 1964–70 was hardly broken by the General Election of March 1966 although it turned a tiny House of Commons majority into a massive one. But the crisis of July 1966 had been forecast in January of that year and would have been faced much earlier had it not been for electoral considerations.
6. For the pledge and its consequences, see Philip Williams, *Hugh Gaitskell* (London: Jonathan Cape, 1979) pp. 526–8.
7. Anthony Downs, *An Economic Theory of Democracy* (New York: Harper and Row, 1957).
8. See above, p. 3.

9. Occasionally even extending back to the 14th Century Lollards, which would have surpr.sed John Wycliffe and other mediaeval heretics.
10. As she did with great conviction in the 1983 General Election.
11. For a useful brief discussion of these themes see James Douglas, 'The Conservative Party: From Pragmatism to Ideology – and Back?', in *West European Politics*, vol. 6, no. 4, October 1983.
12. See R. A. Butler, *The Art of the Possible* (London: Hamish Hamilton, 1971) pp. 126–53 for an account of the adaptibility of the Conservative party in the post-war years by one of its most accomplished practitioners.
13. Williams, *Hugh Gaitskell*, pp. 537–73.
14. William Rodgers, 'Government under stress. Britain's Winter of Discontent 1979', *The Political Quarterly*, vol. 55, no. 2, April–June 1984.
15. See above, p. 10.
16. A bold attempt was made by a Member of Parliament, Leo Abse, to study the relationship of personality to politics by examining the psychodynamics and psychopathology of some of his colleagues. It was not popular with them but *Private Member* (London: Macdonald, 1973) explored some interesting ideas.
17. Anthony King, 'The Rise of the Career Politician in Britain – and its Consequences', *British Journal of Political Science*, vol. 11, no. 3, July 1981, is a wider discussion of the shift in the personal structure of British politics.
18. The pattern of voting is extremely complex and this is not the place for a sophisticated analysis of voting decisions. For a study of political attitudes in Britain over fifteen years, including the implications of the creation of the SDP in 1981 (see below in this chapter), see Hilda T. Himmelweit and others, *How Voters Decide* (London: Academic Press, 1981).
19. Cmnd 7321. Cripps owned much to the support of Ernest Bevin whose authority with the trade unions ensured that they supported a wage freeze by more than 2-to-1. Kenneth O. Morgan, *Labour in Power 1945–51* (Oxford: Clarendon Press, 1984) p. 372.
20. This is not to diminish the factor of patriotism. Patriotism is love of one's own country; a belief in its virtues; a willingness to defend it. No political party can afford *not* to be a patriotic party, however internationalist it claims to be and however inter-dependent it sees the world. In essence, it might be regarded as self-interest but this is complicated by emotion. The Falklands War brought forth a great burst of patriotism although the Falklands are 7000 miles away, bring no benefits to Britain and could only be re-taken at great risk and, as it turned out, with tragic loss of life. It remains to be seen how long voters will regard an expenditure of £500 million a year as a reasonable price to pay for staying on.
21. Ivor Crewe, Bo Sarlvik and James Alt, 'Partisan Dealignment in Britain 1964–74', *British Journal of Political Science*, vol. 7 (1977).
22. Downs, *An Economic Theory of Democracy*, p. 49.
23. Ibid, p. 96.

5 The Relationship between Economics, Politics and the Law in the Formation of Public Policy

CHARLES ROWLEY

1. INTRODUCTION

Since the seminal article on social cost was published by Ronald Coase in the 1960 issue of the *Journal of Law and Economics*,[1] tremendous strides have been made in legal scholarship incorporating economics and, in particular, in relating legal institutions to the pattern of resource allocation in the advanced economies. US legal scholars and economists have given the lead in this development, but Britain is now following hard on their heels not least via the Centre for Socio-Legal Studies, Wolfson College, Oxford. Economists have been appointed to tenured positions in many US law schools and even in a few British law schools and research centres specializing in law and economics have been established, for example, at Chicago, Emory, Columbia, Miami, Pennsylvania, and University College, London. Leading textbooks by Posner[2] and Hirsch[3] have been published in law and economics and several innovative specialist journals have achieved academic and commercial success.[4] Moreover, conventional law journals now publish articles which contain substantial inputs of economics.[5] In many ways, this developing interest in law and economics has signalled the emergence of a new institutional economics which has led the subject back from the wilderness of abstract theory and from the more extreme applications of positivist econometrics.

Simultaneously, though independently, pioneering work by Buchanan, Tullock[6] and Downs[7] in the field of public choice linked economics and political science in a new political economy which developed a theory of government failure to counterbalance the theory of market failure which had been developed during the early postwar period from conventional welfare economics. A major journal, *Public Choice*, has emerged as a vehicle for publication in this field but public choice articles also find their way regularly into the leading journals of economics. In addition to the 'Virginia School', located at George Mason University, important groupings of public choice scholars now are located at the University of Texas at Austin and at Washington University, St Louis.

It is my contention in this paper that the combining of law and economics and public choice offers a powerful mechanism for analysing public policy formation under democratic conditions.[8] In subsequent sections, the relevant theory is briefly outlined and applications are then made in analysing the evolution of British labour laws during the postwar period and in assessing the public policy significance of this process.

2. THE NEW LAW AND ECONOMICS

The term 'law and economics' is here defined as the application of economic theory and empirical method to examine the formation, structure, processes and impact of law and legal institutions. Veljanovski,[9] in his survey paper, divides the study of law and economics somewhat arbitrarily into 'old' and 'new'. The 'old' law and economics is concerned with legal subject matter that affects the operation of the economy and markets, encompassing such areas as conventional antitrust, regulation, labour law and tax law. The subject-matter of the 'new' law and economics is the entire legal system and the doctrines and procedures of the civil, criminal and public laws whether or not they regulate explicit economic relationships. It is this wider application of economics that constitutes the essence of the new approach and which makes the subject relevant to all legal scholarship.

Inevitably, the new law and economics draws upon advanced neoclassical economic theory and statistical techniques in much of its application. But its distinctive feature is the application of market economics to legal institutions, rules and procedures which in some cases (notably in tort and crime) are not conventionally seen to influence market behaviour, but which are predicated on notions of market failure. Commencing with the economic analysis of the law of tort (the Coase theorem) the technique has now been applied to every aspect of the legal system, including contract law, property law, civil and administrative procedure, and theories of punishment, law enforcement and legislation.

The new law and economics has exerted a powerful impact both in its positive and in its normative dimensions. The techniques of positive economics have proved to be most effective in what Veljanovski[10] has labelled 'legal impact studies' or what Hirsch[11] has called 'effect evaluation'. Such studies seek to identify and to quantify (to the extent possible) the effects of law on measurable economic variables. In essence, this is the approach utilised subsequently in this paper in analysing the economic impact of changing British labour laws.

Positive economics, following for the most part Popperian[12] methodology, employs as a generative assumption (the protected core in the sense of Lakatos) the notion of expected wealth maximisation by all individuals in society and in conjunction with other relevant *ceteris paribus* assumptions, deduces falsifiable predictions concerning economic consequences of changes in the law. The extent to which lawyers who are accustomed to an inductive approach which moves from singular to universal statements, who move from facts to theories, and who tend to make total rather than conditional judgments, have shifted to deductive analysis is quite remarkable.

Because of the pre-eminence of Richard Posner in the normative analysis of the law, there is a widespread misapprehension that such economic analysis is concerned exclusively with the achievement of economic efficiency, somewhat loosely and inaccurately referred to as wealth maximisation by Posner himself. Indeed, a central aspect of Posner's thrust is the notion that the common law is an 'efficient' legal institution systematically rectifying market failure when called upon to adjudicate by litigants. Of course, this assertion has generated considerable controversy, not least because Posner frequently is forced back upon dubious transaction cost assumptions in defence of his hypothesis.[13] Since his elevation to the US Court of Appeal (Seventh Circuit) Posner himself has demonstrated a less certain faith in the 'efficiency of the law' hypothesis.[14]

The efficiency objective, whether achieved or not by common law, is not endorsed by all scholars engaged in law and economics analysis. For, as Sen has demonstrated, Paretian efficiency objectives well may be at variance with libertarian objectives thus forcing scholars to choose between these alternative approaches, whenever they conflict, in their normative evaluation of the law. Certainly, many British judges (most notably Lord Denning as Master of the Rolls) have publicly espoused libertarian principles when passing judgment upon the cases brought before them. Posner in contrast has never demonstrated high regard for libertarianism nor any belief that US courts would ever support liberty at some price in efficiency in their effected judgments.

Much of the economic analysis of law has ignored issues of distributive justice (or equity). This thrust has been criticised by economists like Burrows[15] who urge others to take 'a different view of the cathedral', and to emphasise the paradigm of 'law as justice', especially in the important field of the law of tort which has been the heartland of the new law and economics research.

To those (perhaps like Burrows) who are willing to employ an egalitarian social welfare function to drive out distributive consequences, the alternative view of the cathedral is obscured by relatively few pillars. To others, the view is shrouded by conflicting special interests and by a consequential absence of universal (or even near-universal) Wicksellian consent. For the issue of primary distribution of rights has not proved to be amenable to the Paretian calculus, despite the major attempts by Rawls[16] and by Buchanan[17] so to render it.

Rawls introduced the notion of a constitutional settlement on rights effected by individuals negotiating in the 'original position' behind a 'veil of ignorance' which precluded from all constituents any knowledge of their future endowments, positions in society, etc. By invoking the notion that all individuals bargaining in such circumstances would demonstrate infinite risk-aversion, Rawls was able to manipulate the minimax criterion of game theory to produce firstly a lexicographic constitutional preference for liberty over wealth and secondly the famous 'difference principle' concerning distributive justice which would provide a veto power over economic change for the 'least advantaged' members of society.

This outcome, which naturally was well-received by egalitarians, has been severely criticised in logic. In games against nature, such as this game is, individuals are not coerced into the minimax game, as they may be when playing against other risk-averse individuals. But once the infinite risk-aversion assumption is abandoned, there is only a low probability of universal consent behind the veil, and of the Rawlsian solution being endorsed. A major danger of this approach is that scholars can pull out from behind the veil almost any solution they themselves desire. There is no evidence of courts applying the difference principle in their judgments of common law. There is a much greater emphasis in such judgments upon liberty, but not lexicographically in the sense of Rawls.

An alternative approach, by Buchanan, attempts to justify existing distributions of rights in some sense as constitutionally endorsed – the outcome of a rejection by society of Hobbesian anarchy with its plundering of the weak by the strong and with its efficiency losses implicit in the diversion of enterprise away from production and into predation and defence. Even under the most favourable of environmental circumstances – notably the constitutional settlement in the USA by the Founding Fathers following victory in the revolutionary war – this interpretation is suspect. For, although a constitution may define property rights within society, and may establish a government 'as referee' to police such rights, typically it cannot constrain such government to that limited role.

Thus rights that have been constitutionally endorsed, in some sense, may well be subverted by special interest groups operating via the political process, or even by a vote majority which tyrannises minorities within society. This aspect of public choice cannot be ignored in the post-constitutional phase. It weakens significantly the thrust of the constitutional paradigm, and re-emphasises the conflict aspect of the issue of distributive justice.

3. PUBLIC CHOICE

Following early contributions by Downs, Buchanan and Tullock, a very considerable literature has now developed in the field of public choice. At one level, theories of spatial politics centre attention upon the equilibrium properties of political markets in which the motivating assumption is that politicians seek to maximise expected votes or expected pluralities. On the assumption that issue dimension(s) can be determined, that the distribution of voters' preferences over such dimension(s) is single-peaked, that all voters vote, that full information exists, and that two parties compete for elections and are mobile in issue dimension space, both parties are predicted to move to the median of the voter distribution – the famous median voter theorem of Downs.

However, once the above-mentioned auxiliary conditions are relaxed – notably single-peakedness, two party competition, party mobility and vote frequency – the existence, uniqueness and stability of spatial political equilibrium are all in doubt. Although Enelow and Hinich[18] recently have argued forcefully that centrist forces nevertheless dominate in political elections, they are hard stretched to maintain this position as the Downsian assumptions are seen to crumble. In recent years, essentially two-party democracies, notably in the United Kingdom and in the USA, have not been characterised by consensus policy platforms for election purposes nor is it evident that the leftist party in either country has shown itself to be spatially mobile in response to evident rightist shifts in voter preference distributions. In such circumstances, the median voter theorem has encountered increasing scepticism as a political market predictor.

In any event, elections are only periodic incidents in a continuous political market process, and indeed are incidents which many public choice analysts now are inclined to down-play as relatively unimportant in view of the near zero expected impact of individual votes upon electoral outcomes. Much more importance in the political market is currently attached firstly to the behaviour of special interest groups in their attempt to extract rents that privately would be unavailable and secondly to the behaviour of senior bureaucrats in their attempts to wrest discretionary power from their legislator principals and to exercise such power in pursuit of their own objectives.

In his book, *The Logic of Collective Action*,[19] Mancur Olson stressed that the result of special interest group collective action, if successful, typically is a public good available to all within the group irrespective of their rates of individual contribution. For this reason, such collective action tends to be eroded by the free-rider problem in the absence of advantageous conditions. Specifically, the collective interests of such groups will be less than fully served unless membership coercion is economically feasible and/or unless private membership benefits can be made available to the active membership. Even then, organising large special interest groups for the first time is seen to require gifted entrepreneurial leadership, high expected rents, and 'favourable' conditions. In his later book, '*The Rise and Decline of Nations*'[20] Olson further elaborated on these requirements, suggesting that stable democracies such as the United Kingdom, with unchanging national boundaries and an absence of defeat in wars, were particularly vulnerable to wealth destruction by successful, well-established special interests.

Special interest groups thus defined are *rent seekers*[21] whose principal objective is that of transferring wealth from others in society to themselves. Essentially, such groups are not engaged directly in productive activity, which fact distinguishes them sharply from *profit seekers* in the unregulated marketplace, whose behaviour usually is viewed to be wealth-enhancing.

Rent seeking, in contrast, occurs in institutional settings where individual efforts to maximise value generate social waste rather than social surplus, not infrequently as a consequence of government-imposed entry barriers and market regulation. It is the essence of Olson's thesis that such interventions do not occur in a political vacuum, but arise rather in response to effective political rent seeking by special interest groups, who recognise their significance for market rent seeking. The political basis, once granted, may not easily be wrested back from successful rent seekers even by a determined majority government.

Senior bureaucrats, it has been argued by Niskanen and others,[22] maximise a utility function defined with reference to output, the size of staff and possibly on-the-job leisure. They serve as agents to their government principals, though with some discretion as a consequence of the latter's truncated property rights (truncated that is by comparison with the entrepreneur in the classical capitalist firm who can hire and fire factor inputs at will and who can dispose easily of his equity in the residual status of the firm).

Inevitably, therefore, tension exists between any government and its bureaux both in the formulation and in the implementation of public policy. Indeed, according to Breton,[23] the resolution of the bilateral monopoly game is to be seen as decisive in many election situations, since bureaucratic discretion typically will not be exercised in sympathy with the vote-seeking aspirations of government. For this reason, governments determined to discipline their agents typically erode discretion by setting bureaux in competition with each other; by collapsing intransigent bureaux; by reducing the tenure of senior bureaucrats and by directly monitoring their behaviour. Rowley and Elgin[24] have analysed this principal-agent problem as it manifests itself in the USA. Although they infer a greater power for the legislator than is usually conceded, nevertheless scope for independent bureaucratic interventions undoubtedly exists, arguably with significant implications for public choice.

Public choice theory, as expounded above, offers little confidence that unconstrained political markets will reflect the preferences of the median voter, and still less that they will satisfy the necessary conditions for some kind of social welfare optimum. Rather, in the absence of restrictions, political markets are seen to respond to rent-seeking pressures mounted by the more effective special interest groups, often from a minority vote position, and to the manipulation of discretionary power by self-seeking bureaucrats in areas where legislative monitoring is lax.

In such circumstances, the question arises whether political markets should be reined in by constitutional constraints designed to eliminate minority group manipulations, and to protect the majoritarian position. Buchanan,[25] and others of the 'Virginia School' persuasion have argued strongly the 'reason' of such rules, most especially within the context of the US federal budget. Similar arguments have been advanced with regard to the troubled British labour markets, though as yet without practical success. Nevertheless, there are evident dangers in pursuing this constitutional solution.

Firstly, it is by no means self-evident that those special interest groups which successfully plunder the unconstrained political market would not prove to be equally successful in manipulating the constitutional settlement, thus further indemnifying themselves against potential majority vote reactions. For, unlike the secluded negotiations which culminated in the US Constitution in the eighteenth century, late twentieth century constitutional amendments are negotiated in the glare of media publicity against a background of interest group lobbying similar in nature to that evidenced in the ordinary business of the legislature.

Secondly, it is not clear that the bureaucrats called upon to draft the constitutional clauses would not seize the opportunity so provided to incorporate discretionary powers coveted by their respective bureaus, thereby further loosening the principal-agent relationship. Legislators pre-occupied with campaign considerations well may fail to identify self-seeking clauses thus inserted and their special interest constituents may recognise own advantages in allowing bureaux discretionary power which they subsequently will usurp.

Thirdly, constitutional rules are vulnerable to adverse judicial interpretation. It is a surprising fact that even economists like Posner, who view individual behaviour for the most part as being predicated on self-interest, are prepared to make an exception for Supreme Court Justices. In fact, political penetration of the Bench is a long-seated aspect of the US separation of powers, with successive Presidents seizing such opportunities as arise for nominating to the Court individuals of a sympathetic political persuasion. The liberal-biased Court has, over the past twenty years, significantly reinterpreted the Constitution in favour of the socialist perspective. It is rumoured that the Republican victory in the 1984 Presidential Election may result in the establishment of a Republican-biased Supreme Court for the remainder of the twentieth century with some five vacancies expected in the Court between 1984 and 1988.

In any event, in countries like the United Kingdom, which have no written constitution and a long tradition of parliamentary sovereignty, formal constitutional rules effectively are not feasible. Instead, the concept of the 'big Bill' has been developed simultaneously to legislate over a whole range of related policy issues. Such indeed was the ill-fated 1971 Industrial Relations Act passed by the Conservative Government in an unsuccessful attempt at root-and-branch labour market reform. An obvious problem with 'big Bills' is that once enacted they may be overturned by a simple Parliamentary majority, as indeed occurred in 1974 when the 1971 Act was completely repealed.

4. BRITISH LABOUR LAWS 1906–84[26]

The Trades Dispute Act 1906 provided British trade unions and their members with unique immunities from tortious actions for acts done in contemplation or furtherance of a trade dispute. This Act established the basic framework of immunities within which the law in relation to industrial actions was to operate for the best part of three quarters of a century.

It is important to note the difference between immunities at common law and positive legal rights, even when the direct consequence of the two methods of protection are essentially the same. Immunities admittedly form part of the legal framework, for after all they have to be legislated at public law. But they place those individuals and organisations, so immunised, effectively above a common law which still exists and which impact upon non-immunised individuals and organisations. Common law rights are thus abruptly destroyed by such a system of governance, since actions for infringement simply cannot be brought.

In contrast, positive legal rights, such as those legislated in the USA, in France and in West Germany, which regulate labour union behaviour, replace the common law in the areas of their domain and do not *in the same sense* inculcate notions of privilege antipathetic to the whiggist liberal tradition of the rule of law. By defining more sharply the precise areas in which positive rights hold jurisdiction, this latter approach also provides an opportunity for governments to more finely tune their regulation of labour markets. For blanket immunity from the law of tort is a crude and indivisible mechanism, ill-suited to changing styles in trade union behaviour as evidenced in Britain during the decade of the 1970s and beyond.

In any event, whether viewed from the perspective of immunities or of rights, British trade unions operated within a very much more protected environment from 1906 onwards than did their counterparts in the USA, France and West Germany. For example, following the Taft Hartley Act 1947, US unions have no absolute right to strike either in public or in common law, with stringent Federal law restrictions concerning strikes called during the period of a collective agreement; strikes involving 'unfair labour practice'; strikes employing unlawful means; strikes where the dispute is not between employer and employee, and strikes of public servants. Unions are liable for damages if their members take unlawful industrial action. Unlike the British case, collective agreements in the US, which typically contain elaborate grievance procedures and 'no-strike' clauses, are legally enforceable. In the US, picketing is unlawful if it blocks access, is secondary and/or if it interferes with employees of another employer located at a common site.

Several states in the US require ballots prior to strike action and Federal law requires the use of secret ballots in union elections. The pre-entry closed shop is prohibited by the Taft Hartley Act, although union shops or post-entry closed shops are legal save in the 28 'right to work' states which have overriden Federal law. Evidently, unions in the USA are more closely controlled via the legal process than those in the UK, especially prior to 1980. Not surprisingly they are relatively weak, comprising less than 22 per cent of the US work force, and organisationally they are more divided. The US situation is closely reflected by French and by West German labour laws.

The trade union privileges established in Britain by the 1906 Act remained substantially in existence despite periodic attempts of reform, until repealed by the 1971 Industrial Relations Act. This latter legislation, the result of a 'big Bill' designed by the Conservative Government to radically redesign the troubled British labour markets, was a British near-equivalent to a constitutional amendment, given the absence of a written Constitution. Rejected by the trade union movement, and supported by the very voters who had earlier mandated the legislation, the Act quickly fell into disrepute and, eventually, triggered the electoral defeat of the Conservative administration in 1974.

The newly-elected minority Labour Government repealed the 1971 Act as part of the 1974 Trade Union and Labour Relations Act which returned British trade unions to the system of immunities which the 1971 Act had attempted to replace. Section 13 provided individuals with basic immunity from liability for civil conspiracy, inducement to break a contract of employment and interference with business, trade, or employment, all of which had been provided by the Act of 1906. Section 13 also reenacted the Trade Disputes Act 1964, declaring that an inducement to break a contract of employment and an actual breach of contract were not to be regarded as 'unlawful means' for the purpose of establishing liabilities in tort. Section 14 reenacted the immunity in tort for trade union funds in a clearer and more extended form than the 1906 Act. Section 29 reenacted and extended the scope of 'trade dispute'.

The minority 1974 Government failed to extend trade union immunities to the breaking of all contracts, however remote from the contract of employment. However, following reelection with an overall majority in 1976, the Labour Government, in a 'nasty little Act', effected this extension, threatening to invoke the Parliament Acts 1911 and 1949 to prevent obstruction by the House of Lords, and thus rendering immune from legal redress all trade union industrial 'action', however remote from those involved in the original dispute. The consequence of this legislation, of course, was the 1979 Winter of Discontent, the pathetic pleas of Prime Minister Callaghan that he and his Government were 'prostrate' before the union movement, and the culminating crushing electoral defeat of the Labour Government.

The 1979 Conservative Government pursued a cautious piecemeal approach to the reining in of trade union immunities – a policy which has continued since reelection in 1983. The legal changes introduced by the 1980 Employment Act and by the 1982 Employment Act provided the setting for an impact study of subsequent labour market behaviour which forms the basis for Sections 5 and 6 of this paper.

The Employment Act 1980 restricted trade union immunities in three ways. Section 16 provided that immunities do not apply to acts occurring whilst picketing unless such picketing occurs at the pickets' own place of work. Section 17 withdrew immunities from secondary industrial action unless such action was undertaken by employees of customers or suppliers to the employer in dispute, with a principal purpose of interfering with those market relationships and with a reasonable likelihood of achieving that objective. Section 18 withdrew immunities where a person induces an employee of one employer to break contract in order to compel workers of another employer to join a particular union, unless those persons are employed by the same organisation. No attempt was made in the 1980 Act to weaken trade immunities or to narrow the definition of a trade dispute.

The 1982 Act addressed these latter issues. Section 15 withdrew immunity for trade unions and employers' associations from actions in tort, although maximum damages ceilings were imposed and the unions' political funds and provident benefit funds were protected from enforced recovery. Section 18 significantly narrowed the scope of a trade dispute to issues arising wholly or mainly between workers and their employers. Immunity also was restricted to disputes arising within the United Kingdom.

Although each such withdrawal of privilege was limited and piecemeal in nature it is here hypothesised that, in combination, these Acts non-trivially have shifted the labour market environment, with important implications for trade union behaviour in the United Kingdom. They have also shifted the political environment by reducing union leaders' powers.

5. A THEORY OF TRADE UNION BEHAVIOUR

Trade unions are essentially labour cartels whose principal objective is that of extracting rent from employers and transferring such rent to their own organisations. They are a very special kind of cartel since they raise member incomes not only by restricting the ongoing flow of labour services below competitive market rates but, periodically, by employing the strike weapon as an indivisible mechanism for closing down completely the supply of unionised labour. Rent seeking, in the sense here defined, is a socially wasteful activity, involving the expenditure of resources not in wealth-enhancing but in wealth-transferring and in wealth-destructive ways.

It is here suggested that British trade unions, uniquely protected in such cartel activities by the 1906 Act (and its successors), further buttressed by the relative growth of government commodity monopolies, and by the systematic refusal of postwar British governments to liquidate non-viable enterprise, became between 1964 and 1980 the most significant rent-seeking wealth destroyers in the British economy. Even after 1975, when the union membership became aware that their own prospective earnings were being jeopardised by union leaders who had diverted their activities from pecuniary to political rent seeking, the principal-agent relationship posed for them a prisoners' dilemma from which there appeared to be no escape.

British trade unions are non-proprietary organisations. Their members and elected leaders do not hold private property rights in the member/leadership status, nor do they own alienable rights to the net assets of individuals. For the most part, unions refrain from competing directly between themselves for membership (though this now is changing in the post-1980 environment). Leadership mobility between unions (other than via merger) is unknown. For these reasons, labour unions are characterised by a much attenuated monitoring mechanism by comparison with corporate enterprise where capital and labour market pressures are exerted to maintain monitoring control by the principals (equity shareholders) over their agents (management and shopfloor workers).

Labour unions depend for their success upon attracting large numbers of members willing to commit resources to the objectives of the organisation. Such investments are in the form of initiation fees, dues assessments, and the expected income sacrificed in strike and picketing activities. Expected wealth maximising members require a positive net expected return on such investments, in the form of a positive union/non-union wage differential. In this respect, members are principals, imbued with residual claimant status and the (albeit truncated) counterparts of equity stockholders in corporate enterprise. However, since such residual claims are distributed over a large number of principals/members, without reference to individual contributions to the rent seeking exercise, there is a public good problem, with an in built incentive for members to free-ride on the rent seeking exercise.

The free-rider problem generates a collective membership demand for monitoring services in the form of management agents equipped with such disciplinary powers as the power to expel, to fine or to demote those who evade their rent seeking duties. In addition, the agents (leaders) are commissioned to exercise managerial expertise in the collective bargaining process. Inevitably, managerial discretion emerges in the conduct of these duties.

Because membership rights for the most part are non-transferable (the licensed dockers are a notable exception) two control mechanisms available to stockholders in corporate enterprise are precluded in the case of trade unions. Firstly, trade union members cannot withdraw the capitalised value of their expected rent streams from their investments in response to inefficient leadership policies, thereby exposing the leadership to the threat of outside acquisition. Secondly, they cannot concentrate their vote power in the hands of a few representatives endowed with proxy powers as a means of ousting inefficient leaders from within. These factors, given the public good problem in monitoring deviant union leaders, reduce the expected net returns to individual monitoring typically into the negative range (although the 'Silver Birch' phenomenon in the 1984 coal-miners strike is an interesting signal that even this may be subject to change in the new legal environment).

Thus, the non-proprietorial nature of trade unions, in all Western economies, implies the existence of a non-trivial degree of discretion via which trade union leaders may pursue their own objectives at the expense of the pecuniary interests of their membership. Where the union leadership faces periodic reselection ballots (as is the general case in Britain as a consequence of 1984 labour legislation) deviant incumbents may be constrained by the threat of electoral defeat. However, leadership control over relevant information channels, campaign finances and voting procedures, when combined with membership free-riding, will make it very difficult to displace determined incumbents.

The existence of a principal/agent problem in no sense guarantees divergence in the goal pursuits of the parties concerned. For divergence typically is triggered by differences in the reward-cost structure with which individuals are confronted. In the case of trade unions, however, such differences exist almost universally. The membership benefits directly from rents ceded by employers via the collective bargaining process – and indeed it benefits incrementally from each successful labour market settlement. The leadership usually is salaried and although salary levels may reflect long-term rent-seeking success for their membership, certainly they do not vary with incremental success. The leaders do not hold stock-options in the net present value of their union, and thus are not economically motivated to maximise membership rents.

Since leadership budgets tend to be correlated more directly with due income, and since the latter tends to be directly correlated with trade union size (though exceptions occur where high dues are exacted from a declining membership in industries subject to secular decline), union leaders typically pursue policies designed to increase membership size, even at some cost in sacrificed pecuniary rents. Whether such policies take the form of union-sponsored over-manning or of union-induced employment expansion via overt wage restraint will vary according to union leadership predilections, membership monitoring efficiency, and the exigencies of the outside economic environment. Where union leaders sense opportunities for future income and/or career advancement from arranging settlements favourable to the company or government bureau with which they are negotiating they may enter into 'sweetheart contracts' suppressing membership rents in return for negotiated personal benefits. Although this phenomenon is uncommon in Britain, for reasons outlined in Section 6, yet it is not unknown for trade union leaders who have delivered settlements favourable to government labour market policy in sensitive markets to find themselves honoured with peerages or with non-titled equivalents (the CH) even by Conservative governments. To the extent that such potential rewards moderate socially wasteful rent-seeking, the principal-agent problem in its general form may even be welfare-enhancing. In general, unfortunately, such is not the recent British labour market experience.

6. BRITISH TRADE UNIONS, IMMUNITIES AND POLITICAL RENT-SEEKING

A combination of extensive legal immunities, a large and growing public sector and a close association with one of the two major political parties (Labour) has induced a number of British trade union leaders to invade the political process directly, in part to strengthen pecuniary rent-seeking on behalf of their principals, but in part also to pursue ideological objectives of their own, even via the destruction of members' pecuniary rents. Throughout the period 1968 to 1980, Parliamentary sovereignty was itself placed in jeopardy in the United Kingdom as a consequence of such political rent-seeking, and the rule of law, such as it was in British labour markets, was systematically infringed.

Legal immunities provided to trade unions and their individual members from suits in tort and in contract, in connection with trade disputes, catholically defined, provided union leaders with very wide discretionary powers. For the membership saw little or no threat to their own or to their union funds from supporting leadership-sponsored activities which, in any other walk of life, would have invoked successful legal actions. Because of the generalised contempt for the law encouraged by legal immunities in labour markets, even overtly criminal behaviour was allowed to go unpunished by a demoralised legal system. Members disinclined to accept an alienated leadership were often obligated to do so by the ruthless application by leaders of closed shop provisions and of intimidatory threats.

Within an essentially free enterprise economy, such rent-seeking, even based on legal immunities, must be moderated by fears of liquidating otherwise viable enterprises. In Britain, after 1945, however, the rapid growth of public enterprise and of government bureaux, both protected from market competition and both able to finance their accounting deficits by systematically successful invasion of Exchequer subsidies, significantly abated union membership apprehension of redundancies. From 1971 onwards, with the decision by the Conservative Government to protect a bankrupted Rolls-Royce Company from liquidation, even the private sector became imbued with a subsidy expectation. In such circumstances, the bankruptcy constraint on trade union rent-seeking was removed with respect to extensive sectors of the British economy.

The above-mentioned factors, serious though they were in Britain in exacerbating an inevitable principal-agent problem, were in combination no more damaging than the historical association between the trade union movement and the British Labour Party – an association which became extremely close during the early 1970s and which has remained so through the time of writing this paper. The trade unions sponsor a significant number of Labour Party Members of Parliament (125 in the 1976 Administration), they finance more than 75 per cent of the Labour Party's general expenditures and approximately 95 per cent of its general election campaign expenses. Unless individual trade union members specifically opt out of the political levy (and the cost of so doing may be non-trivial) it is deducted from their pay and utilised at the discretion of the union leadership. Financially, therefore, the relationship is tightly bonded.

Politically, the link is closer still. The union leaders nominate by block membership votes more than 50 per cent of the National Executive Committee of the Labour Party, the principal policy-formulating body. Similarly, the union leaders control almost 90 per cent of the vote at the Labour Party Conference and hold a 40 per cent vote in the selection of the Leader and Deputy Leader of the Labour Party. In addition, of course, they also influence the behaviour of the Labour Party via the vote power of members, though since 1979 a growing proportion of the membership has defected to the Conservative and to the Alliance parties.

The median voter model suggests, of course, that such financial and political bonds would tend to be washed aside by convergence forces within the political marketplace which propel vote-seeking politicians into centrist policy platforms and which relegate into Opposition political parties locked into non-centrist political space. Essentially, this latter outcome *has* dominated the British election process since 1979, largely as a consequence of trade union behaviour over the period 1974 to 1979. Such, however, was not the case in the elections of 1974 and 1976 which propelled Labour Governments into office on labour market policy platforms well to the left of the underlying voter distribution, at least as evidenced in national opinion polls.

In essence, many British trade unions from 1971 onwards utilised the logic of collective action, exerting the influence of powerful special interest groups to arrest political market pressures for trade union reform. Voters who had mandated the 1971 Act retracted their positions, in response to labour market disruption, in sufficient numbers to elect Labour governments both in 1974 and 1976, committed to the extension of trade union political protection. Reinforced by closed shop and employment protection legislation, as well as enhanced legal immunities, politically motivated union leaders from 1976 onwards then sought to subvert the political process in pursuit of ideological objectives far removed from the contract of employment. In so doing, they placed the potential rents of their members in jeopardy, thereby sowing the seeds of May 1979 electoral disaster.

7. TRADE UNIONS IN THE COURTROOM: THE POST-1979 IMPACT

The legislation of 1980 and 1982, outlined above, limited and piecemeal though it may have been, significantly changed the legal status of trade unions and their members, and arguably impacted discernibly (the miners excepted) upon their behaviour. Selected legal cases illustrate this phenomenon.

The zenith of post-1976 trade union legal protection was achieved early in 1979 when the House of Lords reversed the December 1978 decision of the Court of Appeal in the case of *Express Newspapers Ltd v. McShane and Another*.[27]

In 1978, a dispute over pay arose between the proprietors of provincial newspapers and their employees, who were members of the National Union of Journalists (NUJ). In an attempt to bring direct pressure to bear on the proprietors, the national executive council of the union called out on strike all the union's journalists employed by provincial newspapers. This 'primary' strike failed to immobilise the provincial newspapers since the latter enjoyed access to news copy supplied by the Press Association. To render the primary strike more effective, therefore, the NUJ called out on strike all Press Association journalists who were union members (the 'secondary strike').

The Press Association supplied not only provincial newspapers but also national newspapers and other organisations with news copy. Thus the secondary strike affected these latter bodies, and also the Press Association itself, none of which were involved in the pay dispute at issue. The NUJ executive was empowered to fine or to expel members who failed to comply with their objectives in which latter case they would lose their jobs as a consequence of the closed shop. Even so, 50 per cent of its journalists at the Press Association continued to honour their employment contracts, thereby weakening the impact of the secondary strike. In retaliation, the NUJ instructed union members working on the plaintiff's national newspaper and other National newspapers to refuse to use news copy sent out by the Press Association. Though this breached their employment contracts, the union's journalists complied with this instruction.

The plaintiffs brought an action against the defendants, who were members of the NUJ national executive council, seeking (i) an injunction restraining the defendants from inducing or procuring its employees to breach their contracts, and (ii) damages for inducing or procuring breach of contract. The defendants claimed that their action was done 'in furtherance of' a trade dispute, because they genuinely and honestly believed that the blacking would advance the cause of the provincial journalists and that their action was accordingly protected by S. 13(1) of the 1974 Act as amended by the 1976 Act. The judge rejected this defence on the ground that the defendants' action did not advance the provincial journalists' interests in a concrete way. The defendants appealed.

The Court of Appeal held that those who sought the protection of S. 13(1) of the 1974 Act (amended) had to establish not only that they had a genuine intention to achieve the objective of a trade dispute but also that acts done pursuant to that intention were reasonably capable of, or had a reasonable prospect of, achieving that objective. It determined that there was no reasonable prospect of the latter outcome and, for that reason, the appeal was dismissed with leave to appeal to the House of Lords refused. The leading judgment in this case was that of Lord Denning, Master of the Rolls, a libertarian judge not well-disposed to the use of coercive power by special interest groups. Lord Justice Lawton and Lord Justice Branden wrote concurring judgments, though without the libertarian references.

Despite the resistance of the Appeal Court, the case eventually reached the House of Lords in late 1979, and the Court of Appeal's decision and its interpretation of the relevant Act was overturned. Four of the Law Lords found that the test of 'in furtherance' was subjective and that it was a sufficient defence to show that the perpetrator of the act genuinely believed that it might further the trade dispute, though discretion for 'objective' correction by the court existed where the 'belief' was obviously unreasonable. The fifth Law Lord determined that there was an 'objective' element in 'in furtherance' which the court must appraise, but suggested that the court would be reluctant to substitute its own judgment for the judgment of experienced trade union leaders initiating the action.

The practical effect of this judgment was to prevent the courts from applying criteria of 'remoteness' or 'capability' to decide whether an act was in furtherance of a trade dispute, confirming the worst fears of those who had opposed the extension of immunity to all contracts in 1974 and 1976.

By the time the House of Lords had given judgment in the MacShane case in December 1979, the Conservative Government had already published the Bill which was to become the 1980 Employment Act, making secondary picketing illegal and removing immunity from trade union officials who organised certain secondary strikes (as outlined above). The 1980 Act, which was widely criticised as being weak, was buttressed by the 1982 Employment Act which placed controls on the closed shop, narrowed the definition of a trade dispute, and removed the immunity for actions in tort from trade unions in certain specified circumstances (as outlined above).

These Acts dramatically shifted the balance within the trade union principal-agent relationship, sharply raising the incentives of trade union members to restrict the political rent-seeking of their leaders, and generally weakening the coercive powers of the trade unions as special interest rent-seekers both in political and in pecuniary markets. A number of behavioural adjustments to the new institutional framework have now been evidenced as the following important court cases clearly indicate.

The crucial importance of the trade dispute redefinition became apparent in November 1983 when, in *Mercury Communications Ltd v. Stanley and Another*,[28] the Court of Appeal granted Mercury an injunction against a strike called to prevent the linking of its telecommunications with British Telecom. This strike, which was politically motivated against the privatisation proposal of the Conservative Government, would have been lawful prior to the 1982 Act and, if successful, would have induced a major trade union assault on the entire competition and privatisation programme of that Government. In the event, the injunction proved successful in eliminating strike action and the telecommunications link was effected as part of the privatisation policy. Other privatisation programmes were subsequently not impeded by trade union resistance.

The importance of the tortious liability of trade unions for deflecting illegal strike behaviour became apparent in 1983 in *Stockport Messenger Group v. National Graphical Association*.[29] The union had illegally engaged in secondary picketing in 1983 at the plant of the Stockport-based Messenger Group in an attempt to prevent the owner of a 'free' news-sheet from employing thirteen non-NGA employees to operate computer printing technology which had effectively rendered NGA craft skills obsolete. The NGA encouraged mass picketing of the plant, thereby infringing both the 1980 and the 1982 Acts. The newspaper proprietor successfully sought an injunction restraining such illegal behaviour, but the injunction was violated on successive occasions, despite the imposition of fines initially of £50 000 but rising eventually to the legal maximum of £250 000 against the union.

Messenger Newspapers then brought a suit for contempt of court against the NGA which was adjudicated upon in the Court of Appeal by Sir John Donaldson, Master of the Rolls. The entire assets of the NGA (approximately £10 million) were sequestrated by the court despite a vain attempt by the union to avoid seizure by using auditors as a third party and claiming that the auditors were under no duty to disclose information.

The combination of rising incremental fines and the sequestration order induced wild strike behaviour in which the NGA sought to close down Fleet Street, thereby exposing themselves to further (and massive) claims for damages. Following a vain attempt to pressure the TUC into a general strike, the NGA called off the illegal action and conceded defeat, an outcome that would have been inconceivable throughout the 1970s. In July 1984, the plaintiff was awarded £125 000 damages, for the episode of unlawful picketing against the NGA.

The importance of the 1980 Act in rendering secondary action by trade unionists in furtherance of a dispute illegal is clearly outlined in the case of *Dimbleby and Sons Ltd v. National Union of Journalists*.[30] The dispute reached the Court of Appeal in December 1983 under the 1980 Act and remains unresolved (as at early 1985), with an appeal pending to The House of Lords.

In 1979, a newspaper publishing company (TBF Ltd) refused to re-engage a number of journalists whom it had dismissed for taking strike action. The journalists, some of whom remained unemployed, were members of the defendant union, which blacked TBF Ltd and instructed its members to refuse to work for or to supply copy to the company. TBF Ltd continued to publish newspapers printed by an associated company, TBF (Printers) Ltd. The plaintiffs, sellers and distributors of a number of local newspapers, contracted with TBF (Printers) Ltd to print their newspapers in August 1983. Journalists employed by the plaintiffs refused to supply copy to the printers for fear of being expelled from the union and, in consequence, were suspended. The plaintiffs successfully sought an injunction restraining the union from inducing its members to breach their employment contracts and from interfering with the plaintiffs' printing contract.

The NUJ appealed, claiming immunity under S. 13(1) of the 1974 Act. The plaintiffs contended that any such immunity had been removed by S. 17 of the 1980 Act because the union's action amounted to unlawful secondary action. The Court of Appeal rejected the NUJ appeal holding that the dispute between the plaintiffs and their journalists was not a 'trade dispute' within S. 29(1) of the 1974 Act, although the dispute between TBF Ltd and *its* journalists was such a 'trade dispute'. Any immunity which the union might have had under S. 13(1) of the 1974 Act had been removed by S. 17 of the 1980 Act and was not saved by S. 17(3) because the printer, TBF (Printers) Ltd, was not an employer party to the original dispute. Once again, Sir John Donaldson, Master of the Rolls, was party to this judgment, though he refrained from presenting the leading judgment. Leave to appeal to the House of Lords was refused, although later this refusal was overturned by the Appeal Committee of the House of Lords.

Most recently, the issue of the tortious liability of trade unions for illegal picketing has been central to the longstanding strike by certain mineworkers, instigated by the National Union of Mineworkers.[31] Despite unprecedented violence by the pickets, intended to intimidate miners from exercising their right to work, the 1982 Act has been invoked only in a very limited way. In one significant case, however, the courts have moved to decisively uphold the rule of law.

In April 1984, the High Court issued an injunction to stop pickets attached to the South Wales area of the National Union of Mineworkers (NUM) from interfering unlawfully with the trade of two small hauliers running supplies into the Llanwern and Port Talbot steel works. The pickets, nevertheless, continued to harass the lorries of these hauliers. In July 1984, the hauliers returned to court for the enforcement of the injunction. The court obliged, fining the South Wales area of the union £50 000 for contempt.

The union refused to pay and attempted to move its assets outside the control of the British courts. Writs of sequestration were issued to seize the union's funds and the sequestrators, Price Waterhouse, successfully tracked down the funds and sequestrated them, establishing that any person or organisation, whether principal or agent, trying to evade the order would be in contempt of court. The road haulage companies proceeded with damage suits against the NUM. Failure to pay damages, if awarded, could lead to further fines for NUM contempt of court. If others should seize upon this precedent, the miners' funds could be drained away much more quickly than they currently appreciate.

8. PUBLIC CHOICE AND THE LAW: THE 'PRISONER'S DILEMMA' PROBLEM

The trade union example illustrates a significant prisoners' dilemma problem for public choice and the law. Rent-seeking involves social waste. Resources that might have been devoted to value-enhancing activity engage instead in competitive effort over wealth transfers. Yet, despite the welfare losses imposed, such distributive struggles cannot be ignored by vote-seeking politicians and self-seeking bureaucrats in attempts to reform a special interest group dominated society.

The contractual (catallactic) theory of politics embraced by the 'Virginia School' and others suggests that, if rent-seeking imposes sufficiently large net losses upon society, a public choice solution should be forthcoming, with the gainers compensating the losers from constitutional reform. Yet, evidently in the British experience, attempts at such constitutional reform of labour markets, following decades of significant welfare losses, failed both in 1968 and 1971, under Labour and Conservative administrations respectively.

An important reason for the failure of constitutional reform in British labour markets lay in the particular pattern of potential payoffs available to the various parties involved in the reform attempt. Notably, certain powerful public sector trade unions (e.g., the miners, the dockers and the power workers) had been fairly consistent winners during the 1960s and early 1970s and stood to lose significantly from labour market reforms designed to weaken the coercive power of the closed shop, to loosen commodity market monopolies and to restrict the strike behaviour of British trade unions. The situation is illustrated for a two person game in Table 5.1.

In Table 5.1 the agents are not identical with respect to anticipated

TABLE 5.1 *Prisoners' dilema with asymmetric payoffs*

		B	
		(1)	(2)
A	(1)	10.14	2.16
	(2)	16. −2	16.0

payoffs. Agents initially in the prisoners' dilemma situation (Cell 4) do not each view unambiguous potential gains from a shift to Cell 1, despite the latter's higher total return. Thus, unless B is willing and able to make a side-payment to A in excess of six units, A will not contract out of the prisoners' dilemma. Such arguably was the case both in 1968 and 1971 when constitutional reform was offered to resolve endemic labour market problems.

In essence, the piecemeal approach of the Conservative Governments of 1979 and 1983 is to be viewed as an attempt to adjust the values in the matrix so as to create a more symmetric payoff matrix, in which case contractual reform is more feasible. It is not at all surprising that the greatest test for this policy has come from the National Union of Mineworkers, the long-time consistent winner from trade union immunities now exposed to a real threat of constitutional reform.

NOTES

* An earlier draft of this paper was delivered at the British Association, Section F meeting held at the University of East Anglia in September 1984. I am grateful to Anthony Ogus, Robin Matthews and other participants for helpful comments. Part of the paper was presented at a seminar in the Center for Study of Public Choice and the help of participants is gratefully acknowledged.

1. R. H. Coase, 'The Problem of Social Cost', *Journal of Law and Economics*, vol. III October 1960, pp. 1–44.
2. R. A. Posner, *Economic Analysis of Law* (Boston, Mass: Little, Brown, 1972).
3. W. Hirsch, *Law and Economics: An Introductory Analysis* (London: Academic Press, 1979).
4. See, for example, *The International Review of Law and Economics, The Supreme Court Economic Review* and the *Oxford Journal of Legal Studies*.
5. A good example is *The University of Chicago Law Review*.

6. J. M. Buchanan and G. Tullock, *The Calculus of Consent* (Ann Arbor: University of Michigan Press, 1965).
7. A. Downs, *An Economic Theory of Democracy* (New York: Harper and Row, 1957).
8. See also C. K. Rowley, 'Social Sciences and Law: The Relevance of Economic Theories', *Oxford Journal of Legal Studies*, vol. 1, no. 3, Winter 1981, pp. 391–405.
9. C. G. Veljanovski, *The New Law-and-Economics* (Centre for Socio-Legal Studies, Oxford, 1982).
10. Ibid.
11. See Hirsch, *Law and Economics*.
12. See K. R. Popper, *The Logic of Scientific Discovery* (New York: Harper and Row, 1968).
13. See Posner, *Economic Analysis of Law*.
14. See W. J. Samuels and N. Mercuro, 'Posnerian Law and Economics on the Bench; and R. A. Posner, 'Wealth Maximization and Judicial Decision-Making' in *International Review of Law and Economics*, vol. 4, no. 2, December 1984.
15. P. Burrows, *The Economic Theory of Pollution Control* (London: Martin Robertson, 1979).
16. J. Rawls, *A Theory of Justice* (Oxford University Press, 1973).
17. J. M. Buchanan, *The Limits of Liberty* (Chicago UP, 1975).
18. J. M. Enelow and M. J. Hinich, *The Spatial Theory of Voting* (Cambridge University Press, 1984). See also C. K. Rowley, 'The Relevance of the Median Voter Theorem', *Journal of Institutional and Theoretical Economics*, March 1984.
19. M. Olson, *The Logic of Collective Action* (Harvard University Press, 1965).
20. M. Olson, *The Rise and Decline of Nations* (Yale University Press, 1982).
21. See J. M. Buchanan, R. D. Tollison and G. Tullock (eds), *Toward a Theory of the Rent-Seeking Society* (Texas A & M, 1980).
22. W. A. Niskanen, *Bureaucracy and Representative Government* (Chicago: Aldine, 1971).
23. A. Breton, *The Economic Theory of Representative Government* (London: Macmillan, 1974).
24. C. K. Rowley and R. Elgin, 'Towards a Theory of Bureaucracy', in G. K. Shaw (ed.), *Public Choice, Public Finance and Public Policy* (Oxford: Basil Blackwell 1985 (forthcoming)).
25. G. Brennan and J. M. Buchanan, *The Reason of Rules* (Cambridge University Press 1985 (forthcoming)).
26. For a more detailed analysis see C. K. Rowley, 'Towards A Political Economy of British Labor Laws', *University of Chicago Law Review*, Autumn 1984.
27. (1979) 2 ALL ER pp. 360–8.
28. (1984) 1 ALL ER.
29. (1984) 1 ALL ER pp. 293–6.
30. (1984) 1 ALL ER pp. 117–28.
31. See *The Economist*, 4–10 August 1984, pp. 41–2.

6 Legislation, the Courts and the Demand for Compensation

ANTHONY OGUS

The appropriateness of including the subject of law and economics and indeed the participation of myself, an academic lawyer, in a book devoted to the theme of 'Economy and Democracy' requires, perhaps, some initial explanation. Law and economics has been a flourishing area of interdisciplinary study in North America for the last two decades or so. It has taken some time to reach these shores and only now is it beginning to establish itself on a secure basis.[1] The benefits to be derived by the two disciplines involved are mutual: lawyers, if they are to understand and evaluate the workings of the legal system, must recognise the economic functioning of legal rules and institutions; economists, for their part, in analysing the behavioural aspects of resource management, must appreciate the critical importance of those rules and institutions. I trust that this chapter will serve as a useful illustration of both propositions.

I take the aim of this collation to be an exploration of how the constitutional and political ordering of our society can influence the allocation and distribution of resources. Since law has a profound impact on the latter, we must investigate the arrangements for making law, notably by courts and the legislature. A comparison between the respective functions of these two institutions is my general theme. By way of illustration, I shall consider how the two law-making institutions respond to one highly problematic task: determining rights to compensation for losses.

A CONVENTIONAL MODEL OF JUDICIAL LAW-MAKING

I begin with a conventional account of judicial law-making, one which I anticipate would reflect the views of most lawyers. Apart from their duty to interpret and apply legislation, English judges have developed their own system of legal principles, known as the common law. This is a network of rights conferred on individuals, in theory since time immemorial; in practice, the rights evolve and are modified in the light of social and economic developments.[2] The system aims at a balance between stability – through the doctrine of precedent – and flexibility – previous decisions are not binding on the highest court, the House of Lords, and even lower courts find ways of escaping from strict adherence to unpopular precedents. The core of the system is the protection of certain fundamental interests, attaching to the person, property and liberty and the rights of protection are complemented by correlating duties of others (including governments) not to interfere with those interests.[3] The remedies available through the common law are predicated on notions of corrective justice: a plaintiff may claim redress, usually in the form of compensation, where the defendant has infringed a protected interest.[4] It should be noted, however, that some interests are the subject of absolute protection – any interference is actionable – while in others the protection is relative – the interference is actionable only where the defendant is in some sense 'at fault'. The implication is that the formulation of the interest, or the notion of corrective justice itself, often imports a moral element.[5]

In Britain, as in most jurisdictions though not in some of the United States, judges are appointed by the government and are not democratically elected. If there is a 'democratic' influence on their law-making powers, it arises from the mere fact that the judicial process is open to all who can prove that they have a direct interest in the subject of the proceedings.[6] The latter criterion is not widely construed but it is arguable that in constitutional terms this does not involve a denial of the usual democratic values. It is always open to the democratically elected legislature to reverse any judicial decision. Moreover, in Britain, the courts do not have the power to quash legislation – Parliament is sovereign. Calls for a Bill of Rights which would confer such powers on judges have, so far, gone unheeded.

THE PUBLIC INTEREST MODEL OF LEGISLATION

To complement this conventional account of judicial law-making, there exists an equally traditional but, as we shall see in due course, also much disputed model of the legislative process which is based on the notion of public interest. According to this, the deficiencies of the common law are corrected by legislative intervention.[7] Since the legislature is a democratically elected institution, it reflects social values held at any point in history and thus its actions are determined by the 'public interest'. The deficiencies of the common law may be economic in character: market failure, for example, may result from the lack of information available to the courts in formulating, and to the relevant parties in enforcing, rights; or they may result from problems of transaction costs – where the benefits to be derived from the individual enforcement of rights are outweighed by the administrative costs involved. Intervention may also be justified on distributional grounds: the network of common law rights protects a pre-existing wealth distribution and expectations which arise from such distribution. By invoking 'social justice', a value presumed to be in the 'public interest', the legislature may redistribute resources from, for example, those with common law rights to those without.

THE COMPENSATION PROBLEM AND THE CONVENTIONAL MODELS

These models are undoubtedly simplistic and much light has been shed on their inadequacies by recent law and economics analysis. Before we consider this analysis, it is first necessary to state the compensation problem and the mode of resolution implied by the conventional models.[8] Wherever there are interactions between individuals and groups, losses will always occur. Some result from physical injury to the person or to property: road, industrial and home accidents; sickness and disease; damage to premises or goods from careless workmanship; natural events, such as floods, or acts of terrorism. With or without any such injury, an individual may suffer a loss to his reputation, his privacy or his emotional well-being. Finally, there is an infinite variety of ways in which 'economic' interests may be harmed – individuals may lose jobs, firms' trade may be captured by competitors, capital assets may decline in value. The permutations are endless, but the question always arises: In what circumstances should losers be compensated? Where such rights exist should they be enforceable in private law against the inflictor of the loss or some other who gained at the loser's expense? Or should claims be satisfied by a centralised fund, established under public law?

It is difficult to summarise in a short space the intricate solutions which the common law has given to these questions but, at the risk of some oversimplification, it may be said that the judges have sought to balance two variables: the nature of the interest to be protected and the conduct of the inflictor of the harm. As regards the first of these, the more tangible the interest, the greater the protection; there is thus a hierarchy of interests extending from physical property (land and goods) and physical personal integrity through intangible aspects to the personality (liberty and reputation) to pure 'economic' interests (trade and profits). As regards conduct, liability to compensate is a function of the degree of fault or wrongfulness, ranging from the intentional infliction of harm through carelessness (the legal action for negligence) to innocence (legal claims based on strict liability). The ranking of interests may reflect normative ideas associated with social stability – the protection of existing capital assets – and individual autonomy.[9] The concern with wrongdoing indicates a moral basis to corrective justice: individuals are to be encouraged to make their own arrangements to deal with hazards which are an inevitable feature of social and commercial life, for example, by insurance, and the burden of protection is to be shifted to another only when that latter creates the hazard by behaviour which deviates from socially acceptable standards of conduct.[10]

It should be evident that the common law, by resolving the compensation problem in this way, eschews a redistributional role. Its concern is with the preservation of the *status quo ante*; the wealth position of the victims of risks – and thus also their ability to protect themselves – is regarded as irrelevant. It must be acknowledged that this image of the common law is to be discerned most completely in the nineteenth century. In more recent times, judges, consciously or unconsciously, have allowed some redistributive elements to enter into their decisions.[11] In cases of road and industrial accidents, they have not ignored the fact that defendants (drivers and employers respectively) are generally in a better position to make the appropriate arrangements for dealing with the risk; they are said to be better 'loss-distributors'. Nevertheless, this may be seen more as the implementation of goals established by the legislature – liability insurance being mandatory in these situations – than a deviation from the fundamental principles of the common law. And it is to the response of the legislature to the compensation problem that we must now turn. The difficulties of locating general principles here are even more pronounced. In the first place, our law contains no constitutional rights to compensation to which legislation must adhere, unlike, for example, the United States of America where there can be no taking of private property for public use 'without just compensation'[12] and France where compensation is payable if legislation or administrative action imposes an unequal sacrifice on some individuals or firms.[13] Secondly, the existence of Parliamentary sovereignty and the very absence of constitutional constraints mean that legislation, unlike the common law, is untrammelled by precedent and principle. How then are we to generalise in the face of a large number of apparently diverse schemes providing compensation? These cover, among many others: the expropriation of property; damage from public works; losses arising from public health measures, such as the destruction of livestock, and from the refusal of a licence; from riots, war and crimes of violence; and, of course, social security and other schemes governing sickness, injury, death, and unemployment.

Application of the public interest model of legislation might enable us to rationalise these measures under a number of categories. First, some schemes, such as those for property expropriation and damage resulting from public works, involve principles essentially akin to those of the common law – corrective justice and morality – and the reason for legislative intervention was simply to overcome the legal-technical problems of suing organs of the state at common law.[14] A second group may also be loosely consistent with these principles and justified on economic grounds: reduction of the high transaction costs involved in using the ordinary courts to process compensation claims, especially where it is difficult to secure evidence against the wrongdoer (compensation for industrial diseases) or force him to pay damages (criminal injuries and riots); and where there is a failure of the insurance market to provide potential victims with adequate cover (war damage). It is, however, the third category, the overt pursuit of redistributional goals, which most clearly distinguishes legislative measures from common law principles. Intervention is thus a response to the conviction that the risk of accidental loss is not distributed equitably but tends to fall on those sections of the community least able to protect themselves against the consequences.[15] While the activities which generate the risks may be in no moral sense wrongful and, in aggregate, may benefit society, 'fairness' implies that those unharmed and who benefit from the activities should share the burden of the losses. On a narrower view, this can be seen as a deliberate attempt to assist the socially and economically disadvantaged (as with social security schemes); on a broader view, it can justify compensation for losses which are inflicted arbitrarily on some individuals or groups, whatever their wealth position (e.g. the vaccine damage payments scheme).

ECONOMIC THEORIES OF LEGISLATION

The public interest model of legislation has been increasingly attacked, particularly by economists, as a convincing hypothesis of behaviour. In the first place, it either takes no account of the motivation of individual legislators or it assumes, unrealistically, that they are wholly altruistic and are thus different from other individuals who are assumed to be predominantly self-interested. Secondly, there is considerable empirical evidence to suggest that the legislature does not succeed in fulfilling the ostensible public interest goals. Insofar as these are economic, that is, the correction of market failure and the pursuit of social efficiency, there are many instances where interventionist measures have led to greater inefficiency. Insofar as the aims are redistributional, in broad terms from the richer and more powerful to the poorer and less powerful, again there has been only partial success; many measures in fact turn out to the advantage of those whom they were not intended to benefit. These failures might result from technical incompetence, poorly drafted laws, inadequate information, or lax enforcement. More convincing, perhaps, is the view advanced by Hayek, that there is an inherent fallibility in legislative attempts to control human behaviour by *specific* rules.[16] For our purposes we should, however, focus on an alternative, economic hypothesis, based on traditional supply and demand analysis.[17] Legislators and potential legislators (i.e. parliamentary candidates) are self-interested and seek power. The commodity which they supply, or promise to supply, is votes for particular legislative measures which benefit particular groups. These groups demand the commodity, the price being electoral support.

One problem arising from this analysis should immediately be apparent. Individual members of groups seeking legislative protection will appreciate that they will benefit from an interventionist measure whether or not they contribute to the payment of the 'price'; they can be 'free riders'. This suggests that the effectiveness of the demand for legislative favours will depend more on the cohesiveness of pressure groups than on the size of the numbers who may potentially benefit.[18] The plausibility of this proposition is reinforced by the success with which tightly organised professional, trading and labour associations have sought legislative protection of various kinds (e.g. licensing systems, property right allocations, immunities to legal liability claims). I shall suggest, in due course, that there are further problems with this analysis, and that it requires substantial modification, particularly in a British context, if it is to provide a complete model for a positive explanation of legislative behaviour. However, for the present, we should acknowledge both an intuitive attractiveness of the theory and the fact that the theory has (to lawyers) an honourable pedigree: Dicey in his *Law and Public Opinion in England* attempted a systematic correlation between the character of legislative change in the second half of the nineteenth and early twentieth century and the extension of the franchise.[19]

What are the implications of the theory for our understanding of how the compensation problem has been resolved?[20] It may be envisaged that there is a potential demand for compensation from all those who have suffered or may suffer losses. The effectiveness of that demand will depend on a number of variables among which the following would appear to be the most significant: the ability of those suffering a given loss to coordinate political pressure at low cost and control the free-rider problem, to persuade legislators, potential or actual, of the marginal value of their electoral power, to characterise their claims to compensation in such a way as to be the subject of specific legislative rules (and thus to reduce the transaction costs involved in the implementation of the claims), and to postulate methods of financing and compensation that will minimise the cost to those groups or sections of the community which command equivalent or greater electoral power.

If these are, indeed, the critical variables, it is evident that legislative rights to compensation will diverge significantly from those implied by the public interest model. Historical examples provide some support for this. Powerful trading associations have been able to secure compensation and other financial benefits for their members.[21] The growth of highly organised pressure groups representing the disabled has been shown to have been primarily responsible for the very significant developments in compensation which occurred in the 1970s.[22] Perhaps the most compelling illustration is the Pneumoconiosis (Workers Compensation) Act 1979, whereby a group of predominantly Welsh quarrymen were granted rights to compensation when their claim for special treatment of this kind had been summarily dismissed a year earlier by the Royal Commission on Civil Liability and Compensation for Personal Injury.[23] The legislative measure was introduced by the Callaghan government in a desperate attempt to secure the support of Welsh Nationalist MPs and thus to maintain a tiny majority in the House of Commons. On the other hand, there are many interventionist measures providing compensation which do not fit so easily into the economic theory, at least as traditionally stated. I shall return to these cases to suggest how the theory may be modified to accommodate them.

ECONOMIC THEORIES OF JUDICIAL LAW-MAKING

Economic analysis of the judicial process constitutes an even more radical challenge to the traditional legal model than does the economic theory of legislation. As such it has generated much hostility from lawyers in particular. In order to understand why this has occurred and whether or not the criticism is justified, it is necessary to consider the analysis as a series of independent propositions.

1. **It is appropriate to apply economic theory to judicial decisions positively to consider their effects in terms of the allocation and distribution of resources and normatively to evaluate them (typically, whether or not they are socially efficient).** This might appear to be self-evident but social scientists may be surprised to learn of the resistance displayed by some lawyers to it. This attitude may be traced to one or more of a number of misconceptions commonly held: law is concerned with 'rights' or 'justice' which have nothing to do with economics; the common law represents a set of fundamental norms, derived from time immemorial, which cannot be 'evaluated' by economic or any other scientific criteria; since law must respond to a variety of social values, efficiency analysis is inconclusive and therefore useless. Comment is probably only required for the last of these misconceptions: it is true that one of the leading exponents of economic analysis of law, Richard Posner, has argued for efficiency as *the* ethical basis of law,[24] but the great majority of economists of course accept that economic efficiency must be weighed and traded-off against other normative criteria, for example, distributional and corrective justice. For policy evaluation of the law, economic efficiency constitutes an important but not exclusive input.
2. **'(T)he rules of the judge-made law are best explained as efforts – however unwittingly – to bring about efficient results'.**[25] This proposition is evidently of a different order than that of (1). It is a hypothesis

which requires empirical verification and yet any attempt at such verification must surmount almost insuperable obstacles: the effects of common law rules would have to be compared with those that would have resulted from alternative institutional arrangements, and, since parties can typically vary common law rules by contract, judgments on their alleged efficiency would involve consideration of all market phenomena which are affected directly or indirectly by those rules.[26] Is the hypothesis inherently plausible? Why should judges be motivated to formulate efficient rules? In a sense it may be the case that the tenured nature of their appointment and the fact that they are not remunerated according to output mean that they are insulated from the pressures which are exerted against legislators.[27] But we are still left with the problem of giving a positive content to a judge's utility function which is consistent with the efficiency thesis. The best answer that can be given – and not everyone would accept it – is that judges are driven to their conclusions by some innate and usually unconscious utilitarian sense.[28]

3. **The litigation process generates a natural tendency for common law rules to evolve towards efficiency**. This proposition has become increasingly fashionable in recent years and the reasoning behind it can be re-stated briefly as follows:[29] as with biological phenomena, 'good' rules survive and 'bad' rules are corrected, in this context because parties will have incentives to challenge and thus eventually to secure the overturn of inefficient rules, while they minimise transaction costs by settling out of court claims based on efficient rules. There would seem to be powerful objections to this argument. It ignores the likelihood that the parties to a particular dispute may be content with inefficient rules (or conversely, motivated to challenge efficient rules) on distributional grounds; and a rule may be efficient primarily because of the benefits it confers on third parties – in such circumstances it will be in the interests of litigants to replace it by an inefficient rule.[30]

Whatever doubts we have as to Propositions (2) and (3) we should, nevertheless, inquire as to how an efficiency-based set of common law principles would resolve the compensation problem. We should observe, in the first place, that if social welfare is to be measured only in monetary terms, arrangements obliging one individual to compensate another do not increase social welfare; they are simply transfer payments which are, indeed, costly to administer. Conventional economic analysis, however, is concerned less with reasons why we should compensate individuals who suffer losses than with reasons why we should impose the liability to compensate on those who cause the losses. This is because, by forcing potential harm-inflictors to bear the cost of their activities, we can ensure that only welfare-increasing activities are undertaken. Two corollaries should be mentioned: we should not impose the liability to compensate in cases where that would deter welfare-increasing activities (that is, where the aggregate social gains exceed the aggregate social losses); and we should formulate the liability rules to minimise transaction costs, those costs incurred in acquiring and processing relevant information and administering the rules. A considerable literature exists which attempts to evaluate the common law principles of liability in the light of these objectives.[31] The results of the analysis are often inconclusive but at least some are persuaded that the principles are, by and large, consistent with the efficiency criteria.[32]

THE LEGISLATIVE AND JUDICIAL PROCESSES COMPARED

It may be helpful if I summarise the position which emerges from this economic analysis of legislation and judicial decision-making respectively. Legislation is 'democratic' but unless subject to constitutional or other constraints it allows benefits to be conferred on those who can wield effective electoral power, with results that are consistent with neither efficiency nor distributional objectives, as conventionally formulated. Judicial decision-making is 'undemocratic'; judges are insulated from political pressure and, in theory, do not respond to distributional objectives; in the view of some, their decisions do generate economic efficiency.

Such bold conclusions have major implications for our constitutional and legal arrangements. Since they also contradict, as we have seen, the conventional view taken, at least by British lawyers, it is necessary to consider further the assumptions on which the analysis is grounded and their plausibility in the British context.

Let us take, first, the legislative process. The economic analysis assumes that individual legislators are able to respond to the demand for favours by supplying legislation. How is this to be achieved, given that each legislator commands only a single vote in the legislative process? The answer is through what is known as 'log-rolling': the process by which one member of a voting body trades his support for a particular measure with another – X agrees to vote for an amendment sponsored by Y if Y votes for an amendment sponsored by X.[33] This is unexceptional in the American political system where legislative voting is by no means tied to party lines. In Britain, on the other hand, party discipline is strict and while backbench revolt on particular issues is not unknown it is far from common. Several consequences flow from this. First, the content of most Acts of Parliament is controlled exclusively by government which, because of its voting power in the House of Commons, can afford to ignore sectional interests represented by individual MPs. The Welsh quarryman incident is significant not as an example of general legislative behaviour but rather as illustrating what can occur when the normal situation of government control of the parliamentary processes no longer pertains. Secondly, an individual cannot use the ballot box to express preferences for individual measures which will benefit him, since trading with the elected representative will not ensure the desired result. It follows, thirdly, that the demand for legislative favours must be communicated to government or a political party which may form a government. Such communication may be to the government (or political party) directly through, for example, the processes of consultation, or it may be filtered indirectly through a number of alternative or cumulative channels: pressure groups, bureaucrats, party members, backbenchers.

Given these features of the British political system, it is not surprising that though history may indeed reveal that legislative intervention is a response to public opinion, as sharpened by political power, in the loose sense adopted by Dicey, many measures would not seem to satisfy the specific hypothesis of the economic analysis that they confer material benefits on marginal voters.[34] Compensation schemes provide a good example. We have seen that the disabled benefited under a number of statutes passed in the 1970s. No doubt, this was, in part at least, due to the increasing power of pressure groups but it is highly unlikely that the disabled were able to pay, in terms of electoral votes, a price which exceeded that payable by those who were disadvantaged by the measures – taxpayers and national insurance contributors. There are several ways of dealing with difficulties of this kind. Consistently with the economic analysis, it may be there is often an informational asymmetry between the gainers (the disabled) and the losers (taxpayers and national insurance contributors): the former can clearly perceive the benefits, while the latter are less fully aware of the burden they will have to bear.[35] Alternatively, it may be argued that there exists an implicit form of trading or logrolling between some of the losers who agree to withhold opposition if the gainers agree to support some other measure from which they will benefit. This is more plausible than at first sight may appear. Individuals form allegiances to particular political parties whose policies involve a package of proposals each of which benefits some proportion of the parties' supporters. The condition for support is that the individual will gain more, or lose less, from the package compared with that offered by any other political affiliation. On this view, then, 'ideologies' play an important part in the legislative process but can be viewed simply as a device for economising on the communication of information to politicians.[36]

We should consider finally the possibility that voting behaviour may be motivated by altruism: some may support particular measures because they derive satisfaction from the knowledge that other groups, notably those otherwise disadvantaged, will benefit materially.[37] Such behaviour is not, of course, economically 'irrational'; it involves attributing a non-monetary element to the utility function of individuals. Economists, it would seem, tend to underplay or ignore the possibility not because they consider it unrealistic but because it is difficult to estimate and consequently to derive reliable predictions from it. Whatever difficulties it causes, we should not, however, dismiss altruism lightly. It would seem to be the most likely explanation for some legislation which has had clear redistributive effects.

It is thus possible to adapt the economic model to accommodate social, redistributional values. But what of efficiency? For it is failure in the pursuit of this goal which, according to the economic analysis, most sharply distinguishes legislative from judicial rulemaking. The problem we observed with the public interest theory was its inability to explain why legislators should be motivated to correct market failure. One way of solving the problem, which is compatible with the economic analysis, is through conventional public goods theory. As is well known, decisions on the production of these goods cannot be left to market transactions, but have to be made through political processes. Unanimity is unlikely to be achieved (or is any event too costly) so typically majority voting is employed. This enables majorities to impose costs on minorities, but members of the minority might be expected to appreciate that in the long run their gains will exceed their losses.[38] Another possibility is that pressure groups will in some cases be motivated to seek reform of inefficient rules where they will benefit, even though the demand will to some extent be blunted by the free-rider problem.[39] It may be cheaper, in terms of transaction costs, for them to organise lobbying than to resort to contractual devices to modify or avoid the inefficient commonlaw rules.[40] The clearest illustration of this may be found in property law. The common law method of defining interests in land were notoriously inefficient: alienability was hindered by the power of owners to tie up property over several generations and by the expense of establishing title where the interests were fragmented. The legislation at the end of the nineteenth and beginning of the twentieth centuries solved most of the problems.[41]

There are other ways of explaining public interest legislation. One important theory asserts the possibility of public, objective values as an alternative to individual, subjective values. The legislature is the forum for identifying and pursuing these values; legislators are presumed to possess a moral insight rather than mere self-interest; communal goals are achieved through 'rational' discourse based on sociological understanding.[42] No doubt, this view is naïvely idealistic; on the other hand, the economic view may be naïvely cynical. The reality of either is a matter for individual impression.

We come finally to the alleged efficiency of the judicial process. There are a number of difficulties with this thesis; as will be seen, some of them have reference to the particular character of British institutions which distinguishes them from their American counterparts, the subject of much of the economic analysis. First, British judges are traditionally conscious of constraints on their own lawmaking powers; they appear to be much concerned with preserving a system of certain and stable rules. While this may be consistent with efficiency goals in that it reduces litigation and thus transaction costs, it also makes them less open to arguments for modifying inefficient rules. This is in accordance with a widely-held constitutional norm, that judicial adjudication should be based on 'principles', which are statements of rights emerging from the network of previous judicial decisions, and not on 'policies', which express collective goals, economic or distributional, and which are the province of the legislature.[43] There are, indeed, clear instances where judges have not been prepared to sacrifice individual rights to goals of aggregate social welfare.[44]

Secondly, there is no reason to expect that they will respond to the task of dispute-settlement exclusively, or perhaps even predominantly, from an innate, or unconscious, utilitarian perspective, as is claimed. If, as is conceded, judges have no self-interest in reaching particular decisions, then like any other individuals they will reflect a variety of different social and political values.[45]

Thirdly, even if, contrary to this, they may be assumed to pursue efficiency aims, at least in some areas, albeit in an inarticulate and unconscious way, the judicial process itself presents formidable obstacles to their reaching correct conclusions.[46] Private law adjudication is, essentially, a bipolar confrontation between two individuals or two unitary interests. Third parties, and thus society generally, have no standing, and yet if the common law is to be efficient, all such interests must be taken into account. The judge has no easy way of obtaining information as to general social effects and even if he can acquire it, is not always able to process it.

These arguments should not, of course, lead us to ignore the efficiency implications of common law rules but only to treat with caution claims that the inherent characteristics of the judicial process, in contrast to those of the legislative process, are likely to generate efficiency. My general conclusion is that economic analysis has seriously exaggerated the differences between legislatures and judges as lawmakers. The common law may concentrate on the enforcement of (relatively) stable rights, and legislation may reflect unduly the interests of those with marginal electoral power, but judicial rules are not necessarily efficient and statute law is not necessarily inefficient. One might legitimately expect both processes to reflect, in varying degrees, different social and economic values. It is not impossible to employ economic models to predict and explain how and when these values will be fed into the lawmaking process[47] though there are evidently great difficulties in accomplishing this with any precision.

THE COMPENSATION PROBLEM REVISITED

We may briefly reconsider the compensation problem in the light of this conclusion. As should be clear from the account given above, the solutions provided both by common law and statute law are highly complex and not easily to be forced into a meaningful pattern. An economic analysis which confines itself to explaining common law liability rules by the efficiency goal of minimising social costs and statutory schemes by the ability of groups of losers to 'purchase' rights to compensation in the political market place is inadequate. Both lawmaking processes may be seen to respond to a variety of values and influences. Judges, in formulating rules requiring defendants to pay compensation to plaintiffs, take account not only of economic-deterrence arguments (the creation of incentives to induce socially optimal behaviour) but also of moral ideas (how blameworthy was the defendant), correct justice ideas (the protection of individual autonomy and liberty) and perhaps even distributional ideas (which party was in the best position to absorb the loss). For their part, legislators, more particularly governments and political parties, may seek to preserve or obtain power through the granting of rights to compensation to those able effectively to communicate demand to them, and to pay the appropriate 'price', but we are entitled to assume that such rights can achieve efficiency objectives (e.g. corrections of market failure arising from the common law) or distributional objectives (e.g. alleviation of hardship). There may be good reasons why such objectives are included in the demand communicated by voters; alternatively, we may prefer to view the legislative process as responding not merely to subjective, individual interests but also to objective, collective values.

NOTES AND REFERENCES

1. C. G. Veljanovski, *The New Law-and-Economic: A Research Review* (Oxford: Centre for Socio-Legal Studies, 1982).
2. B. N. Cardozo, *The Nature of the Judicial Process* (Yale UP, 1921).
3. R. Dworkin, *Taking Rights Seriously* (London: Duckworth, 1977).
4. R. Epstein, 'Nuisance Law: Corrective Justice and its Utilitarian Constraints', *J. Legal Stud.*, 8 (1979) 49.
5. C. Fried, *Right and Wrong* (Harvard UP, 1978).
6. Technically known as *locus standi*, on which see P. Craig, *Administrative Law* (London: Sweet & Maxwell, 1983) pp. 418–60.
7. E. Freund, *Standards of American Legislation* (University of Chicago Press, 1917).
8. Cf. W. J. Samuels and N. Mercuro, 'The Role of the Compensation Principle in Society', *Research in Law & Econ.*, 1 (1979), p. 157; A. I. Ogus, 'Do We Have a General Theory of Compensation?', *Current Legal Problems* (1984) 29–45.
9. R. Pound, 'Interests of Personality', *Harv. L. R.* 28 (1914) pp. 343, 445.
10. O. W. Holmes, *The Common Law* (Boston: Little Brown, 1881), Lecture III.
11. P. S. Atiyah, *Accidents, Compensation and the Law*, 3rd edn (London: Weidenfeld & Nicolson, 1980) ch. 22.
12. US Constitution, Fifth Amendment.
13. On which see L. N. Brown and J. F. Garner, *French Administrative Law*, 3rd edn (London: Butterworth, 1983) pp. 124–5.
14. Craig, *Administrative Law*, ch. 15.
15. R. M. Titmuss, *Social Policy: An Introduction* (London: Allen & Unwin, 1974) esp. chs 5–7.
16. F. A. Hayek, *Law, Legislation and Liberty* (London: Routledge & Kegan Paul, 1973) vol. 1.
17. The literature is now immense. The leading studies are: G. J. Stigler, 'The

Theory of Economic Regulation', *Bell J.*, 2 (1971) 3; R. A. Posner, 'Theories of Economic Regulation', *Bell J.*, 5 (1974) 335; S. Peltzman, 'Towards a More General Theory of Regulation', *J. Law & Econ.*, 19 (1976) p. 211.
18. Posner, *Theories of Economic Regulation*.
19. A. V. Dicey, *Law and Public Opinion in England*, 2nd edn (London: Macmillan, 1962).
20. Cf. W. J. Samuels and N. Mercuro, 'The Role and Resolution of the Compensation Principle in Society: Part Two – The Resolution', *Research in Law and Econ.*, 2 (1980), p. 103.
21. See, generally, G. Alderman, *Pressure Groups and Government in Great Britain* (London: Longman, 1984) and for a particular example, National Farmers' Union and compensation for slaughtered livestock, J. J. Richardson and A. G. Jordan, *Governing Under Pressure* (Oxford: Martin Robertson, 1979) p. 150.
22. B. Frost, *The Tactics of Pressure* (London: Galliard, 1975) p. 87.
23. Cmnd. 7054, 1978, vol. 1, paras 888–92.
24. 'The Ethical and Political Basis on the Efficiency Norm in Common Law Adjudication', *Hofstra L. R.*, 8 (198) p. 487.
25. W. M. Landes and R. A. Posner, 'Salvors, Finders, Good Samaritans and Other Rescuers: An Economic Study of Law and Altruism', *J. Legal Stud.*, 7 (1978) pp. 83, 128.
26. A. I. Ogus, 'Social Costs in a Private Law Setting', *Internat. Rev. Law & Econ.*, 3 (1983) pp. 27, 28.
27. R. A. Posner, *Economic Analysis of Law*, 2nd edn (Boston: Little Brown, 1977) pp. 409–10.
28. W. M. Landes and R. A. Posner, 'The Positive Economic Theory of Tort Law', *Georgia L. R.*, 15 (1981) pp. 851, 863.
29. See the papers and bibliography collected in *Research in Law and Econ.*, 4 (1982).
30. L. Kornhauser, 'A Guide to the Perplexed Claims of Efficiency in the Law', *Hofstra L. R.*, 8 (1980) 591, pp. 627–34; R. Markovits, 'Legal Analysis and the Economic Analysis of Allocative Efficiency', *Hofstra L. R.*, 8 (1980) 811, pp. 849–56.
31. See the papers and bibliography collected in A. I. Ogus and C. G. Veljanovski, *Readings in the Economics of Law and Regulation* (Oxford UP, 1984) ch. 3.
32. Landes and Posner, 'The Positive Economic Theory of Tort Law'.
33. See D. C. Mueller, *Public Choice* (Cambridge UP, 1979) pp. 49–57.
34. J. P. Kalt and M. A. Zupan, 'Capture and Ideology in the Economic Theory of Politics', *Am. Econ. Rev.*, 74 (1984) p. 279.
35. J. A. Brittain, *The Payroll Tax for Social Security* (Washington: Brookings Institute, 1978) pp. 6–13.
36. A. Downs, *An Economic Theory of Democracy* (New York: Harper, 1957) pp. 98–103.
37. See, generally, E. S. Phelps (ed.) *Altruism, Morality and Economic Theory* (New York: Russell Sage, 1975).
38. J. Buchanan and G. Tullock, *The Calculus of Consent* (Ann Arbor: University of Michigan Press, 1962).

39. G. Tullock, 'A (Partial) Rehabilitation of the Public Interest Theory', Law and Economic Center, University of Miami, Working Paper 82-2 (1982).
40. P. H. Rubin, 'Common Law and Statute Law', *J. Legal Stud.*, 11 (1982) p. 205.
41. R. A. Epstein, 'The Static Conception of the Common Law', *J. Legal Stud*, 9 (1980) 253, pp. 267-9.
42. F. Michelman, 'Political Markets and Community Self Determination: Competing Judicial Models of Local Government Legitimacy', *Indiana L. J.*, 53 (1977-78) pp. 145, 148-52.
43. Dworkin, *Taking Rights Seriously*, ch. 4.
44. The law of nuisance provides perhaps the best examples: see A. I. Ogus and G. M. Richardson, 'Economics and the Environment: A Study of Private Nuisance', *Camb. L. J.* 36 (1977) pp. 284, 308-311.
45. Epstein, 'Static Conception of the Common Law', pp. 271-3.
46. Ogus, 'Social costs', n. 26.
47. Elsewhere, I have attempted to show how the pursuit of general social values can be incorporated into a model of utility maximisation. See Ogus, 'Do we have a general theory of compensation?'

7 Economy, Democracy and Bureaucracy

PETER JACKSON

> The phenomenon of abdication to bureaucratic directives in corporations, in trades unions, in parties and in cooperatives is so widespread that it indicates a fundamental weakness of democracy. (Selznick, 1949, p. 9)

Public sector bureaucracy is regarded by many to be a major social problem. It is often regarded in pejorative terms to represent inefficiency, wastefulness, a haven of privilege, and a threat to the ideals of a democratic society. The growth of bureaucracy is viewed with suspicion; stimulates much political debate and generally receives a bad press. Bureaucracy is the object of ridicule; the subject of investigative journalism; and forms the subject matter of polemical tracts on the future direction of society. The growth of bureaucracy has brought forth charges of unrepresentativeness and demands for a reduction in the size of government. Even those sympathetic to the ideals of government have criticised bureaucracy for failing to carry out legislative intent and for being insensitive to the needs of the average citizen.

Liberal academics fear and mistrust the bureaucratisation of society, regarding this trend as a threat to democracy. They express concern about the alienating and depersonalising effects of an organisational form characterised by the minute division of labour. There is also concern about the citizen (consumer) abusing powers of bureaucracy which makes impersonal decisions on behalf of society without paying sufficient attention to the specific needs of the individuals who come into regular contact with it. The role played by bureaucracy in the formation of elites in society has also received much attention and comment.[1]

Despite the ubiquitousness of bureaucracy it has surprisingly, until recently, received very little attention from economists.[2] The major contributions to the literature on bureaucracy have come from political scientists, sociologists and social philosophers generally. In this essay I will consider the more recent developments and awakening interests that are taking place in the 'economics of bureaucracy'. After considering fundamental questions such as what is meant by the term 'bureaucracy' (i.e. just what is it that we are referring to) I will turn my attention to the economist's modern treatment of bureaucracy as illustrated through the seminal contribution of William Niskanen's (1971) *Bureaucracy and Representative Government*. This is followed by an examination of specific topics such as bureaucratic efficiency and the link between bureaucracy, accountability and democracy. Within the space of a short essay one must be selective, not only in the topics chosen for discussion but also in terms of the depth of treatment. More extensive discussions of the economics of bureaucracy can be found in Jackson (1982), Breton and Wintrobe (1982), Hess (1983), and Hoenack (1983).

WHAT IS BUREAUCRACY?

Niskanen does not dwell upon the problem of defining bureaucracy. He proceeds on the assumption that bureaucracy is synonymous with the agencies of government, central and local, i.e. bureaucracies are 'not for profit organisations' whose finances do not come from market transactions but, instead, from periodic grants-in-aid approved by some politically elected chamber. This definition was appropriate for Niskanen's purposes which were to study the overall conditions of allocative efficiency in an economy which contains the presence of a *public* sector bureaucracy. For the purposes of a more general analysis of bureaucracy, however, Niskanen's definition is insufficiently precise.

To gain insight to the more fundamental properties of bureaucracy there is no better place to begin than with Weber (1947) whose seminal contribution remains the cornerstone of all analysis of bureaucracy. Weber defined bureaucracy as a particular form of organisation which is characterised in structural terms as possessing; a hierarchy of authority; fixed and official jurisdictional areas; written rules; tasks demanding loyalty and full capacity of vocationally oriented workers. These characteristics defined for Weber an 'ideal type' of organisation which possessed the qualities of rationality (i.e. a consistency in its functioning over time) and efficiency. Weber's use of the ideal type in this context is very similar to the economist's construct of the perfect market. In both cases there is no prior claim that the ideal type exists in reality.[3] Rather it is a datum line against which performance criteria might be calibrated. It should be remembered that Weber had studied government organisations which were rotten and corrupt in their operations. Decisions were frequently inconsistent, favours were bought and sold, and promotion decisions were often based on nepotism rather than the criterion of finding the best person for the job.

Defining bureaucracy as an efficient and rational form of organisation might seem a bit perverse to the critics of bureaucracy who generally play up its inefficiencies. Perrow (1979), however, points out that as an organisational form, bureaucracy is an improvement over the complexity of organisational structures in pre-industrial society and that it has, therefore, much to commend it. Nor should it be forgotten that Weber was only too aware of the dysfunctions, failings and imperfections of real live bureaucracies. He did not believe that his prescriptions were a description of reality. Just as markets are imperfect, so too are bureaucracies.

As an organisational form, bureaucracy is not confined to public sector agencies. It is characteristic of most private sector corporations, trades unions, political parties and even cooperatives that they are organised on bureaucratic lines. This raises a number of interesting questions, including that of whether the economist's analysis of bureaucracy which has been developed for the public sector can be used to give some insights to private bureaucracy. Moreover, it would be interesting to know if alternative modes of financing (market raised revenues in the case of private bureaucracies and grant appropriations for public bureaucracies) influenced bureaucratic performance. Finally, it also means that much of the behavioural theory of the firm which has been developed in the context of studying intra-organisational behaviour in private enterprises might, in fact, be imported to the analysis of public sector bureaucracy.

There is much variability in the form of organisational structures both across space and time. Bureaucracy as an organisational form does not, and has not, existed in all places at all times. How then, did bureaucracy as an organisational form evolve? Some theories explain the emergence of bureaucracy as the end product of a struggle to cope with increased size and complexity.[4] This is not, however, an entirely satisfactory explanation since there are historic examples of human activities carried out on a large scale which were not organised along bureaucratic lines, for example the construction of the Egyptian pyramids (Bendix, 1947). Also, many small-scale activities were organised on a bureaucratic pattern, for example the Boulton and Watt factory 1775–1805 (Bendix, 1954). Since bureaucracy is not necessarily the inevitable outcome of increasing size of activity or operations it is wrong to conclude that many of the problems associated with bureaucracy will simply disappear if production units are returned to a smaller scale – it might be a necessary condition to do so but it is not sufficient.

Technological change brings with it an elaborate division of labour and, therfore, the need for an elaborate form of organisation to coordinate the diversity of individual actions.[5] With a large organisation the 'distance' between decision makers can be great, giving rise to a demand for the formalisation of routines, procedural rules etc. These rules play a coordinating role which is similar to that of the invisible hand in market exchanges. There is, however, a great deal of technological determinism in this explanation. Very early on, management scientists demonstrated that it was not a necessary requirement of modern technology to break tasks down into finely specified operations. Less specialisation was found to be just as efficient and not so alienating (Drucker, 1946, pp. 183–4).

Technology is not a sufficient explanation for the emergence of bureaucracy since other forms of organisation are capable of coping with the issues involved in coordinating activities performed in complex and uncertain environments (e.g. see the Miedner plan in Sweden). One way of trying to find out why bureaucracy has a survival value over other forms of organisation is to ask, whose interests are being served by that form rather than another? Organisational structures cannot be judged or considered to be neutral in their impact upon the distribution of rights in society and, therefore, are not passive in terms of their impact upon human welfare. Just as the initial distribution of property rights in society will determine the distribution of financial rewards from market exchanges, so will the rights conferred by the role one occupies in a bureaucracy determine the distribution of pecuniary and non-pecuniary benefits.

A finely specified division of labour arises from management's need to *control* workers. Bureaucracy is, therefore, an agent of social control placing individuals in a network of subordinate and superordinate positions. At the same time, specialisation and the division of labour minimises management's dependence upon any specific worker or group of worker. Workers who are highly specialised will find it more difficult to find alternative employment and will obey if threatened.

This raises more questions than can be answered here. What, for example, is the origin of the rights of a superordinate to control the activities of a subordinate; what are the limits to these rights; what rules govern access to these rights; what determines the means of control; why do individuals enter into contractual arrangements in which they voluntarily subordinate their rights; whose interests are served by these rights; who controls/determines the menu of rights on offer? To these moral or social philosophical questions can be added those relating to institutions such as the trades union which presents a countervailing power to protect and enhance the rights of their members. Economists interested in the distribution of welfare in society must, therefore, be interested in how these questions are answered.

Finally, specialisation might, in fact, confer power upon certain classes of workers if they hold a strategic position within the organisation such as controlling information or some other resource which is vital to the functioning of the organisation. These workers essentially regulate in part the amount of uncertainty which the organisation faces which, in the event of there being no immediate substitute, grants them power within the organisation (Crozier, 1964; Pfeffer and Salancik, 1978).

When this approach is applied to the public sector, bureaucracy is then seen as a mechanism of social control in a modern state. As an apparatus of the state it is a form of self regulation rather than coercive control but this assumes the legitimation of such control. That is, it assumes a set of values that provide the rationale for 'applying the apparatus of the state on behalf of the welfare of persons as individuals'. (Janowitz 1977, p. 19). Social philosophers such as Hayek (1960) and more derivative libertarian economists like Friedman question the nature of this legitimacy asking if such values do exist today and if they do, who regulates the regulators and how do the regulatory functions of public sector bureaucracy conflict with individual liberty and freedom, which are regarded as the primary goods of any democratic society.

For the purposes of the remainder of this essay we will concentrate upon the economic dimensions of public sector bureaucracy defining it as a non-profit organisation which receives revenues from sources other than the per unit sale of output on the market. At the same time we recognise that profit-seeking firms and partnerships within the private sector may be organised on bureaucratic lines whilst private non-profit organisations that receive periodic income from a grant or trust fund fall into the definition of bureaucracy reserved for the public sector.

WHY STUDY BUREAUCRACY?

Why should the study of bureaucracy, a particular form of organisation, be of particular interest to economists when the field has been dominated by political scientists, sociologists and organisation theorists for so long? What contributions do economists have to make to this traditional topic? I have attempted to answer these questions at much greater length in my *Political Economy of Bureaucracy* (Jackson, 1982). Economists are primarily concerned with the way in which society's scarce resources are allocated and distributed amongst different activities and individuals. The efficiency of an economy depends upon the institutional mechanisms employed to allocate resources, as too does the distribution of welfare (material and non-material) amongst the members of society. A cursory glance at any standard text book on economics will, however, reveal that the institution which is most frequently studied is the allocative mechanism of the market place with the formation of prices, output, employment, investment and other decisions being compared in efficiency and welfare terms across alternative market structures. Non-market allocations and decisions have generally been ignored.

The 'public choice' school pioneered in the USA by Professor James Buchanan and his associates, in particular Gordon Tullock, has emphasised the importance of studying non-market decision-making, especially decisions made within public sector bureaucracies. This gives a more complete understanding of how agents within society do, in practice, go about allocating and distributing resources.

Members of the public choice school perceive government and its agencies (bureaux) as the product of individual behaviour. It is individuals who make choices and who, therefore, shape and guide the outcomes of government. This view is very different from that commonly held which sees the public sector as some kind of super-individual making decisions in the 'public interest' (however defined and by whom). It means that there is scope for the decision makers (politicians and bureaucrats) to form decisions which will enhance their own welfare and that of the elites to which they owe allegiance.

These remarks might seem a little strange to an anthropologist, but to economists brought up in the strict neoclassical tradition of market centred micro and macro economics, it represents a development. When we add up all of the allocative decisions which are made, few of them take place in markets. There are allocative decisions and exchanges made within the household: who is going to work, how is the household budget going to be spent? Many important decisions are made *within* organisations (public and private; voluntary and non-voluntary). How much of the education budget will be allocated to primary, secondary or university education; how much of a university budget will be allocated to physics as compared to economics; how much of a firm's budget will be allocated to research and development or to marketing? These decisions might be made with reference to signals generated by markets (including prices) but in order to understand how decisions are arrived at, and therefore how they might be improved, it becomes necessary to open up these areas of non-market decision-making as legitimate study and enquire into the rules and constraints which govern their behaviour.

Moreover, it is problems of individual decision-making within collective or group settings which are more often than not presented by this approach. Collective decision-making is a particularly interesting analytical problem with its various impossibility theorems (Arrow, 1951). However, to the economist engaged in positive analysis what is of interest are the various collective choice decision rules which exist in practice. The properties of these decision rules are of particular interest, especially those properties which determine the distribution of the net benefits of the collective decision.

Alongside developments made in the public choice school, microeconomists have turned their attention to a study of the intra-organisational behaviour of the private sector firm.[6] Behaviour within an organisation, which results in an allocation and distribution of resources, is best viewed as a series of political exchanges in which power politics plays a vital role in any explanation of how resources come to be allocated in the way in which they are. This moves the traditional economist in search of a new vocabulary and a new set of concepts including the slippery notion of 'power'! In effect, it reintroduces old-fashioned 'political economy' but now dressed up in a more formal and analytically more appealing garb.

It would be a mistake to conclude as so many do that public choice theory and a political economy based study of intra-organisational behaviour stand in conflict to the neoclassical study of market allocations and distributions. That is quite the wrong way of viewing these developments which are best seen as being complementary, filling in the decision-making process of the organisational black boxes of the neoclassical general equilibrium system. However, it would be totally misleading to suggest that anything approaching a synthesis of the two approaches has been effected.

Neoclassical economics has made major intellectual achievements in studying the equilibrium properties of the heuristic fiction of the perfectly competitive market system. Attempts at synthesis are likely to illuminate why real economies do not come into equilibrium. Many of the reasons for Keynesian sticky prices and, hence, quantity adjustments might be found within non-market organisations, including public sector bureaucracy. Recognition of the institutional constraints form part of the basis of post-Keynesian economics, especially that in the Kaleckian spirit.[7]

Finally, decision-making within bureaucracies is of importance in accounting for both the design and implementation of policies. Whilst economists have devoted much of their attention to the design of policy they have been somewhat cavalier in their attitudes to the translation of these policies into concrete actions through the medium of complex organisations. One weak defence might be that policy implementation is the province of other specialists. However, an understanding of the implementation process and the organisational constraints which it contains will very often provide useful information which can be incorporated into the policy at the design stage. Too often policies are prescribed without any appreciation of the difficulties involved in implementing them – they are often designed with perfect or idealised organisations in mind. What are the organisational problems of implementing a control of the money supply or effecting an incomes policy? Do changes need to be made to the set of incentives faced by individuals in order to obtain their compliance? As I have argued elsewhere (Jackson, 1982, 1984), this is an area in which economists and policy analysts must get together to minimise the wasteful and often distressing unintended consequences of policies. Moreover, within the context of the political economy model the ability of any person to ensure compliance with a decision is constrained by time, distance, organisational complexity and the self-interest of the principal actors involved. For example, bureaucratic resistance to the withdrawal of US missiles from Turkey despite President Kennedy's directive prejudiced the American position during the 1962 Cuban missile crisis.

THE ECONOMIST'S ANALYSIS OF BUREAUCRATIC BEHAVIOUR

For so many years the analysis of public bureaucracy remained in the province of political science and public administration. Economists took the budget decision-making process as given and were more concerned to examine the impact of government spending and taxation decisions upon private sector economic activity. At the normative level of analysis, economists established prescriptive rules for budget decision-making with regard to the design of tax systems and how best to make public investment decisions (especially the body of rules incorporated in cost-benefit analysis). This highly prescriptive approach was criticised, with less than sufficient care and attention being paid to the purpose of the economist's analysis, by, amongst others, Wildavsky (1964, 1969). However, where Wildavsky's criticisms did score points was that economists had paid insufficient care and attention to considering how their prescriptive rules might be implemented in practice within real live bureaucratic organisations. Elaborate planning procedures designed to achieve efficiency and improved effectiveness in resource allocation such as Programme Planning and Budgeting Systems (PPBS) or output budgeting or the UK system of Programme Analysis and Review (PAR) not only required the cooperation of all parties to the decision but also rested upon a centralisation of authority within the bureaucracy. Wildavsky and his followers passionately believed in the virtues of pluralistic democratic systems and feared the concentration of power in a central authority within the bureaucracy whilst also pointing out that the new planning systems would be unworkable since they would be frustrated and opposed by powerful intra-organisational groups who would object to the redrawing of constituency boundaries inside the organisation.

The first major attempt to produce a strict economist's perspective of bureaucratic behaviour is found in Niskanen (1968, 1971, 1973). Niskanen's view is that bureaux can be modelled in ways similar to those employed by economists studying private sector firms (Baumol, 1959; Williamson, 1964; Galbraith, 1967). The main features of Niskanen's neoclassical model are:

(a) bureaucrats seek to maximise budgets rather than profits;
(b) a public sector bureau is a non-profit-making organisation which receives its finance from sources other than per unit sale of output on the open market;
(c) when dealing with the legislature, bureaucrats have an effective monopoly over information about the true costs of supply.

The principal conclusion which Niskanen arrives at is that budget maximising bureaucrats use their monopoly powers in order to secure budget and output levels that are above the socially optimal level. During the past fifteen years Niskanen's approach has been influential in shaping economists' thinking about bureaucracy (Ahlbrandt, 1973; Breton and Wintrobe, 1975 and 1982; De Allesi, 1974; Hoenack, 1983; Jackson, 1982; Migue and Belanger, 1974). Niskanen's model has, however, also fueled an ideological movement which argues against the bureaucratic supply of public services in favour of greater privatisation and stricter constraints placed upon bureaucrats' discretionary behaviour.

The approach to the study of bureaucracy employed by Niskanen is within the public choice mould and, therefore, based on the behavioural assumption that bureaucrats are motivated by factors similar to those that influence decision-makers in the private sector. That is, bureaucrats are assumed to act primarily out of self interest. They do not necessarily subordinate their self interests to some nebulous higher order concept such as that of serving the 'public interest'. Nor are they treated as neutral actors in the policy formation or implementation processes. They are not administrative eunuchs. Bureaucrats employ their resources so as to maximise their utility as they perceive it. The factors which influence a bureaucrat's utility are power, prestige, job security, expected future salary, intensity of work effort, and attractiveness of working conditions including perquisites (such as index linked pensions). Thus, utility-maximising bureaucrats will advocate and campaign for larger rather than smaller budgets.

A bureau's budget is the outcome of a series of bilateral negotiations between the budget head and the legislature. In the UK these budgeting games are played out within the context of the PESC system (Public Expenditure Survey Committee).[8] Each central government department puts up a bid for funds. These bids, which are supposed to reflect the costs of continuing the bureau's set of activities plus the costs of any new activities, are debated and discussed (frequently with much heat and passion) by the Cabinet which decides upon final allocations and the structure of planned public expenditure. Finally Parliament grants its approval of the Government's decision, again after debate.

The PESC process can be illustrated within the context of the Niskanen model. Demand for the bureau's output is articulated via the legislature. Voters elect politicians who represent their preferences in a parliamentary democracy. The legislature places a value on different levels of output. This produces a schedule of budgets (B) equal to this evaluation such that:

$$B = aQ - bQ^2 \quad (a \text{ and } b > 0)$$
where Q is the level of bureau output
a and b are constants.

This budget function defines the legislature's total evaluation curve for bureau output.

Output is produced by a monopolistic bureau whose head is a budget-maximising bureaucrat. The cost (C) of producing the output is given by:

$$C = cQ + dQ^2 \quad (c \text{ and } d > 0)$$

It is assumed that the cost of producing output is specialist knowledge known only to the bureaucrats, i.e. the distribution of knowledge is asymetric or in Williamson's terms it is 'impacted'. The bureaucrat acts in such a way as to maximise B subject to the constraint that he must be able to deliver the Q which is promised.[9]

As clearly indicated, Niskanen regards the bureau to be a monopoly supplier whilst the legislature is a monopoly buyer (monopsonist). The relationship between the two groups is, therefore, best seen as one of bilaterial monopoly.

The way in which the problem is presented can trivially be formulated as a standard neoclassical constrained maximisation problem. That is, the budget is to be maximised subject to the constraint that the budget must cover the costs of production:

$$\max B = aQ - bQ^2$$
$$\text{subject to } aQ - bQ^2 = cQ + dQ^2$$

Solving this gives the following results:

(a) the maximum budget corresponds to $A = a/2b$
(b) the largest budget which just covers cost is $Q = (a-c)/(b+d)$ (this is referred to as the cost constrained budget)
(c) if the budget and cost curves do not intersect at some $Q = a/2b$ then the budget $B = a/2b$ provided by the legislature will be just enough to cover the supply costs. Under these conditions the rational bureaucrat will simply make the unconstrained choice and go for the maximum budget $Q = a/2b$ (this is budget choice within the demand constrained region).

There are two solutions to the budget output decision depending upon whether cost or demand constraints are in play. These are illustrated in Figure 7.1. To complete the analysis two further assumptions are

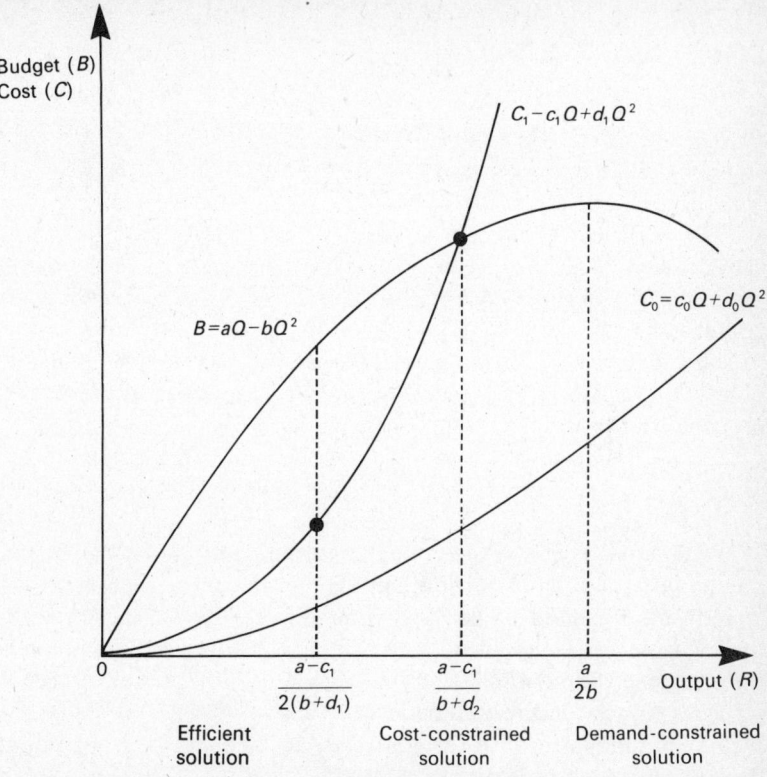

FIGURE 7.1

required. First, assume that the legislature's total evaluation of Q is a true reflection of society's evaluation. That is true representative democracy is assumed. Second, it is assumed that the cost curves used represent technologically efficient costs of producing the different levels of output. In other words, these are the minimum costs of producing Q for a given state of technical knowledge. From this it is a simple matter of deducing the socially optimal level of bureau output. This occurs where the marginal valuation (dB/dQ) of the output to the legislature just equals the marginal cost (dC/dQ) of supply. In terms of Figure 7.1 this is where the slope of cost curve C_1 equals the slope of the budget curve B. At this point the socially optimal level of output is

$$Q = \frac{a-c}{2(b+d_1)}$$

Niskanen's analysis demonstrates that the cost constrained solution

$$Q = \frac{a - c_1}{b + d_1}$$

exceeds the socially optimal level – indeed, it is easily seen to be twice the social optimum. The consumer's surplus (the difference between the total budget and total cost curves) is appropriated and allocated to socially inefficient uses – namely a budget and a level of output (and hence a level of public employment) which is greater than the social optimum. The demand constrained solution produces an even greater amount of social waste.

This rather simple, but insightful model has provided the ammunition for those who believe that government is too large. It provides a proof of the proposition that when public services are supplied by monopolistic bureaux the level of public output and the budget size (public expenditure) will be higher than that which is socially optimal. Niskanen's result is of the same genre as that which is applied to private sector monopoly. Simple static analysis demonstrates that the output of a private sector monopolist is half that which would be produced by an industry organised via perfectly competitive markets. The output of the public sector monopolist being twice that of the social optimum is the private sector monopolist's mirror image. Finally, Niskanen's result provides a more secure foundation to those who wish to see public sector monopolies broken up and made to face greater competition from privatisation programmes.

These results do, however, stand in sharp contrast to the claims of deteriorating public services (public squalor amidst private affluence). In a pluralistic democracy those who consume public services might not be those who, through taxation, finance the services. If those who consume public services face a set of subsidised prices, then their effective demands may be greater than the level of output actually supplied. Unfortunately this is a complex issue which the Niskanen model in its original form is unable to handle. The problem is that the Niskanen model is a supply determined model of bureaucratic output. Demand plays a relatively passive role despite all the problems of collective choice posed by representative democracies.[10] This severely limits the usefulness of Niskanen's analysis for policy analysis and places a question mark over those prescriptions derived from it, especially those which favour a limitation or a reduction in the scope of government activity. Demand for bureaucratic outputs can be incorporated into the Niskanen model in a variety of ways. First, bureaucrats (the suppliers of public services) might lobby the legislature on behalf of the consumers of the services, presenting warnings of falling standards of service provision and their consequences if a larger budget is not forthcoming. Not only is this congruent with Niskanen's notion of budget-maximising behaviour, it is also a traditional criticism of bureaux that they will act in order to preserve and maintain their continued existence and hence their jobs (the gory immortality of the bureau). Bringing demand into the analysis in this way forces us to question the welfare significance of Niskanen's result. If the level of output supplied is that which satisfies the preferences of the client group which the bureaucracy serves, then how can it be too large or non-optimal to that particular client group.

Looking at an individual bureau on its own can give a misleading picture. Welfare analysis requires that we take a more general approach by considering all public bureaux together, along with the output of the private sector. The second way of incorporating demand into the analysis is to look much closer than Niskanen did at decision-making by the legislature, especially the way in which it expresses its demand for public services. This, however, throws into relief many more problems than can be dealt with here. In particular it would require a close scrutiny of the Westminster model of democratic decision-making including Cabinet decision-making.[11]

Having pointed out that the relationship between the legislature and the bureaucracy is one of bilateral monopoly, Niskanen then proceeds with his analysis by almost totally ignoring the role of the legislature and the complexity of the bilateral relationship. The budget outcome is not a purely bureaucratic decision as Niskanen at times seems to imply – with the legislature passively accepting whatever outcome emerges. The budget is the product of a joint decision between bureau and legislature and the analysis is enriched if this is modelled formally.[12]

Decisions about public expenditure in the UK are essentially cabinet decisions. Each year central government departments present their budget requests to the central coordinating committee referred to as the PESC. The committee comprises the chief finance officers of each department and is chaired by the Treasury. The budget requests are made at constant prices for a number of years ahead and are scrutinized by the Treasury to ensure that they are consistent with the conventions established over the years. At the same time items in the requests will be debated with some eventually being dropped. The PESC then makes a report to the Cabinet in which the requests for public spending for the next and subsequent years are presented, along with information about the availability of resources over the short to medium term and the likely tax costs of financing those levels of public spending. Cabinet then discusses the PESC report and makes its decisions about public spending over the medium term during the summer recess.

In Cabinet, Government Ministers will vigorously defend the budget request of the department of which they are the head. It is the task of the Treasury, the Chancellor of the Exchequer, but more especially the Financial Secretary to the Treasury to trim the total of requests bringing them in line with what the nation can afford in terms of resources available. This means taking from one department relatively more than from another. Rational action does not always prevail as the diaries of many political actors who participated in this budgetary game testify. Very often the Chancellor will seek cuts from the weakest of his colleagues in the knowledge that to do otherwise might cause a split in the Cabinet. This is likely, therefore, to result in a non-optimal mix of public spending between services.

Once Cabinet has decided upon the total and composition of public expenditure the annual Public Expenditure White Paper is drafted, published in the autumn of the year and then discussed by Parliament which votes the supply of resources to Government to carry out its activities for the next year.

Deciding upon the optimal level and mix of public and private expenditures and upon the private composition of public spending is, analytically, not a trivial task. In a world of perfect competition and lump sum taxation the problem is the relatively straightforward one of equalising marginal benefits across the set of public and private goods whilst using non-distortionary lump sum taxes to solve the income distribution problem. The real world, however, does not offer such convenient solutions. Imperfect competition in a variety of forms abounds; externalities exist; some markets do not exist because of the high transaction costs of organising them and whilst most of the publicly supplied goods are not pure public goods in the technical sense of the term, nevertheless they are supplied on a fixed quantity basis. This last point is important and often overlooked. It means that the consumers of publicly supplied goods are quantity takers. They are unable, by their own individual actions, to vary the amount or quality of the good, unless they opt out of the public sector completely and consume private sector substitutes, which are not always available. School children must stay on at school until they are 16 years old whilst their parents – short of moving to another geographical location (assuming they had information about the quality of education across different area) – will find it difficult to change the quality of education consumed.[13] Similar arguments apply to health care, personal social services, police, fire and defence.

In an imperfectly competitive world, judging the optimal mix of public and private expenditures must also take into account the impacts of public expenditure and its financing instruments upon private sector decisions. In the absence of lump sum taxes, income and expenditure taxes can have distortionary impacts upon private sector decisions regarding how much work effort and savings to supply to the economy, or upon the amount of risk-taking individuals are willing to engage in. A bond (deficit) financed public spending increase could crowd out private sector spending if interest rates were to rise or if the economy was at near full employment. Consideration of these issues compounds the complexity of an already complex question, especially since there is little agreement amongst groups of economists about just how important these distortionary impacts are in practice.

It is insufficient to blame bureaucracy alone for a non-optimal total and mix of public output (expenditure). The legislature (in the UK the Government and Parliament) must also accept responsibility. If public expenditure is judged to be too large then one must ask why did the legislature allow it? Thus, discussion of the efficiency of public output decision-making needs to look not only at the nature of bureaucratic decisions, but also at the way in which the legislature makes decisions, and the relationship between legislature and bureaucracy, especially the degree of accountability and control which the legislature exercises over the bureaucracy. These issues are developed in the next section.

Before leaving this discussion of Niskanen's model, a few more reservations about it should be expressed. First, Niskanen formulated his model with the American system of bureaucracy very much in mind. In that system chief bureaucrats' salaries are related to the size of the bureau's budget. This is not the case in the UK. A permanent secretary's salary is fixed irrespective of the size of his department's budget. This implies that caution should be exercised when importing Niskanen's model into an institutional system which has a significantly different incentive structure. It is still possible to retain the public choice framework by assuming that UK bureaucrats like all other individuals are motivated by self interest but the incentives and constraints which they face need to be specified for the particular institutional conditions which prevail in the UK.

An understanding of behaviour or action requires that the incentives and constraints which individuals face, be specified. If promotion within the UK civil service depends upon making sure that mistakes are not made then this will, in all probability, spill over into bureaucrats' being over cautious and risk averse in their decisions. The result will be that the nation is denied the greater social product that more adventurous decision-making might have produced (equally, it is protected and safeguarded against dramatic and costly mistakes). In this case the incentive structure might stultify bureaucrats, preventing them from using their imagination in seeking novel solutions to problems which would be more efficient to the extent that for the same resources (cost) society would obtain a greater net social product.

The importance of incentives in the public sector has been recognised and recent discussions, especially those relating to the new 'ministerial information system' such as 'MINIS', which was designed by Mr Michael Heseltine when he was Secretary of State for the Environment, have suggested that bureaucrats should be paid a bonus which would be related to the achievement of their objectives – such as when their decisions result in resource savings. If there is no cash reward for making savings then, it is argued by some, management will not search and seek out new routines. Why bother if there is no reward for doing so? It is, under these circumstances, much easier to continue with the old routines, avoid the disruptive costs of change and pursue the quiet life.

The last remark raises an important question-mark over Niskanen's specification of the bureaucrat's utility function. As originally set out by Niskanen, the type of person which occupies the bureaucrat's role, of his world, is a 'thruster': a get up and go individual who is motivated to expand his empire and increase the size of his budget. But if salary and general satisfaction are not related to budget size some bureaucrats might prefer to maximise their leisure time – in particular their 'on the job leisure'. This organisational slack or economic rent will be taken out in the form of long lunch breaks, unnecessary and lengthy committee meetings and an avoidance of change. It will result in a lower productivity of bureaucrats and higher unit costs for the bureaucracy.

EFFICIENCY, ACCOUNTABILITY, BUREAUCRACY AND DEMOCRACY

Niskanen's model demonstrated that for a given set of assumptions it is possible that a bureaucracy will produce a level of output that is allocatively inefficient in the sense that it will supply services above the socially efficient level. This is, however, only one of a number of possible sources of inefficiency arising from the presence of bureaucracy.

For some considerable time now social philosophers and economists from both ends of the ideological spectrum have argued that the presence of government results in inefficiencies, reduces personal freedoms and threatens democracy. In recent times these voices have captured the minds of the electorate with the result that in the UK and the USA governments have been returned whose intentions are to reduce the size and scope of government, to roll back the state and transfer activities from the public sector back to the private sector.

The notion of big government is usually associated with a large all-pervasive bureaucracy in which the right of decision-making is transferred from individuals acting on their own behalf and in their own interests to politicians and bureaucrats who make decisions in the name of the 'public interest'. This transfer is regarded by many to result in a reduction in the freedom and the liberty of the individual. These ideas are not new. Conservative economists whose roots are to be found in the writings of J. S. Mill express concern about the erosion of libertarian ideals. Von Mises (1944) and his student Von Hayek (1960) have been consistent advocates of the superiority of free market decision-making over the centralised system of bureaucratic allocations. This debate reached its heights at the LSE in the 1930s with Hayek (1935, 1948) and Lange (1938) taking opposing views. In more recent times Friedman (1953) in the same libertarian tradition along with public choice economists such as James Buchanan have persistently argued that the welfare state bureaucracy is a misguided way of organising society, giving way to the emergence of large and powerful organisations. They are, therefore, strong advocates of greater privatisation and the use of market forces in order to improve the efficiency of the whole economic system.

Alongside the libertarian tradition many Marxist economists, who spend their time considering the practical issues of the organisation of the economic processes of allocation and distribution, have become very critical of the Soviety type model of organisation which is characterised by centralised control over the economy and most parts of social life (e.g. the demise of the Solidarity Movement in Poland). Today many of these economists are advocating a greater use of market mechanisms in their systems (Sik, 1972; Horvat, 1976) in order to counteract the wasteful and inefficient elements of the system of bureaucratic centralised planning. In both these cases the Conservative and the Marxist critiques are based upon the fundamental question 'how should a modern society or economy be organised?' Marxists seeking to emancipate humanity from repressive conditions (as do liberal economists) want a greater role for the market but thereafter the details of the two visions diverge.

The crucial element in all of these debates is the role played by the individual when it comes to deciding about what the bureaucracy does – what it produces, for whom it produces etc. This also plays a central role in any discussion of democracy. Rousseau's *Social Contract* was based upon the Greek model of direct participation. This differs from John Stuart Mill's *Representative Government* which was an ideal type in which a representative national and accountable government was assumed to improve individual welfare. This was a utopian view of democracy. Dahl (1961) who represents the modern view of democracy argued for an elite theory of democracy on the grounds that the average citizen was not 'by nature a political animal' (p. 225) capable of governing. Government falls to the most competent to do so – that is the elites. To the question 'is this democracy?' Dahl would argue yes, to the extent that the elites agree about the democratic method and compete with one another to gain office. Schumpeter (1954) argued that 'the democratic method is that institutional arrangement for arriving at political decisions in which individuals acquire the power to decide by means of a competitive struggle for the peoples' vote (p. 269). This view as with that of Dahl assumes the existence of competent leaders who will represent the voters' views accurately.

Michels (1915) and Selznick (1949) have suggested that idealised democracy is an impossibility in reality. In his 'iron law of oligarchy' Michels argues that a system of leadership is incompatible with the most essential postulates of democracy. The reality is an emergent oligarchy which derives from the tactical and technical necessities which result from the consoldiation of every disciplined political aggregate whether it is socialist or anarchist. Whilst Michels and Selznick see these as outcomes that cannot be avoided, Gouldner (1955) asks if it is inevitable that bureaucracy acts against the achievement of democratic ideals? Gouldner's argument is that there is every reason to assume that the tendencies which frustrate the democratic process are just as likely to impair authoritarian rule. Oligarchic tendencies which threaten democracy are challenged and overturned.

'There cannot be an iron law of oligarchy, however, unless there is an iron law of democracy' (Gouldner, p. 506).

Discussions of the representativeness (and hence allocative efficiency) of democracy are similar to those over the degree of consumer sovereignty which exists in market systems. Who is powerful – the producer or the consumer – in deciding what is produced? It has been pointed out by Walker (1967) that if voters become too active this might make a representative democracy based on pluralist elitism unstable since the elites would find it more difficult to bargain amongst themselves. Bell (1973) argues that society is increasingly characterised by rising entitlements and an increase in the number of interest groups. In earlier times politicians were likely to operate across a multitude of issues whereas today there are more single issue politicians who campaign on behalf of specific interest groups. One result of this is an increase in the probability that government will grow as politicians trade votes with one another for their own pet schemes. Another of Bell's arguments is that if there are too many people competing for political power and influence then this results in frustration – everyone's demands cannot be satisfied (p. 469).

Bell (1973) along with others such as Huntington (1974, 1974, 1976) represent the new conservative counter-revolution. Post-industrial citizens *demand* greater participation which they see will herald in a new social order, whereas Bell (*et al.*) want to change such expectations of greater participation. In particular, Huntington argues that democratic systems cannot handle the increased participation which has occurred in democracies over the post-war following extensions of the franchise. Increased participation implies greater decentralisation which upsets the efficiency gains to be obtained from centralisation. It is Huntington's view that the needs of society require greater centralisation and bigger forms of organisation along with a need to accept the authority of big organisations. According to Huntingdon, increased participation will impair the function of society.

Neo-conservative political theorists such as Bell and Huntingdon clearly believe in an idealised or perfect representative democracy just as libertarian economists assume that markets will operate perfectly. Neither position can be sustained empirically, whilst on a theoretical level the conclusions of Bell and Huntington can be challenged. First, extreme neo-conservative economists tend to ignore the interdependence of production and consumption functions (externalities and spillovers) and public goods problems. Second, the claim by Huntington that efficiency is improved by centralisation is an assertion that cannot be supported unambiguously by theory.

These issues can be illustrated by means of some elementary economics. One of the features of public sector supply is that individual consumers are quality and quantity takers. Individuals generally cannot vary the education or the police services etc., that they consume. Different individuals will have different preferences for different public services. Individuals whose preferences are distributed around the median voter's preferences, which dominate,[14] will be dissatisfied and will voice this. As an aside it is worthwhile noting that whilst public sector supply will generate, as a by product, much 'voice' of dissatisfaction, this is not necessarily an indication of inefficiency. If the median voter's preferences are satisifed then the deadweight loss of inefficiency has been minimised. One means of further reducing the inefficiency would be to set up a system of decentralised governments with each catering for a more homogeneous set of preferences.

This is illustrated in Figure 7.2. Assume that there are two local governments. The preferences of those in local government 1 are shown by the demand curve D_1 whilst those in local government 2 are given by D_2. Given uniform costs of supply in both local governments the most preferred output for local government 1 is Q_1 and for local government 2 is Q_2. In a system of centralised government a simple uniform level of public output Q_3 would have been produced. A centralised system results in welfare losses shown by ABC to group 1 and by CDE for group 2.[15] The neo-conservative solution for more centralisation would, therefore, result in less efficiency and not more as they claim.

Recent trends in the UK towards a greater degree of centralised control over local authorities flies in the face of the efficiency gains to be obtained from decentralised choice. A change in the financing of local government services in the UK so that the local electorate are made aware of the costs (e.g., via a local income tax) coupled with decentralised choice would improve public sector allocative efficiency considerably. The present trend towards increased central control has the possible perverse effect of reducing efficiency because any efficiency gains obtained by reducing wasteful expenditure can be eliminated by increases in allocative inefficiency.[16]

Another trend by governments today in an attempt to improve efficiency is to privatise more and more activities which had been previously supplied via the public sector. There is much sense in this programme. Many of the activities organised in the public sector have more in common with private goods than with public goods and public

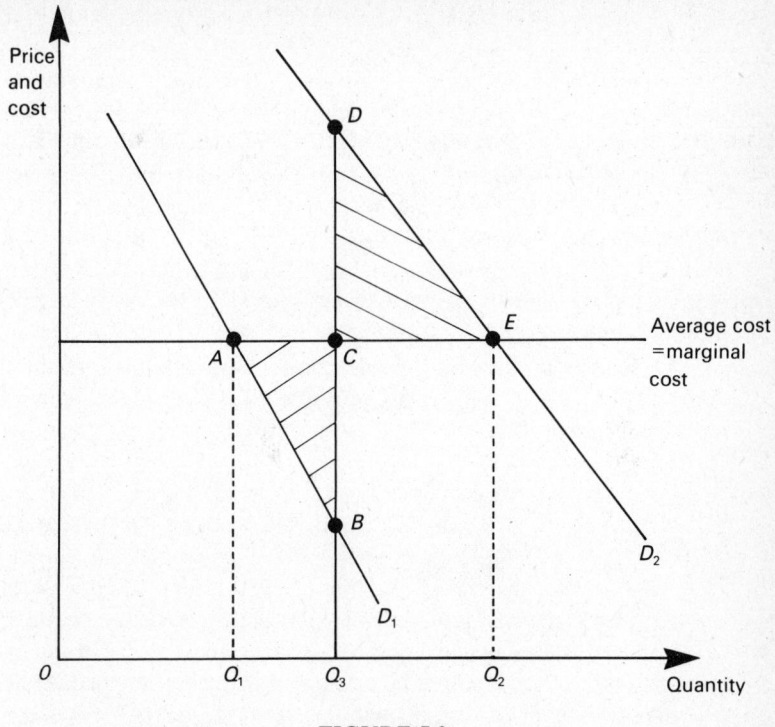

FIGURE 7.2

sector supply does not imply public sector production. However, whilst efficiency gains might be obtained from privatisation by improving consumer choice, too much is being claimed by some who have a naive view of how private markets work.

Unless the privatisation programme is backed up with strong anti-monopoly legislation then one is simply replacing a public sector monopoly with a private sector monopoly. A new set of allocative inefficiencies will replace the existing ones, Moreover, original thoughts that private finance could be used to fund public sector capital projects such as roads have been dashed. The main stumbling-block seems to have been the price to be paid to private investors for the risk that they will face for such programmes. The risk premia demanded have been so high that most projects have proved to be uneconomic. If public finance is provided for these same projects then smaller sums are required because society is, in effect pooling any risks.

X-EFFICIENCY AND BUREAUCRACY

Allocative efficiency is only one dimension of a broader definition of efficiency which will also include technical or X-efficiency.[17] That is, are bureaucrats using the most efficient production function available and hence producing output at minimum cost? The standard treatment of production decisions is to assume the existence of internal technical efficiency and hence the absence of X-inefficiency. This follows from the assumptions of profit maximisation and from the notion that the managers of production units (firms) are also the owners. If on the other hand, there is a separation of ownership from management there then arises scope for discretionary decision-making by management who may or may not act to serve the interests of the owners (shareholders) of the organisation – i.e. they may not go out to maximise profits. Instead they might pursue the maximisation of their own goals whilst returning a satisfactory rate of profit that will keep shareholders happy and not cause them to ask embarrassing questions at shareholder's meetings.

The scope for managerial discretion and the maximisation of a managerial utility function will depend upon the distribution of information about the details of production and management[18] within the firms and also upon how sheltered the firm is from external threats such as a competitive environment. Obviously there is greater scope for managerial discretionary behaviour in monopolistic environments. Since managers are those who possess the detailed information about the internal workings of the firm, it is difficult and costly for shareholders to challenge the decisions made by managers, unless they commission an independent consultant's review of the company. These factors combine to form the basic conditions for X-inefficiency in which managers, living in sheltered environments, can pursue their own interests without the detailed control of shareholders whose countervailing power is limited by the extent of their detailed knowledge. To the extent that managers take economic rents out of the firm in the form of larger salaries, big empires working for them, perquisites, on-the-job leisure, then costs will be higher than they would otherwise be.

The idea of X-inefficiency draws together a number of the points that have already been raised. Unless the internal incentive system is correct; unless there is a system of accountability and review, then bureaucrats who already enjoy the sheltered environment of a public sector monopoly will exercise their managerial discretion and take out of the bureaucracy economic rents which will show up as a higher public expenditure. X-inefficiency is illustrated in Figure 7.3 by modifying figure 1. The cost curve C_0 assumes no X-inefficiency whereas C_1 does. It is seen that the efficient solution falls from Q_0 to Q'_0 and the cost-constrained solution falls from Q_1 to A'_1. This lost output represents a welfare loss to the consumers of the service – in the case of public services it is the citizen/taxpayer who loses.

Again it is worthwhile paying particular attention to the efficient solutions Q_0 and Q'_0 in Figure 7.3. Transferring public sector programmes to the private sector through a privatisation programme will not, in itself, reduce X-inefficiency and produce welfare gains for society, especially if the newly established private sector organisation enjoys the sheltered environment of monopoly. Indeed, without the scrutiny of Parliament it might be that a private sector monopoly will

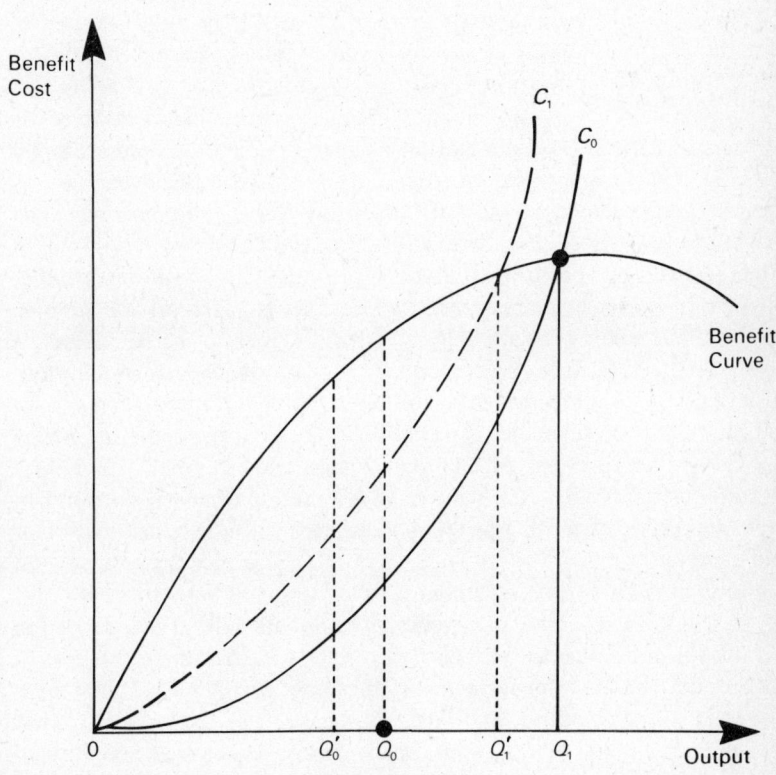

FIGURE 7.3

enjoy an even more sheltered environment resulting in an increase in X-inefficiency after privatisation!

Discussions of efficiency in the public sector raise a number of almost insoluble problems. First, the outputs of the public sector (education, police, defence, health, etc.) are very difficult to identify and to define – what do policy statements 'we will improve the standard of education – or we will improve health care or the defence of the realm' really mean; how can they be verified or refuted? This problem is not confined to the public sector – it would still exist if the services were given over to profit-maximising private sector firms. Problems of this kind mean that it is extremely difficult to design internal incentive systems that will improve productivity and efficiency. Classic examples of the application of simple-minded incentive systems abound. For example, if the productivity of the police force is measured in terms of the number of arrests per policeman then this can be easily improved by picking up anyone and arresting them. The quality of the police system would fall as too would the clear-up rate (a more meaningful indicator of efficiency). In education, if efficiency and the pay of teachers was to be related to the attainment of students then this could be fixed by showing students the examination papers in advance. These examples are, of course, contrived but they show some of the deeper issues involved. There is no reason to believe that these problems would go away through more privatisation. Indeed, the quality of service might deteriorate since profit-maximising firms competing with one another would be keen to demonstrate results. Unless these private services were to be heavily regulated (again an infringement of personal liberty) then there would be every reason to fear the private sector's solution.

The Thatcher Government instituted a number of internal reviews of public sector performance referred to as the Rayner scrutinies. These reviews were intended to eliminate waste and, therefore, to reduce public spending. But the way in which they have been carried out throws into relief another problem associated with the interpretation of efficiency. A typical Rayner review has as its objective the reduction of inputs – it is an input budgeting exercise. But what happens to output? If the response to a reduction in inputs (especially labour) is a reduction in output or a fall in the standard of the service then surely this cannot be claimed as an improvement in efficiency. But it has already been pointed out that output is difficult to measure, so that we must view with caution any recent claims made to the effect that the Rayner reviews have improved the efficiency of the public sector. They have reduced public spending but have they increased efficiency?

Another problem with discussions of efficiency in the public sector is that it is only one of a number of objectives which public sector managers face. Whatever their objective they should perform it at minimum cost – that almost seems axiomatic – but if one of their objectives relates to the distribution of welfare (benefits/income) this often comes into conflict with the notion of efficiency. Efficiency criteria and rationality are only one set of values drawn from a much wider set. For example, cost benefit analysis and other managerial techniques seek to find that alternative that will maximise the net benefit to the members of society. These techniques are based upon utilitarian ethics, and mimic the profit objective of the private sector. But they are morally suspect because they tend to ignore minorities since to allocate resources to the problems faced by minorities tends to be expensive (given the nature of the problems they face) which will reduce the size of total net benefits and dramatically reduce the net benefits per consumer. For these reasons, policies aimed at solving or alleviating minorities' problems seldom reach the agenda.

Agenda setting is another potential source of inefficiency. Who decides what alternatives are to be discussed? There has been much discussion about the use made of rational calculation techniques such as cost benefit analysis, and much effort has gone into refining such techniques but the political dimension of deciding upon the list of alternatives (the agenda) to which these techniques will be applied in arriving at a policy choice (outcome) has been left relatively ignored. Modern decision theory following the work of Simon (1947) has shown that because of the transactions costs of decision-making, the choice set will be bounded and search for the most satisfactory alternative will only take place over a limited number of possible candidates. But the problem remains who decides upon the alternatives that will be considered?

Bureaucrats pursuing their own or professional interests will attempt to influence the agenda, as too will pressure groups and their representative politicans. The neglected issue of agenda setting not only captures the issues of X-inefficiency, but it also highlights an important source of allocative inefficiency.

Agenda setting also forces us to consider more carefully a number of the more practical issues which are either neglected or ignored by neo-conservative political theorists such as Bell and Huntington. In their elitist theory of democracy they assume that elected representatives act in the best interests of the electorate. At no time are the complex issues of demand articulation in a social choice setting, or the problems of aggregation of a set of diverse individual preferences ever tackled. Instead, there is an implicit faith that politicians are well informed, that they know the preferences of the electorate and that democracy has somehow solved these technical problems. Indeed, many authors in this school argue that politicians know better than the electorate so that the outcome is, by definition, best. This approach, however, ignores all the issues raised by a close consideration of how agenda are set. Whose preferences are being served – are they those of the median voter (which maximises the probability of the election of the politician); those of the politicians or some elite group; or those of the bureaucrat?

These problems are illustrated in Figure 7.4. The median voters' demand curve is shown as D_M whereas an elite preference function is given as D_E (which could be to the left or the right of D_M). The allocative inefficiency (and welfare loss) is shown by the difference between Q_M and Q_E. The way in which agenda are set and, therefore,

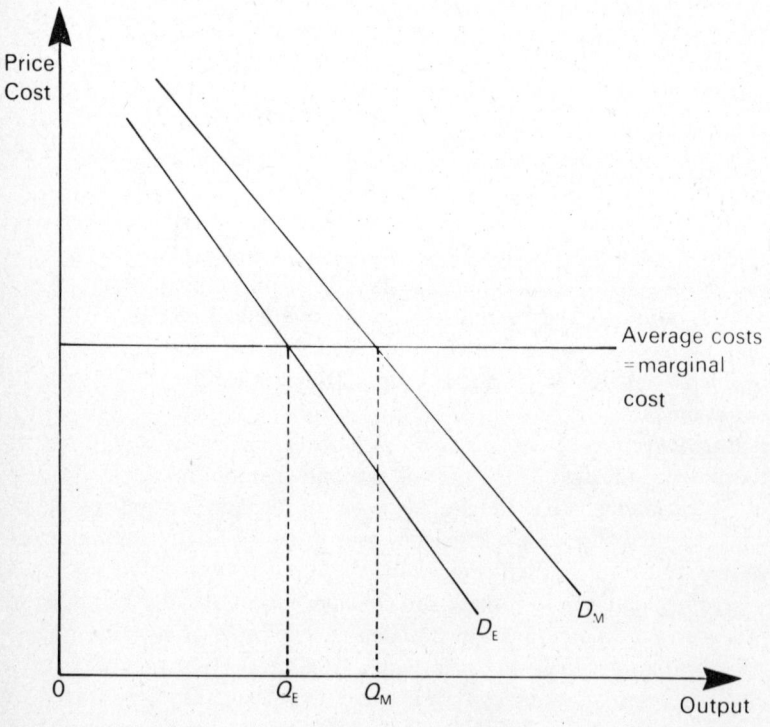

FIGURE 7.4

whose preferences are being satisfied is central to the issue of economic efficiency and cannot be assumed away.

The study of agenda setting promises to be one of the most exciting areas of future study. One of the sources of X-inefficiency referred to above was the asymmetric distribution of information between the producer of a service and the consumer. In the case of a public sector bureaucracy the consumer (including politicians) do not know the technical detailed information about alternative means of producing the service. They, therefore, have to trust that what is being provided is the best available at a given cost. This relationship, which is often referred to as the *principal-agent relationship*, is, however, open to abuse in which case trust breaks down.

In the economic theory of agency there are two parties (a) the principal and (b) the agent. The relationship is such that the principal seeks to motivate or to control the agent so that the agent will choose activities that are most advantageous to the principal. This is not a trivial relationship and gives rise to problems because (a) the agent's activities are only known to himself and (b) there is no reason for the agent to truthfully reveal these activities to the principal. An example of the principal/agent relationship is that which exists between a patient and a doctor. The patient (principal) seeks the advice of a doctor (agent) because the doctor is the expert. It is a relationship in which information is not distributed equally between the two parties. If the doctor advises the patient to have surgery then the patient trusts that the doctor is giving advice that is in the best interest of the patient, but is it?

In an unregulated private medical system a doctor motivated by self-interest (maximisation of his income) could end up advising the patient to have expensive and unnecessary surgery or some other form of treatment. How is the patient to know without going to the expense of seeking a second opinion from another doctor who might be similarly motivated?

Within the context of the public sector there are at least two main sets of principal/agent relationships. The first is that between voter and politician – do politicians represent the interests of the voter – and the second is between politician and bureaucrats – do the bureaucrats give the best advice to politicians? Defining the problem in the context of the principal/agent relationship forces one to think carefully about the structure of incentives as well as the constraints which characterise the relationship. Systems of accountability and control are attempts to break into the principal/agent relationship and to give to the principal greater access to the information held by the agent. How adequate are these accountability systems?

Before answering that question specifically, it is again worthwhile pointing out that the principal/agent relationship is all pervasive, it is not just confined to the public sector. It is the relationship which characterises most economic exchanges. Transferring public services to the private sector will not eliminate principal/agent problems. Indeed, it is this problem which lies at the heart of the escalating costs of the American private health care system. Because insurance companies pay out to doctors and hospitals whatever is charged there is no effective constraint placed upon X-inefficient practices. Also, doctors have scope to act in such a way that they can increase their earnings by reaping the rents charged by prescribing unnecessary treatments. The privatisation of health care does not eliminate this problem.[19]

Public sector systems of accountability lie at the heart of any attempt to improve public sector efficiency.[20] They are the public sector's equivalent to the discipline of the market place but they have the potential (if used) to go much further than the market does to tackle the inherent difficulties in the principal agent relationship. But there is every evidence in the UK that our system of accountability is weak on a number of different levels.

In order to illustrate the problems which the UK institutions of public sector accountability face, the statements of two leading politicians, who have been closely associated with the system, are presented. First, Mr (now Lord) Joel Barnett:

> I do not see why there could not be more openness about whether a particular marginal piece of expenditure should be cut or not cut as the case may be and why there should not be open discussion about it. It would be helpful both to Parliamentary control and general democratic discussion of the way expenditure should be decided. (para. 719)[21]

Second Mr (now Sir) Edward Du Cann:

> Our systems are complex, archaic, and are a denial of democracy. There is not the opportunity to look at or discuss money that there should be. We who have the honour to be the peoples' representatives in Parliament are not carrying out the work which the electorate believes and trusts us to do ... The way in which we fail to examine expenditure in my opinion is a disgrace in a modern Parliament – the

sooner we make a start on getting a better control of expenditure and examining expenditure, the healthier democracy will be.[22]

Whilst Barnett and Du Cann have formulated their critique in terms of public expenditure, they are implicitly seeking to control and to make more accountable the formulation of policies which give rise to these expenditures. But note where they level their critique. It is in the Mother of Parliaments that the problem lies. Is Government sufficiently accountable to Parliament; are the present arrangements wide enough and do they cover adequately notions of efficiency and effectiveness? The general view seems to be that they do not and the main fault is that Parliament is too often denied the relevant information which it requires to make Government accountable. British Governments are too secretive and in terms of freedom of information Britain must be ranked as one of the most closed and centralised systems in the world. This lack of information and hence, absence of informed debate must result in much inefficiency.

There is, therefore, not just a need to make bureaucrats more accountable to Government, there is equally a need to make Government more accountable to Parliament. This has been seen in recent years with the leaking of information by civil servants to the press and to Members of Parliament on the grounds that such actions will improve efficiency and serve the national interest – the implicit assumption behind these actions is that Government is not. The paradox is that instead of reducing efficiency, bureaucrats now become a possible source of improved efficiency. In a complex system of multiple interlocking principal/agent relationships old relationships need to be reconsidered and redefined. Whom should bureaucrats serve, to whom do they owe loyalty? Is it their Minister and the Government, or is it Parliament and the 'public good'? These questions can no longer be regarded as settled.

CONCLUSION

This rough sketch has indicated that the question of public sector efficiency raises a number of complex technical and empirical issues which lie deep at the heart of long-standing discussions about democracy and its meaning. There can be no doubt that public sector inefficiency does exist – allocative inefficiency and X-inefficiency. The causes of this are many as has been demonstrated; lack of information;

the presence of uncertainty; complex principal/agent relationships; too high a degree of centralisation; instability in resource allocation formulae; inappropriate incentive systems; failure to use appropriate decision-making techniques; and last but not least, a public financing system (taxation and borrowing) which distorts private sector decision-making either through disincentive effects or through crowding out. In other words, the sovereignty of the consumer/taxpayer of public services is limited and the discretionary decision-making powers of politicians and bureaucrats is enhanced.

But would private sector provision be any better? The answer is lukewarm and unhelpful. In some instances it would be better, but in other cases it would not. The use of the market is unlikely to produce the gains in efficiency which many libertarians suppose. Instead, it is more likely to redistribute economic rents. Minorities will continue to suffer and the distribution of income is likely to suffer. Unless the Government is prepared to strengthen its competition policy then privatisation simply results in the substitution of public monopoly by private monopoly. The consumer is then no better off and many are worse off. Privatisation will not, of itself, eliminate X-inefficiencies unless competition is improved, nor will privatisation dissolve the problems contained in the existing principal/agent relationship.

There is a great need to strengthen the institutions of public sector accountability and control. Bureaucrats need to be made more accountable but equally they need to be given greater incentives to work out more imaginative solutions to society's pressing problems. Government also needs to be made more accountable to Parliament. In both cases this requires opening up Government and its bureaucracy to greater scrutiny. There must be greater freedom of information. This will go some way towards giving more power to the consumers of public services and to the taxpayers who provide the finance.

The economic analysis of bureaucracy is still in its infancy and has only just begun to sort out the basic questions and to formulate models to handle them. We have only just started to understand some of the implications of a bureaucratised society for the individuals within it. If we are to come to terms with issues discussed within this essay then we require more adequate theorising and more innovative research in this area.

NOTES

1. Djilas (1947); Bottomore (1966); Connell (1977) and Kristol (1978).
2. Early studies of bureaucracy by economists include Von Mises (1944); Tullock (1965) and Downs (1967).
3. This is similar in essence to Macklup's (1967) discussion of the theory of the firm: 'to confuse the firm as a theoretical construct with the firm as an empirical concept, that is, to confuse a heuristic fiction with a real organisation like General Motors or Atlantic and Pacific, is to commit the "fallacy of misplaced concreteness". This fallacy consists in using theoretical symbols as though they had a direct, observable, concrete meaning'.
4. See Weber (1947) p. 334.
5. See Parsons (1951) p. 507.
6. See in particular the work of Williamson (1964), Simon (1947), Leibenstein (1966).
7. For an excellent review of the differences between post-Keynesian/Kaleckian economics and the Keynesian-Monetarist tradition see Sawyer (1982).
8. For descriptions and discussions of this process see Heclo and Wildavsky (1974) and Pliatsky (1982).
9. This is rather a strong assumption since information about output might also be impacted. That is, because public sector output is extremely difficult to measure. Only those delivering the service have a detailed knowledge of what is happening to output, and even this is on a qualitative level.
10. The main problem is that of Arrow's possibility theorem (see Arrow, 1951; Sen, 1970).
11. For a flavour of some of the issues involved see Jackson (1984).
12. In a later article Niskanen (1975) paid more attention to decision-making by the legislature but he did not make the link back to his original analysis. Others have tried to model bureau-legislature interaction including Miller (1977), Spencer (1980), Breton and Wintrobe (1975) and Fiorina and Noll (1978). For critiques of the Niskanen model see especially Thompson (1973) and Ott (1980).
13. The education production function is extremely complex and includes the inputs of parents (resources, private tutoring, encouragement, environment) in addition to classroom activities provided by the school.
14. The median voter theorem attributed to Duncan Black is a simple model of public choice – for an explanation see Brown and Jackson (1978).
15. This is the essence of the Tiebout (1956) model and the Oates (1972) decentralisation theorem.
16. See Jones and Stewart (1983).
17. The term 'X-inefficiency' is due to Leibenstein's (1966) seminal work on this notion: see also Leibenstein (1973, 1975, 1976, 1978, 1979) for an application to bureaucracy see Leibenstein (1982).
18. The asymmetric distribution of information is captured in a comparatively new topic in economics referred to as the 'principal/agent' relationship – see Mirrlees (1976), Radner (1981) and Stiglitz (1975).

19. For a critique of privatisation programmes in the USA see Fish, Kiesling, and Muller (1978).
20. The concept of accountability raises a number of problems of definition since there is a variety of different forms of accountability. For an excellent review and discussion of this problem see Stewart (1984).
21. Extract from Mr Barnett's evidence to the House of Commons Civil Service and Treasury Committee H.C. 118 viii, April 1981, para. 719.
22. Extract from Mr Du Cann's evidence to House of Commons Civil Service and Treasury Committee H.C. 118 vi; March 17, 1981; para. 592.

REFERENCES

Ahlbrandt, R. S. 'Efficiency in the Provision of Fire Services', *Public Choices*, vol. 19 (1973), pp. 1–42.
De Allesi, L. 'An Economic Analysis of Government Ownership and Regulation: Theory and Evidence from the Electric Power Industry', *Public Choice*, vol. 19 (1974).
Arrow, K. J. *Social Choice and Individual Values* (Chichester: John Wiley, 1951 (second edition 1963)).
Atkinson, A. B. and Stiglitz, J. E. *Lectures on Public Economics* (Maidenhead: McGraw-Hill, 1980).
Bacon R. and Eltis, W. A. *Britain's Economic Problem: Too Few Producers?* (London: Macmillan, 1976 (2nd edition 1978)).
Baumol, W. J. *Business Behaviour Value and Growth* (London: Macmillan, 1959).
Bell, D. *The Coming of Post Industrial Society* (New York: Basic Books, 1973).
Bendix, R. 'Bureaucracy: The Problem and Its Setting', *American Sociological Review*, vol. 12 (1947) October.
Bendix, R. 'Bureaucratization in Industry' in Kornhauser, Dubin and Ross (eds), *Industrial Conflict* (New York, 1954).
Bottomore, T. B. *Elites and Society* (Harmondsworth: Penguin, 1966).
Breton, A. and Wintrobe, R. 'The Equilibrium Size of a Budget Maximising Bureau: A Note on Niskanen's Theory of Bureaucracy', *JPE*, vol. 82 (1975).
Breton, A. and Wintrobe, R. *Bureaucratic Conduct* (Cambridge University Press, 1982).
Brown, C. V. and Jackson, P. M. *Public Sector Economics* (Oxford: Martin Robertson, 1978) (second edition 1982).
Connell, R. W. *Ruling Class, Ruling Culture* (Cambridge University Press, 1977).
Crozier, M. *The Bureaucratic Phenomenon* (Chicago University Press, 1964).
Dahl, R. A. *Who Governs?* (New Haven: Yale University Press, 1961).
Djilas, M. *The New Class. An Analysis of the Communist System* (New York: Praeger, 1957).
Downs, A. *An Economic Theory of Democracy* (New York: Harper and Row, 1957).
Downs, A. *Inside Bureaucracy* (Boston, Mass: Little Brown, 1967).
Drucker, P. *Concept of the Corporation* (New York, 1946).

Friedman, M. *Essays in Positive Economics* (Chicago University Press, 1953).
Fish, D., Kiesling, H., and Muller, T. *Private Provision of Public Services* (Washington DC: Urban Institute, 1978).
Fiorina, M. and Noll, R. G. 'Voters, bureaucrats and legislators: a rational choice perspective on the growth of bureaucracy', *Journal of Public Economics*, vol. 9 (1978).
Galbraith, J. K. *The New Industrial State* (London: Hamish Hamilton, 1967).
Gouldner, A. W. 'Metaphysical Pathos and the Theory of Bureaucracy', *The American Political Science Review*, vol. 49.
Hadjimatheou, G. and Skouras, A. 'Britain's Economic Problem: The Growth of the Non-Market Sector', *Economic Journal*, vol. 48 (1979) June.
Hayek, F. A. 'The Present State of the Debate', in Hayek (ed.) *Collectivist Economic Planning* (London: Macmillan, 1935).
Hayek, F. A. *Individualism and Economic Order* (Chicago University Press, 1948).
Hayek, F. A. *Constitution of Liberty* (London: Routledge & Kegan Paul, 1960).
Heclo H. and Wildavsky A., *The Private Government of Public Money* (London: Macmillan, 1980).
Hess, J. D. *The Economics of Organisation* (Amsterdam: North Holland, 1983).
Hoenack, S. A. *Economic Behaviour Within Organisations* (Cambridge University Press, 1983).
Horvat, B. *The Yugoslav Economic System* (International Arts and Science, 1976).
Huntingdon, S. P. 'Post Industrial Politics, How Benign will it be?', *Comparative Politics* (1974).
Huntingdon, S. P. 'The Democratic Distemper', *Public Interest* (1975).
Jackson, P. J. *The Political Economy of Bureaucracy* (Oxford: Philip Allan, 1982).
Jackson, P. M. 'Fiscal Crisis and Democracy', in R. L. Borthwick and J. E. Spence (eds), *British Politics in Perspective* (Leicester University Press, 1984).
Jackson, P. M. 'Monetarism and Implementation: Two Primers', in P. M. Jackson (ed.) *The Implementation of a Philosophy: Conservative Government Policies 1979–83* (1985 (forthcoming)).
Janowitz, M. *Social Control of the Welfare State* (University of Chicago Press, 1977).
Jones, G. W. and Stewart, J. D. *The Case for Local Government* (London: George Allen and Unwin, 1983).
Kristol, I. *Two Cheers for Capitalism* (New York: Basic Books, 1978).
Lange, O. 'On the Economic Theory of Socialism', in B. E. Lippincott (ed.), *On the Economic Theory of Socialism* (Minneapolis, 1938).
Leibenstein, H. 'Allocative Efficiency vs X-efficiency', *American Economic Review*, vol. 56 (1966) June.
Leibenstein, H. 'Competition and X-efficiency: reply', *Journal of Political Economy*, vol. 81 (1973).
Leibenstein, H. 'Aspects of the X-efficiency Theory of the Firm', *The Bell Journal of Economics*, vol. 6, no. 2 (1975).
Leibenstein, H. *Beyond Economic Man* (Harvard University Press, 1976).
Leibenstein, H. 'On the Basic Proposition of X-efficiency Theory', *American Economic Review* (1978) May.

Leibenstein, H. 'A Branch of Economics is Missing: Micro–Micro Theory', *Journal of Economic Literature*, June (1979).

Leibenstein, H. 'Note on X-efficiency and Bureaucracy', in R. C. O. Matthews and G. B. Stafford (eds), *The Grants Economy and Collective Consumption* (London: Macmillan, 1982).

Machlup, F. 'Theories of the firm: Marginalist; Behavioural Managerial', *American Economic Review*, vol. 57 (1967).

Migue, J. L. and Belanger, G. 'Towards a Theory of Managerial Discretion', *Public Choice*, vol. 17 (1974).

Miller, G. J. 'Bureaucratic compliance as a game on the unit square', *Public Choice*, vol. 29 (1977).

Mirrlees, J. 'The Optimal Structure of Incentives and Authority Within an Organisation', *Bell Journal of Economics*, vol. 7 (1976).

Niskanen, W. A. 'The Peculiar Economics of Bureaucracy', *American Economic Review*, vol. 63 (1968) May.

Niskanen, W. *Bureaucracy and Representative Government* (Chicago: Aldine, 1971).

Oates, W. E. *Fiscal Federalism* (New York: Harcourt Brace Jovanovich, 1972).

Ott, M. 'Bureaucracy, Monopoly and the Demand for Municipal Services', *Journal of Urban Economics*, vol. 8 (1980) November.

Parsons, T. *The Social System* (Glencoe, Illinois: Free Press, 1951).

Perrow, C. *Complex Organisations: A Critical Essay*, 2nd Edition (Glenview, Illinois: Scott Foresman, 1979).

Pfeffer, J. and Salancik, G. R. *The External Control of Organisations: A Resource Dependence Perspective* (New York: Harper Row, 1978).

Pliatsky, L. 'The Rise and Fall of Public Expenditure Planning: An Essay on the British System of Public Expenditure. Planning and Control' in R. C. O. Matthews and G. B. Stafford, *The Grants Economy and Collective Consumption* (London: Macmillan, 1982).

Radner, R. 'Monitoring Cooperative Agreements in a Repeated Principal–Agent Relationship' *Econometrica*, vol. 49.

Sawyer, M. *Macroeconomics in Question* (Brighton: Wheatsheaf Books, 1982).

Selznick, P. *TVA and the Grass Roots* (University of California Press, 1949).

Sen, A. K. *Collective Choice and Social Welfare* (Edinburgh: Oliver and Boyd 1970).

Sik, O. *Czechoslovakia: The Bureaucratic Economy* (International Arts and Science, 1972).

Simon, H. A. *Administrative Behaviour: A Study of Decision-Making Processes in Administration Organisation* (2nd edition 1965) (Glencoe, Illinois: Free Press, 1947).

Spencer, B. 'Outside Information and the Degree of Monopoly Power of a Public Bureau', *Southern Economic Journal*, vol. 47 (1980).

Stiglitz, J. 'Incentives, Risk and Information: Towards a Theory of Hierarchy', *Bell Journal of Economics*, vol. 6 (1975).

Stewart, J. D. 'The Role of Information in Public Accountability', in *Issues in Public Sector Accounting* (1984).

Thompson, E. A. Review of W. A. Niskanen's, 'Bureaucracy and Representative Government' – *Journal of Economic Literature*, September (1973).

Tiebout, C. M. 'A Pure Theory of Local Expenditures', *Journal of Political Economy*, vol. 64.
Tullock, G. *The Politics of Bureaucracy* (Washington DC: Public Affairs Press, 1965).
Von Mises, L. *Bureaucracy* (Yale University Press, 1944).
Walker, J. L. 'Critique of Elitist Theory of Democracy' in C. A. MacCoy and J. Playfords (eds), *Apolitical Politics* (New York: Thomas Y. Cromwell, 1968).
Weber, M. *The Theory of Social and Economic Organisation* (trans. A. M. Henderson and T. Parsons) (New York, 1947).
Wildavasky, A. *The Politics of the Budgetary Process* (Boston, Mass: Little Brown, 1964).
Wildavsky, A. 'The Political Economy of Efficiency: CBA', *Public Administration Review*, vol. 29, no. 2.
Williamson, O. E. *The Economics of Discretionary Behaviour* (Englewood Cliffs NJ: Prentice-Hall, 1964).

8 Industrial Democracy at Enterprise Level: Problems and Prospects

JOHN ELDRIDGE

Cooperation involves responsibility and responsibility involves power. It is idle to expect that men will give their best to any system which they do not trust, or that they will trust any system in the control of which they do not share. (R. H. Tawney)[1]

I have chosen to begin with the quote from Tawney for several reasons. First, I think it succinctly states a profound truth about industrial relations. Without such a starting point I think the search for high trust relations at work will prove very elusive. Secondly, it makes a simple but necessary connection between cooperation, responsibility and power. To suppose that we can, as it were, put questions of power in brackets when discussing industrial democracy is an illusion. Thirdly, when Tawney wrote *The Acquisitive Society*, he was reflecting on the profound social inequalities of his day. He was prepared to analyse the nature and implications of those inequalities in industry as elsewhere, whilst suggesting alternatives that he thought were morally preferable and administratively practical. The gulf between what he saw and what he wanted to see served as a spur to him. My concern is that those of us who think of industrial relations and how they might be organised might become absorbed in a form of reactionary 'common sense'.

I had meant to write a fairly self-contained paper based mainly on research that my colleagues and I have undertaken at Glasgow University. And I will still refer to it, since it does highlight some of the issues and problems relating to industrial democracy. However, I now think in the light of our present industrial relations crisis that there are other things that need to be said.

Discussions around the idea of industrial democracy can be confusing. There are a variety of perspectives and sometimes different background assumptions. Real differences may be masked by semantic problems or hidden by clichés. Consider the plethora of terms which can and do come into play: worker's participation, employee involvement, industrial partnership, joint regulation, collective bargaining, workers' self-management, workers' control and syndicalism. Some of these concepts may be mutually supportive in thinking about industrial democracy, others mutually exclusive. Some imply that industrial democracy is possible under private ownership, others see public ownership as a necessary prerequisite.

I would suggest that not only are there different vocabularies which may be used when talking about industrial democracy, but also different vocabularies of motive, that is to say, different reasons and justifications for particular proposals. Take, for example, the question of workers' control. André Gorz writes: 'When we speak of workers' control we speak of the capability of the workers to take control of the processes of production and to organise the working process as *they* think best. To organise the work process in such a way as to stop it being oppressive, mutilating, soul-destroying and health-destroying; to organise it to allow for the maximum display of each worker's initiative, responsibility, creativity; to organise it to replace forced labour and authoritarian labour by free cooperation.[2] This is contrasted with existing forms of the social and technical division of labour, which generate social fragmentation and sectionalism and stifle the humanist question: technology, or production, for what and for whom? This was the question that socialists like Cole and Tawney tried to keep on the agenda. Cole, for example, writing late in his life – 1959 – stated: 'I am as convinced as ever ... that Socialism cannot be soundly built except on a foundation of trust in the capacity of ordinary people to manage their affairs – which requires methods of management on a scale not so large as to deprive them of all possibility of exerting any real control over what is done.'[3] At the same time, reflecting on his earlier commitment to Guild Socialism, he thought that he and his freinds had not adequately confronted the problems of power, large-scale organisation and planning in industrial society: 'It surprises me how little thought we gave in those days to the higher ranges of control, and especially to the control over investment, of which we were hardly conscious as a problem.[4]

The vocabulary of workers' control can be used to try and reveal other forms of participation as management strategies designed to incorporate workers into the system. From some political standpoints that may serve as an instructive critique but the positive achievement of its own goals is another matter. The mechanisms by which it is to be effectively accomplished have yet to be spelt out. While the rhetoric of workers' control may have some ideological resonance and may even fuel resistance to the exercise of managerial prerogatives we still await the articulation of a positive strategy based on this commitment. Still, the resistance can point to the possibility of alternatives to whatever currently passes as conventional wisdom in an industry. This is well illustrated in the *Workers' Enquiry into the Motor Industry* (1978) where the position was taken up that: 'Through participation and planning agreements, management are trying to draw convenors, stewards and union officials into the management of problems from the companies' point of view. The real danger here lies in the fact that in the current state of crisis Leyland and Chrysler, the old style of union and rank-and-file activity will not seem to provide solutions to the problems of the industry, thus leaving workers' representatives inclined to accept management's proposals in the absence of a clear workers' alternative.'[5]

Other ambiguities exist when collective bargaining as a form of industrial democracy is considered. The institutionalisation of conflicts of interest between capital and labour in collective bargaining structures has been the most obvious historical development in UK industrial relations, as in many other countries. Originally this was a defensive activity, a bulwark to safeguard members' wages and working conditions. The right to bargain collectively was a hard-won affair, and still today of course recognition strikes are not uncommon. While it has constrained the exercise of managerial prerogatives, not all are agreed with writers such as the Webbs and Clegg that collective bargaining is a form of industrial democracy at all. The unions, after all, are a form of permanent opposition rather than an alternative government. Their oppositional status which inclined them not to take part in managerial decision-making was one of the reasons why worker-director schemes were regarded with suspicion by the trade union movement, although by the time of the Bullock Report there was a modification of attitude on this.

Some trade union leaders came to see that traditional forms of collective bargaining did not really shift the balance of power between management and employees in any deep way. The problem was identified as early as 1969 by Hugh Scanlon: 'The main and most immediate objective which is the starting point for industrial democracy is to oppose the position where organised labour can only react to management decisions and fight a difficult rearguard action to reduce the magnitude of their impact. It must be recognised that conventional bargaining systems are not appropriate for dealing with technological changes, particularly when the time for planning has been reduced from decades to months. It is no longer possible or desirable to wait for the end of a specific contract period to negotiate, when management's decisions are already and quite arbitrarily in the pipe-line. These decisions may threaten technological unemployment, obsolescence of skills, disappearance of the workers themselves. To protect workers adequately, we must be involved with decisions as they occur. We need an anticipatory function at the planning and implementation stages. This is getting to the kernel of our struggle for industrial democracy.'[6]

It is worth recalling that the Labour Government's White Paper, *Industrial Democracy*, also recognised the need to go beyond traditional forms of collective bargaining. If decisions taken by company boards have direct and sometimes major implications for the long term interests of employees, then ways should be found for employees to be involved in the development of corporate strategy and not just be on the receiving end of it. Not only was this seen as important for its own sake but it had instrumental value. It could increase efficiency, utilise shop floor experience and revitalise our economy. Insofar as this kind of thinking goes beyond collective bargaining, involving as it does some collaborative activity between management and employees, then we are approaching the idea of joint regulation.

Joint regulation implies that management and workers together formulate the rules of the enterprise – procedural and substantive. This is clearly something different from simply resisting managements' orders or contesting its policies. A well-established example of joint regulation is the operation of the National Dock Labour Board, which, with equal representation of employers and employees exercises ultimate control over all matters relating to the supply, distribution training, welfare and severance provisions for labour. There are local boards similarly constituted in each port area which have disciplinary powers over workers and employers. This was perhaps the only industry where the post-war Labour Government actually provided for more than nominal participation of workers in management activity. There was much talk of the importance of joint regulation particularly in the 1960s. In order to regain control, management had to share it with employee representatives. This was the way to implement productivity bargains, job evaluation schemes and new forms of work organisation. Management by coercion must give way to management by agreement. Authoritarianism must be replaced by a more democratic ethos. The spirit of this was well captured by Daniel and McIntosh: 'Management must recognise that it manages only with the agreement of the managed. It does not take decisions as of right because of its position, but must justify that right by demonstrating professional and technical expertise, and by demonstrating that the decisions are in the interests of the employees. This involves giving information, consulting, discussing and seeking agreement. It involves recognising employees' interests, ideas and abilities and the possibility that their understanding of the enterprise through their jobs can contribute to better decisions. Thus it is not communication or consultation in a paternalistic or patronising way that are needed but rather talking or listening to people as equals. All too often in considerations of communication it is the critical importance of listening that is ignored.'[7] In a period of full employment where in some sectors of manufacturing industry there was a preoccupation with shop steward organisation and the effects of plant bargaining in terms of wage drift and working practices, joint regulation could be presented as a solution to managements' problems rather than as some form of incipient encroaching control by labour. Indeed, in a sense it was a sophisticated technique for countering it.

The concept of joint regulation does carry with it a broadly pluralist view of industrial relations – the recognition that there are real conflicts of interest in the enterprise which can nevertheless be regulated by mutually agreed arrangements. What has happened to it? Interestingly enough, James Prior, who was Secretary of State for Employment in Mrs Thatcher's first Administration, gave a Granada Guildhall Lecture – 'Industrial Relations – Approaching the year 2000'. This had a pluralist ring about it. He took the view that management, to be really successful over the long haul, must be based on consent not coercion. He emphasised the centrality of employee involvement in contributing to economic recovery: 'I have consistently encouraged employers to seek to foster greater employee participation whether in the more immediate aspects of working life, through financial involvement with the company or by greater involvement in those company policy decisions which affect them.' This, in his view, was an important way of tackling the problem of low productivity and of introducing new technology. This is the way to wealth creation. What are the implications? 'It means moving towards a high-output, high-wage economy, where industry earns the profits it needs for expansion and modernisation. And, above all, it means taking full advantage of the opportunities now going for this country, to reform our old practices, to modernise our approach and to offer our people a new confidence and sense of purpose at their work.'[8] Even today Government ministers are still talking about the need for employee involvement, although the emphasis is much more on joint consultation rather than joint regulation. John Selwyn Gummer in a recent speech said: 'The Government is completely committed to the principle of employees being informed and consulted about matters which affect them. Our future industrial competitiveness and prosperity depend on both employers and employees having that same belief and commitment to make employee involvement work, and that is why organisations must be free to develop systems that match their needs.'[9]

How are we to evaluate such sentiments and their significance for even a weak version of industrial democracy in the light of recent experience? It is necessary here to touch upon the philosophy and practice of the new right. Whatever qualifications may be offered about the performance of post-war governments they did seek to pursue full employment policies and they did demonstrate an awareness of the personal and social consequences of unemployment. So, Lord Butler, in his autobiography, wrote: 'When as post-war Chancellor of the Exchequer I turned to the apostles of old-style economics and said that "those who talked about erecting pools of unemployment should be thrown in them and made to swim", I was still seeing in my own mind's eye the look of hopelessness in the eyes of the men of the thirties standing idly on street corners or queuing drably at the labour exchanges.'[10] It is that old style economics, with its glossy new right label, that is now in business putting the rest of us out of business. For the millions out of work, including thousands of young people who have not yet had a chance to get into work, discussions about industrial democracy coupled with Government claims that it is doing everything in its power to give individuals greater control over their lives must surely sound hollow and unconvincing.

The new right, in a sentence, is for individualism and against collectivism. This has had very considerable implications in the field of industrial relations. There is, of course, a general view within the Conservative party that the unions have too much power. Following the 1979 election the Conservative government neither encouraged or welcomed meetings with the TUC and when they did take place they were not seen as productive by the participants. This cold shouldering of the national trade union leadership by the government could be construed as an attack on the credibility of that leadership. To the extent to which the government urged responsibility on work forces in their actions and wage settlements, this tended at the same time to put union authority in question. Responsibility, that is to say, was defined more in terms of individual responsibility to the employer on his terms, rather than collective responsibility expressed through collective bargaining.

The cold war between the government and the TUC was a fairly predictable outcome of the administration's anti-corporatist stance. If incomes policies and social contracts are dismissed as dangerous nonsense and trade unions are defined as an obstacle to economic regeneration as a result of their irresponsible and restrictive behaviour, then what purpose could encounters between the government and the TUC serve other than to fray tempers further? The possibility of what Crouch has termed 'bargained corporatism' involving the Government, the TUC and the CBI receded. Practically the only corporate part of the structure which remained was the NEDC. That too is now in abeyance as far as the trade unions are concerned following the direct attack by the Prime Minister on trade union rights at Cheltenham GCHQ. Not much sign of industrial democracy there in any shape or form it would seem. Indeed the basic pre-requisite of trust is removed. For if workers having trade union membership are essentially defined as the enemy within our security establishments, then by extension trade unions must be seen by the Government as a subversive force in our society. It is this sense of the matter which I think has soured any prospects for a 'new realism' in industrial relations. There is actually a new antagonism and we see it all around us.

If the TUC is seen as having too much power on the national stage, the unions as institutional groupings were seen as having too much power *vis-à-vis* employers. Although the Government ostensibly supports a policy of non-intervention in industrial relations, this manifestly does not include legal intervention. The Conservative policy both before and after 1979 was presented in terms of the need to use the law to redress the balance of power between trade unions and employers. The Labour Government's Trade Union and Labour Relations Act of 1974 was described in the Tory Manifesto of 1979 as a 'militants' charter' which needed to be repealed. The Conservatives challenged *inter alia*, the closed shop, secondary picketing and the nature of union decision-making. The promise to do something about industrial relations when they came into office can indeed be seen as part of the 'law and order' syndrome. The rhetoric around the 1978–79 Winter of

Discontent from the right contextualised the trade unions as the agents of disorder. Had not von Hayek, one of the new right's heroes, drawn attention to the problem long ago? 'It cannot be stressed enough,' he wrote, 'that the coercion which unions have been permitted to exercise contrary to all principles of freedom under the law is primarily the coercion of fellow workers. Whatever true coercive power unions may be able to wield over employers is a consequence of their primary power of coercing other workers; the coercion of employers would lose most of its objectionable character if unions were deprived of this power to exact unwilling support.'[11]

It used to be the received wisdom that experiment in industrial democracy was to be encouraged in the public sector. This was where the Government could take initiatives and lead the private sector by example. This wisdom no longer holds – first because the government is engaged in a policy of galloping privatisation, and secondly because it has in effect endorsed an authoritarian style of management. The steel, car and mining industries provide us with prominent examples.

Consider first the British Steel Corporation. Leaked documents before the Government took office in 1979 indicated that there were some groups they would be willing to take on: winning against select opposition would perhaps deter the others. The steel workers were considered a weak group. Their first national pay offer under the new Government was 2 per cent. It followed a 22 per cent award to the miners. The steel workers signalled their intention to strike and, with varying degrees of intensity, did so from 2 January to 3 April, 1980. The Government refused to intervene. Not until 24 March was a Committee of Inquiry set up under Lord Lever. The agreed settlement was of the order of 16 per cent.

Sir Keith Joseph, a key member of the new right, was then Industry Secretary. He refused to intervene, whilst, at the same time, informing the world that BSC was bankrupt. What this did for the competitive position of the industry can well be imagined. But, as a Guardian editorial put it, the entire affair was an intervention: 'The Government is involved both as owner (on the nation's behalf) and as banker. It is also involved ... to the tune of hundreds of millions of pounds which the rapid run-down of steel-making will cost this country in terms of redundancy pay, unemployment benefits and supplementary support, lost tax revenues and regional development and job creation programmes. It is involved more immediately because the Government directly precipitated the current crisis by intervening to cut off financial support to steel from this Spring.'[12] In such forms did the arbitrary application of cash limits lurch into being and in a much more unilateral, non-negotiable way than previous Governments' incomes policies, let alone productivity agreements. At the same time, John Biffen thought it appropriate to accuse the steel strikers, on national strike for the first time since 1926, of causing 'spectacular de-industrialisation'.[13] What should have given more pause for thought was the willingness of a strike-free industry, with what the press usually term a 'moderate' (that is non-left wing) leadership, to engage in such activity for a prolonged period.

The MacGregor style of leadership, while at BSC, was to announce his plan, which early on included the six month postponement of a pay increase, plant closures, the loss of 20 000 jobs and then to ballot the work force over the heads of the trade unions. The tactic was to announce the ballot, surrounded by media publicity, and then indicate that if he did not get the necessary support for this plan he would be unwilling to ask the Government for continued financial support. In a situation of rising unemployment, where the preservation of some jobs may be regarded as preferable to the destruction of an industry, the tactic worked. What could be more democratic? After all, everyone had a vote.

British Leyland, on whose Board we may recall Ian MacGregor also sat, also serves as a continuing example of industrial relations by brinkmanship. Michael Edwardes, then Managing Director, had been appointed to office by the previous Labour administration but his aggressive and abrasive style of industrial relations was less inhibited under the Thatcher administration with its explicit anti-union rhetoric. In some respects the ground had been well prepared for him, since media coverage of the company's troubles tended to blame the work force and pay little attention to the structural, organisational and market factors which impinged on the company's performance. Britain entered the 1970s with a car industry that suffered from a chronic lack of investment and a conspicuous absence of new models, yet it was 'the strike-prone work force' which mainly served as the scapegoat.[14]

As early as September, 1979, Edwardes announced his plan for BL. In addition to 18 000 jobs lost in the previous year, another 25 000 losses out of a work force of 165 000 was indicated. The company informed the union leaders that unless the work force endorsed these plans, no further tax-payers' money would be sought from the Government. The plan was endorsed and the style was then set of forcing pay and conditions questions through unilaterally and balloting the work force over the heads of the unions. Ironically, the participation structures which the advocates of workers' control had seen as part of management's incorporation strategy, shrivelled. The Longbridge convener, Derek Robinson, was judged to have deliberately undermined the company's recovery programme by writing a pamphlet on the matter, and was sacked. The AUEW, after an inquiry, called for Robinson's reinstatement, but did not call an all-out strike when BL threatened to sack all strikers and, if necessary, close down the company.

A year after the sacking of Robinson, a year during which a new era of industrial peace was promised, four shop stewards and a number of other workers were sacked in the aftermath of the so-called Longbridge riot. The situation arose when some 500 trim section workers were laid off after a dispute over the increased work rate involving the seat manufacturing teams. BL bought in seats from outside assembly companies to be fitted to the new Mini-Metro cars. But a riot? 'You could not possibly call it a riot', one BL spokesperson said, 'it was a generalised outburst of frustration.' Yet two weeks later, amidst very conflicting reports, dismissal notices were issued. Again, Edwardes played the management prerogative card in a forceful way, insisting that the strikers be dismissed, otherwise BL would not seek further money from the Industry Minister.

I do not think that the examples of British Steel and British Leyland are typical of the way industrial relations are conducted throughout British industry. Nevertheless, it is fair to say that the Prime Minister, in her non-interventionist way, consistently backed MacGregor and Edwardes and was of course personally committed to placing MacGregor at the head of the NCB where he now is. She has therefore encouraged a style of management by confrontation. The new right brings with it the old whip of recession and reduces industrial relations to a very primitive state. Many firms will no doubt recognise the ultimate poverty of such authoritarianism but the new right, in my view, exalting in these exemplars of steel, cars – and now coal – is creating a climate of alienation and social division. Thus, Len Collinson, a management consultant, told his audience of executives and managers: 'We have an opportunity now that will last for two or three years ... so grab it now. In the past we have had a pounding and we are fed up with it. I think it would be fair to say that it is almost vengeance.'[15] This is what the new realism in industrial relations comes to, clothed in the language of 'grabbing' and 'vengeance'. What possible moral stance will those practitioners be able to take if and when there is an upturn in the market and the roles are reversed? Here we see authoritarian solutions imposed in the name of freedom, based on the proposition that we must punish and discipline a recalcitrant work force and make them toe the line in the name of increased productivity. This is what I mean by reactionary 'common sense'.

What about the private sector? In 1981 my colleagues and I reported on the results of a Scottish based survey in enterprises which had more than 500 employees.[16] The 48 enterprises surveyed were drawn from manufacturing, construction and service sectors. It was evident that many of the companies were multi-plant, often with very complex organisational structures and of course including multi-nationals. However, while it was quite common to find some form of worker representation at plant level, this was not so at enterprise level. So at the level of corporate strategy and capital investment there was little evidence of worker representation or involvement. The parameters for worker participation related to conditions immediately surrounding the work situation: pay, health and safety, working conditions and, to a lesser extent, manning and work organisation. The distinction between business-related and job-related matters for the most part separated the participatory and non-participatory areas and does seem to stem from the nature of the organisational structure and the paucity of representation at enterprise level. In general there was a good deal of enthusiasm displayed for the idea of industrial democracy among both managers and worker representatives, but particular schemes, such as board level representation or even the obligation to discuss major proposals before decisions are taken received far less support.

Managers tended to see the merits of participation in terms of educating the work force. Where the company stood in the market, its current performance and what was required of each plant or section: these were the things management wanted to get across to encourage greater realism and a larger commitment to the fortunes of the company. In addition a role for participation was seen in terms of shop-floor expertise and knowledge contributing to the management decision-making process. But all of this was typically seen as complementary to management's right to manage and make decisions, not a challenge to that power. It was noteworthy that most participation schemes or consultation arrangements had been established or revived by management initiatives rather than employee representatives.

Employee representatives naturally thought that employees could contribute their knowledge of the shop floor in a way which could improve organisational performance. But typically they were more prepared to encourage this if they could make an input to the decision-making process that would not simply be subordinate to managerial prerogatives but would take into account what they saw as their specific interests such as job security and working conditions. Moreover, information disclosure and communication had to be comprehensive and early enough to avoid the charge of hypocrisy. Many shop stewards complained and some managers agreed that information about the company tended to flood down in difficult times and dry up when prospects were brighter.

In general terms there was a mis-match of aspirations which was reflected in the fears of the two groups about the dangers of participation. Management tended to fear the prospect of discussions promoting challenges and opposition to their plans, rather than understanding them. Representatives feared that unless they could influence and challenge managements' plans when they were unacceptable to the work-force, then they would be seen by the work force as just another set of managers. In addition, many representatives felt most need of influence where they jduged themselves least qualified to exercise it: in business decision-making. Even though a measure of mutual dissatisfaction seems to be built into many situations, managerially initiated consultation systems were certainly in evidence. Nevertheless from case study evidence we suspect that many arrangements tend to have a short life although other mechanisms may be devised to take their place. It is as though the verdict is: 'participation doesn't come to much but it's better than nothing'.

If management are the initiators of participation schemes then it is not surprising that they are related to defined problems in the running of the enterprise. Management define the forum within which the theatre of participation takes place. They define the agenda and may rehearse the presentation beforehand. It is sometimes suggested that in difficult economic times managers and workers will pull together to ensure survival. The evidence from our case studies does not clearly support this view. In one case the company thought that the existence of consultative committees had helped them through the crisis of the management of redundancy. Nevertheless, most people in the company had not heard of or were not aware of the work of the system and were perhaps more influenced in their acquiescence to redundancy by generous severance terms. Another company, a non-union plant, was very keen to promote a system of joint consultation at plant level. However, as the market position declined, it was the top management from outside the country that intervened to say that the workers must either take a wage cut of the order of 16 per cent or the factory would be closed. They were given 48 hours to decide and agreed by ballot to take the wage cut. But the system of consultation, which local management had carefully fostered, lost all credibility. By contrast, another multinational with a highly developed participative style of management seemed to engender a good deal of commitment from the work force but it was in a growth industry and had real material benefits to offer. The substance of these case studies will be dealt with in a forthcoming book.[17]

Behind all discussions about industrial democracy and participation the issue of authority is to be located. What consultation or participation schemes reveal is the way in which management seeks to legitimate its power. Yet enterprises are notoriously unstable places – subject to changes in investment, technology, product and labour markets. It is easy to see the temptation to relapse into authoritarian management when the labour market is in the buyer's favour. The alternatives are harder to work through. How do you humanise the bureaucracy? How do you balance local control at plant level with central control? How do you organise systems of representation that are effective? How are differences of interest to be acknowledged and regulated? Industrial democracy like political democracy will always be imperfect but worth the struggle none the less when one thinks of the alternatives.

A serious concern with democracy in general and industrial democracy in particular means that questions of accountability and representativeness in large-scale industrial societies will be kept on the agenda and the answers will be continually debated and, from time to time, reformulated. Industrial democracy may be an impossible goal in absolute terms, not least because there are real conflicts of interest. This, of course, is not just a problem for capitalist societies, as Alec Nove has notably shown in *The Economics of Feasible Socialism*.[18] A comparative analysis of different structures of domination – and wherever power or authority is exercised there is domination – may reveal that individual freedom, fulfilment and autonomy may be distributed more or less widely. Constraint, that is to say, is always a reality, but some systems of constraint may allow more breathing space than others.

The new right has sharply reminded us that political economy carries with it moral baggage. We may even recognise that it was able to build upon felt grievances with the state, with bureaucracy and trade unions. Yet there are grounds available for challenging this reactionary common sense. We may recall, as one important example, that Keynes, in the *General Theory* demonstrated a clear awareness of the political and moral implications of economic diagnoses and prescriptions. The avoidance of avoiding unemployment on a large scale without resorting to authoritarian solutions was, for him, paramount:

> The authoritarian state systems of today seem to solve the problem of unemployment at the expense of efficiency and freedom. It is certain that the world will not much longer tolerate the unemployment which, apart from brief intervals of excitement, is associated – and in my opinion, inevitably associated – with present day capitalistic individualism. But it may be possible by a right analysis of the problem to cure the disease whilst preserving efficiency and freedom.[19]

It is this kind of capitalistic individualism, which Keynes was challenging all those years ago, which the new right has now brought into play again. Although Keynes' own perspective was in terms of preserving the mixed economy, it should be remembered that, in his view, for this to be possible a more equitable distribution of incomes and diminution of wealth disparities was required. Those who call for incomes policies, as many Keynesians do, need to remember that. For such policies to work in the long term there must be a sense of moral legitimacy of the distribution of wealth and income, among the population at large. A radical Keynesian approach would utilise an incomes policy where such differences as do exist are generally recognised as 'fair' and provide a basis upon which rational bargaining can take place. It is this advocacy of bargained corporatism which appears to inform Clegg's view that, despite acknowledged problems, governments, employers and unions can become more expert at negotiating and administering incomes policies. In the nature of the case, however, one would expect special attention to be paid to the highest and lowest paid groups.[20] This could provide a context within which schemes for worker participation and joint regulation of decision-making could be developed and evaluated. However eloquent the current political rhetoric about the need for employee involvement, in circumstances of high unemployment, widespread bankruptcies and hostility to the trade union movement in high places, it is difficult to take it seriously.

In a paradoxical way, it is the new right with its non-interventionist philosophy that has developed the strong state. Rather than one which is responsive to the needs of individuals and groups it is exercising power that is tending towards the erosion of the intermediary institutions in our society, shifting us in the direction of a mass society. From such authoritarian populism, good Lord deliver us!

NOTES

1. R. H. Tawney, *The Acquisitive Society* (London: Fontana, 1961), p. 149.
2. A. Gorz, Workers' control is more than just that, in G. Hunnius *et al.*, *Workers' Control* (New York: Vintage Books, 1973).
3. Written in 1959 and cited in Ken Coates and Tony Topham (eds), *Workers' Control* (St Albans: Panther, 1970), p. 80.
4. Ibid, p. 79.
5. IWC Motors Group, *A Workers' Enquiry into the Motor Industry* (London: Spider Web, 1978), p. 53.
6. Cited in IWC Motors Group, *A Workers' Enquiry*, p. 55.
7. W. W. Daniel and Neil McIntosh, *The Right to Manage?* (London: MacDonald, 1972), pp. 209–10.
8. Granada Guildhall Lectures, 1980. 'The Role of the Trade Unions', p. 28.
9. 'Participation, Industrial Relations and the Law', *Topics*, July, 1984, p. 4.
10. Lord Butler, *The Art of the Possible* (Harmondsworth: Penguin, 1973), pp. 61–2.
11. Cited by Tony Lane in Stuart Hall and Martin Jacques (eds), *The Politics of Thatcherism* (London: Lawrence and Wishart, 1983), p. 176.
12. *Guardian*, 15 January 1980.
13. *Guardian*, 16 February 1980.
14. Glasgow University Media Group, *Bad News* (London: Routledge and Kegan Paul, 1976).
15. *Guardian*, 8 January 1981.
16. Peter Cressey, John Eldridge, John MacInnes, Geoffrey Norris, *Industrial Democracy and Participation: a Scottish Survey*, Research Paper, no. 28, November 1981.
17. Peter Cressey, John Eldridge, John MacInnes, *Just Managing* (Open University Press, forthcoming, 1985).
18. Alec Nove, *The Economics of Feasible Socialism* (London: George Allen and Unwin, 1983).
19. J. M. Keynes, *The General Theory of Employment, Interest and Money* (London: Macmillan, 1961), p. 381.
20. Hugh Clegg, *The Changing System of Industrial Relations in Great Britain* (Oxford: Basil Blackwell, 1979).

9 Can Democracy be Tamed?

RALPH HARRIS

As what was still called an 'undergraduate' at Cambridge in 1945, I had an advantage, alas, denied to my more recent successors. The economics faculty at that time was not swamped by a narrow philosophic school, but included powerful exponents of economic freedom in the tradition of Alfred Marshall, including particularly Dennis Robertson, Stanley Dennison and Alan Prest, as well as unconcealed adherents of socialism and communism in Joan Robinson and Maurice Dobb. In between, there were more neutral offerings from such as Harold Kirkaldy, Austin Robinson and Claude Guillebaud.

TOWARDS THE MIXED ECONOMY

Similarly, the reading lists provided a varied menu of contrasting flavours to challenge the standard fare of Marshall's *Principles of Economics*. On the central issue of the agenda for government intervention, there was Pigou's apparently impressive denial of market harmony in *The Economics of Welfare,* reinforced by the seemingly devastating critiques of Edward Chamberlin and Joan Robinson alerting us to the horrors of monopoly, duopoly, oligopoly and other forgotten ailments. More in the Marshallian tradition, there were the spirited essays of Lionel Robbins, especially in *The Economic Basis of Class Conflict*, offset by the Fabian outpourings of G. D. H. Cole and many others. And, of course, on macro-international policy there was Keynes's *General Theory*, buttressed by such impressive state papers as the 1944 White Paper on Employment Policy as well as Bretton Woods and the GATT.

I do not think I was very different from most economics graduates of that time in finding market analysis intellectually satisfying in pure theory, but subject to such severe defects in its practical operation that extensive government intervention was unavoidable. How could we tolerate producers controlling the supply of their product by branding and then influencing the demand by advertising, thereby making nonsense of the consumer's quest for maximising satisfaction? I had not then read Hayek's sizzling essays in *Individualism and Economic Order*, especially 'The Meaning of Competition', which show what sterile, static nonsense the abstraction of 'perfect competition' always was as a model for practical policy.

Certainly my generation of budding economists had no doubt that one of the first duties of government was to manage total demand so as to prevent any repetition of mass unemployment which disfigured the inter-war years. I am ashamed to say that, in all the exciting ferment and popular discussion about the *General Theory*, I – along with others – overlooked the significance of the great man's acknowledgement (in Chapter 2) that 'voluntary unemployment' could be caused by the refusal (or inability) of workers through trade unions (or legislation) to accept what we would now call a market-clearing wage.

This complacent disposition of post-war economists and others to accord large and growing responsibilities to government undoubtedly owed much to the prestige of Churchill and his leading Coalition ministers – 'of all parties and none' – in winning the war. I was even then sufficient of an economic liberal not to fall for the Labour Party's repeated slogan after 1945 that 'planning for peace' followed logically from 'planning for war'. Having thrilled to Robbins' three Marshall lectures, published in 1947 as *The Economic Problem in Peace and War*, I had no illusions about the crucial difference war made to both the ends and means of public policy. Not only is the allocation issue crudely simplified by imposing the single, shared, overriding criterion of winning the war; but even the most democratic government does not shrink from employing draconian methods of conscription, direction of labour, rationing, price and wage controls. Later we were to learn from the writings of Ely Devons, John Jewkes, Robbins and other insiders, that economic planning of war production was made more arbitrary by the suspension of price signals which alone lend economic rationality to the calculation of opportunity costs.

But the general impression that government could be trusted with enlarged powers over the economy was no doubt strengthened by the high repute in which the British civil service was held. In 1945 most people were statistically less likely than today to know anyone employed by central or local government; but they had mostly received an occasional official letter signed 'your obedient servant' to maintain the odour of diligent devotion to public service. For more acute observers of affairs, there were the elevated exemplars of Sir John Anderson (later Lord Waverley), Sir William Beveridge (Lord Beveridge), Sir Arthur Salter (Lord Salter) and others as highly professional public servants in war available to administer policy in times of peace. Above all, for economists contemplating a larger role for government, there was the towering example of Keynes to illustrate how elitist guidance could help stop politicians straying too far from the paths of rectitude.

SEEDS OF DISENCHANTMENT

This is not the occasion to try to recall the precise stages by which hopes turned to scepticism and then to disillusion. Certainly my mind was prepared for what was to follow by Jewkes's *Ordeal by Planning* and Hayek's *Road to Serfdom*. But if they helped innoculate me against giving credence to the Crippsian dream of a comprehensive national plan, or the Morrisonian blueprint for nationalising all 'public services', it was only gradually that I saw the 'mixed economy' as an unstable equilibrium tending cumulatively towards domination by government. As an early admirer and biographer of R. A. Butler, I came to see consolidation of 'Butskellism' into a hardening consensus as boding ill for the health of the free society. Among the earliest signs of danger were the remorseless creep of inflation and recurring 'sterling crises'; the competitive boasts of Labour and Conservative as champions of increased spending on state pensions, the National Health and other 'free' social services; the lack of interest in restrictive practices and other damaging consequences of uniquely privileged trade unionism; the political competition to build more council houses rather than get rid of rent controls introduced as a war-time emergency in 1915 and responsible for the increasing decay of privately rented homes. Not least, there was the perpetuation of such government-made market imperfections as high tariffs, exchange control, feather-bedded agriculture, resale price maintenance and regional policy. Even more liberal-minded politicians in all three parties shrank from radical reform, on the apparently supine ground that radical reform, however desirable, was 'politically impossible'.

The central objection I found to the mixed-economy consensus was that the advancing frontier of the coercive, tax-financed state sector did not correspond to any intellectually persuasive division of labour between politicians and entrepreneurs in the market place. There was no dispute that government had a range of essential duties. Apart from such (predominantly) 'public goods' as national defence and the police, there were also Pigovian conflicts between private and social benefits that could be held to justify judicious intervention, through taxing 'bads' and subsidising 'goods'. Then there was the framework of law to maintain security of property and person – which I have come to regard as the primary public good – without which there is no continuing incentive to work, save or invest. Not least, since the Elizabethan Poor Law, government has accepted the duty of combating poverty by guaranteeing citizens a minimum income in cash or kind.

Of course in a democracy there is wide scope for argument about the scale on which all these duties are implemented, and so about the line between the state and private sectors. The size of national defence, police or poverty policy loom large in political debate. Likewise private production or consumption which imposes significant costs or confers significant benefits upon others, so-called 'third-party effects' or 'externalities', calls for correction by government; but how large is 'significant'? As Robbins warned almost 40 years ago, what he called 'the penumbra of indiscriminate benefit or detriment' is so pervasive that there are few forms of paternalism or even, he said, of 'totalitarian regimentation' that 'could not find some formal justification by appeal to this analysis'.

An even more central difficulty, rarely discussed in standard texts on the functions of government, is how to ensure they are discharged efficiently with some regard to consumer satisfaction. A little-noticed defect of public provision, for example in education or health services, is that government becomes a monopoly supplier with absolute power to compel customers to pay undisclosed prices in the form of taxes. An unintended result is that the majority of people who could pay for choice among private suppliers of education and medical services have their net income reduced to the point where they are compelled to accept whatever services government provides. At the same time, the illusion of 'free' services prompts consumers to demand ever more expenditure, whilst the absence of competition for custom deprives schools and hospitals of both the incentive and the economic calculus to minimise costs or maximise valued output.

GOVERNMENT FAILURE VERSUS MARKET FAILURE

It is surely one hallmark of myopic naïvety or certifiable prejudice for economists to deploy the argument of imperfection competition and market failure as a justification for government intervention, without a moment's thought for the often far worse deformation of efficiency and equity that follows from supplanting competition and obliterating market pricing. Mocking the obsession of so many fashionable economists with Pigou's smokey chimneys, Friedman has observed that every government measure is born with a smoke-stack on its back belching externalities into the market-place. The frequency with which public policies have results quite different from their glowing intentions suggests that in place of Adam Smith's invisible hand – which leads private enterprise to promote the public benefit – we are offered the visible fist of government which inflicts indiscriminate damage on private welfare.

A rough indication of this tendency is the extent to which governments throughout Europe, spending commonly around half of recorded national income, are confronted with widespread evidence of discontent from the supposed beneficiaries, who increasingly take refuge in the 'underground' or 'black' economy. When party men lament the lack of gratitude in policies, the citizen might be forgiven for asking: 'Where's the cause for thanksgiving?' Even when government programmes intend to promote general rather than sectional interests, they often impose massive, uncounted costs by distorting production, destroying choice, retarding economic progress and disrupting the operation of the entire market system through the blinding smoke of inflation. What is the cause of this chronic failure of governments to satisfy their electorates?

Since my argument leads to strong conclusions highly adverse to democracy as it is widely practised, I shall not take refuge in technical jargon about the logical impossibility of constructing a social welfare function. Instead, I must ask indulgence for speaking plainly in popular parlance. After all, any prospect of radical reform will depend on the understanding of people mostly without economic training or life tenure who are the preponderant victims of what now passes as democracy.

Although the differences between parties are often exaggerated in political debate, government is bound to be a continuing focus for deeper and wider conflicts than occur in competitive markets. In other words, the generality of consumers will be more nearly satisfied by their private suppliers than by their 'public' servants. This asymmetry follows from the contrasting mechanisms by which we make private and public choices in the disposition of our income. Thus the economic market has been likened to a perpetual referendum in which we all vote every day with our money between the widest conceivable range of goods and services supplied by myriad competing producers, each with a powerful incentive to meet our individual preferences. In stark contrast, the political market offers us one vote between 2 or 3 dominant political suppliers every 4 or 5 years.

Where competing goods and services in the market are each marked with separate price tags, the rival packages of party policies are coy on costs which in total pre-empt about half of average incomes. In the economic market we can choose the products, services, brands, colours, shapes, sizes that suit our particular tastes. The market-place caters for minorities in a way no government agency could conceivably match. We don't have to lobby or demonstrate. However eccentric our preferences, there is likely to be a supplier, whether for fancy waistcoats, black pudding or the collected speeches of Edward Heath.

In the political market, the rival candidates will appeal to sectional interests with hundreds of policies, many of which voters will not understand and are not intended to understand. Even under the most theoretically perfect system of proportional representation, the outcome of an election is settled by some assessment of majority opinion, whereby at best 50 per cent plus 1 of the voters is sufficient to coerce 50 per cent minus 1. Thus the winning party becomes a monopoly supplier over a range of goods and services nowadays costing about half the national income. In the name of the manifesto, it thereupon engages in full-line forcing of all its dubious wares on 100 per cent of its truly captive customers.

Whilst willing buyer and willing seller both reap gains from trade, for the majority of voters elections are a negative sum game in which losses exceed gains. Where the imperfect market-place enables you to get what you pay for, the incorrigible political market offers no redress against not getting what you voted for – except to vote for the other rascals next time. Alas, while the competitive market invites us daily to switch from an unsatisfactory supplier, the government takes a 4- or 5-year franchise over half the national income. Thus even for 'public goods' that have to be supplied by government, what passes as representative democracy is a crude, clumsy, choice-destroying steamroller. At best, it flattens out individual preferences and caters for average tastes shaped by dominant and unrepresentative pressure groups. At worst, as Hayek and others have taught, the unfettered will of the people exerted through unlimited government produces a result the majority do not want.

PRESSURE FOR MORE GOVERNMENT

If competitive markets have more potentiality to serve us better than overblown government, the question remains why politicians have almost everywhere extended their empire at the expense of consumer choice. There are no doubt many reasons. I used to believe the chief explanation was the intellectual discrediting of free markets by economists who identified theoretical imperfections and simply assumed governments would have both the knowledge and the incentive to implement better if not perfect solutions. This explanation points us in the right direction, but I am now persuaded that it does not sufficiently allow for the spontaneous pressures for more government.

Let us go back to the fundamental economic driving force in a free society. Critics may inveigh against 'self-interest', but I prefer Adam Smith's formulation of the central motive as 'the uniform, constant and uninterrupted effort of every man *to better his condition* . . .'. Who can quarrel with Mill's logic that 'a greater gain is preferred to a smaller'? The rationale of economic analysis is the scarcity of resources in relation to our insatiable demands for more income or satisfaction, whether in material goods, comfort, leisure, security, prestige, charitable impulses or any other self-chosen purpose.

In this light, the overwhelming merit of a competitive market is that all producers, including workers, are denied access to more income unless they can satisfy the consumer. The legal framework on property, contract, trade descriptions, weights and measures and the rest, prevents producers enriching themselves through force or fraud. The availability, or even the prospect, of alternative suppliers – domestic or foreign – exerts a downward pressure on prices and profits. In short, it is the life-force of competition which prevents producers from advancing their interests at the expense of their customers. It is the open market which disciplines self-seeking and brings the prospect of harmony in what would otherwise be a war of all against all.

Whilst everyone generally favours competition in things he buys, producers are ever tempted to seek some relief from competition in what they sell. Adam Smith said it all in 1776:

> People of the same trade seldom meet together even for merriment and diversion but the conversation ends in a conspiracy against the public, or in some contrivance to raise prices.

The virtue of competitive markets and the only justification of profit (or high wages) is that producers (including members of trade unions) are compelled to defer to consumer sovereignty. The consumer interest is, after all, the most widely-shared and therefore the most *impartial* interest in a free society. It will generally prevail against the *partial* producer interest so long as government prevents restrictions on the entry of competing products or services. Alas, throughout this century politicians have everywhere been engaged in obstructing beneficial competition in deference to organised sectional interests. Thus once a tariff, subsidy or legal privilege is conceded to one group – whether of capital or labour – others are tempted to seek similar favours. For each group, the soft option of protection in its various guises appears more enticing than the strenuous efforts of competition. But the wider the process is extended, the more the sectional gains are diluted and the larger the total loss of economic welfare.

The same self-destructive process can be seen in the extension of non-market entitlement to social benefits in cash and kind. Starting from taxes on higher incomes to relieve proven poverty, questionable 'redistribution' has been massively extended to finance generalised benefits and universal 'free' services that weaken the incentive of most people as taxpayers and supposed beneficiaries to exert themselves for market rewards.

The illusory outcome of this scramble for free lunches was nicely predicted as long ago as 1848 by the neglected French economist, Frederic Bastiat, when he warned against the degradation of the state into what he called: 'the great fiction by which everybody tries to live at the expense of everybody else'.

Theory and practice confirm that the result of all such self-seeking outside the competitive market is to reduce the efficiency and flexibility of supply, whilst piling-up inconsistent claims on total output which governments can redeem only with the bouncing cheque of inflation. Even if democratic politicians were stronger and saintlier, they would have difficulty in resisting the demands for favoured treatment by powerful interests in plausible 'special cases'. But it is no recent revelation, say by the two Harolds – (now Lords) Macmillan and Wilson – that politicians are not remarkably saintly or strong-minded, least of all in the run-up to an election. Indeed, Adam Smith again glimpsed the timeless reality when he warned against:

> that insidious and crafty animal, vulgarly called a statesman or politician, whose councils are directed by the momentary fluctuations of affairs.

In the more measured language of J. S. Mill in *Considerations on Representative Government* (1861):

> the very principle of constitutional government requires it to be assumed that political power will be abused to promote the particular purposes of the holder; not because it always is so, but because such is the natural tendency of things, to guard against which is the especial use of free institutions.

ECONOMICS OF POLITICS

It is upon this insight that the new Virginians, led by James Buchanan and Gordon Tullock, have developed 'public choice', or the economic analysis of politics, as an intellectual substitute for blood sports. To match the neo-classical theory of the competitive economic market, with its well-advertised examples of practical imperfections, the Virginians have constructed a theory of the competitive political market, which formally explains the unalluring reality behind all that familiar rhetoric invoking the 'public interest'.

Politicians and parties are revealed as entrepreneurs and firms competing for votes by promising benefits to sufficient lobbies to build-up a winning coalition of electoral support. Deploying all the Galbraithian guile of advertising, packaging, branding, semantics, product differentiation, switch-selling, these seekers after power devise and promote policies to appeal to such sectional interests as businessmen, farmers, trade unions, the professions, owner-occupiers, tenants, the elderly, large families, non-families, and any other sizeable pressure groups.

As a market economist would predict, the response to these competing political bids is the multiplication of hitherto undreamt of minorities, with a fertile invention of new grievances clamouring for urgent redress. The artful calculus of vote-buying rests on the appeal of visible benefits concentrated on grateful minorities but paid for by hidden costs thinly dispersed among the apathetic, because uninformed, majority. Throw in the economics of bureaucracy, which exposes a powerful interest group in favour of almost indiscriminate enlargement of government, and we see why the balance of the mixed economy has shifted remorselessly from the private to the public sector.

The official OECD statistics from 16 Western democracies show that in the quarter century from the early 1950s to the mid-1970s government spending rose from an average of less than one-third of national income to more than half. Unsurprisingly, Japan and Switzerland were well below the average, whilst Sweden, Denmark, Netherlands and UK were well above. Even for the USA, the vaunted home of free enterprise, over almost half a century from 1929 to 1976, total government spending rose from 12 per cent of national income to 42 per cent.

Such numbers do not tell us the whole truth. I recall the present Pope being asked by an investigative journalist how many people worked in the Vatican; to which he replied: 'About half of them'. It reminded me of the free market Pontiff from Chicago, Milton Friedman, who regularly offers up thanks and prayers that we don't get all the government we pay for!

Here is a subject calling for further research, which I commend to the British Association as a theme for another year. What is the true economic cost of government? Can it be measured as a simple proportion of the real wealth produced each year by our national exertions? We know the official measure of national income is sadly deficient in a variety of respects. For me the GNP is not gross national product but 'gross naive 'proximation'. For one thing, it values all government activity, to say nothing of inactivity, at the cost of inputs rather than the more debatable value of resulting output, which may be negative. For another, it ignores the compliance costs imposed on private individuals and industry by all government regulation, taxation, legislation.

On the other hand, official statistics of national income omit the goods and services produced in the underground or cash economy, which has predictably expanded with the increasing exactions of government. At the same time, it ignores the loss of effort and output caused by the damage to incentives of higher taxes. And there are many other defects in government statistics which should keep us alert to the adage that figures don't lie, but liars can figure.

HOW CAN WE LIMIT GOVERNMENT?

The spread of collectivism, which I judge so damaging to individual freedom as well as to economic progress, has been the work of all parties in Britain. Indeed, the Liberal Party, once the champion of competitive enterprise, took a wrong turning after 1906 by granting immunities to trade unions and launching spurious 'national insurance' with the huckster's promise of 'ninepence for fourpence'. Since then the result of clobbering the market is not to be measured by the narrow short-term calculus of misallocated resources. The ultimate cost is the frustration of long-run economic and social progress which depends on what Hayek has called the 'discovery procedure' of competition.

It is the growth of government in all its manifestations that has slowed down or immobilised the adjustment of prices (including wages and rents) and the adaptation of production and employment in the face of massive changes in demand, technology, and comparative costs. The British disease of the 1960s can now be seen as a forerunner of the economic sclerosis since widely diagnosed in most other European countries.

The common virus is the malignant power of trade unions and other sectional interest groups to obstruct policies that would promote the general welfare. In his graphically entitled study, *The Rise and Decline of Nations*, Professor Mancur Olsen has developed a general theory from which Samuel Brittan has distilled the following law.

> Stable societies with unchanged boundaries tend to accumulate collusive organisations and interest groups over time, and thus tend to lag behind in their growth rates and capacity to adapt, in comparison to newer and more dynamic societies.

As an observer of the political process in the House of Lords, I have no doubt that our long continuous history of guilds, trade unions, professional and trade associations account for the respectful awe in which Ministers, faced with a call for radical reform, refer to the need to consult the NEDC, the TUC, the ILO, the CBI, the BMA, the NFU, even the Apple and Pear Development Council and thousands of similar bodies that speak for special interest groups. When the present government has contemplated outright repeal, for example of the Shops Acts, or Wages Councils, or the solicitors' conveyancing cartel, or the opticians' monopoly, it has repeatedly delayed or diluted changes in deference to the orchestrated objections of the entrenched interests. We have seen modest, tentative approaches to reform in education and medical care through vouchers, student loans and health insurance. All have been nipped in the bud by rumblings of resistance from the NUT, AUT, NUS, NUPE and other lobbies chiefly concerned with preserving their easy access to public money or exemption from the unwelcome rigours of competition.

It goes without saying that any effort to withdraw legal privileges, cut subsidies, or reduce tariff and other barriers to imports, would likewise encounter concentrated opposition. The trick of all such resistance to change is that the most blatant defence of sectional self-interest is dressed-up in bogus rhetoric about the 'national interest' or maintaining essential standards. Even when more thoughtful leaders of both the main parties might privately condemn the extortion of the print unions or the NUM or even when they might secretly agree that the tax subsidy on mortgage interest distorts spending and saving, and inflates land prices the party in power shrinks from action in the knowledge that the Opposition would exploit any short-term disaffection for its own electoral advantage. Perhaps for the first time since the Fabians captured the Liberal Party before 1914, the powerful emergence of David Owen as champion of the market economy brings hope that the Social Democrats may prove a third force to help rescue the free society from self-destruction by warring pressure groups.

Almost 40 years ago Henry Simons warned in connection with union monopolies that the danger of disruption was not confined to mixed or market economies but would be quite as lethal for democratic socialism,

> if organised groups persist in exercising that power [of disruption] or if they must continuously be bribed to forgo its disastrous exercise.

FROM IDEAS ...

So we come to the central question for the health or even survival of a free society. How can politicians with nominally unlimited power be freed from the grip of sectional interests which render them practically impotent to pursue radical reform in the general interest? In a famous passage at the end of the *General Theory*, Keynes pinned his faith on the power of ideas to defeat vested interests. Certainly, his own ideas triumphed, with the help of wartime planning, and held the stage until the 1970s. Over the past decade, it was growing alarm about the rising trend of both inflation and unemployment that prepared the way for Friedman's counter-revolution of monetary policy, so proving the power of even an old idea whose time appeared to have come again. Both shifts in policy conform to Dicey's magisterial judgement:

> A change of belief arises, in the main, from the occurrence of circumstances which incline the majority of the world to hear with favour theories which, at one time, men of common sense derided as absurdities.

But 80 years ago Dicey was already haunted by the pressure for collectivism, which he explained in terms that anticipate a central insight of the economics of politics:

> The beneficial effect of state intervention ... is direct, immediate and, so to speak, visible, whilst its evil effects are gradual and indirect and lie out of sight.

It was that asymmetry between short-term sectional benefits and long-run general costs that led Dicey to emphasise the importance of restoring what he called 'a presumption or prejudice in favour of individual liberty – that is, of *laissez faire* ... [and] self-help'.

Just as fears of inflation opened minds to Friedman's stable monetary policy, we may hope that disillusion with governmental excess will bring still more intellectuals to champion the idea of a freer and more flexible market economy, which I have hinted has a wealth of neglected argument in its favour. Such hope is certainly strengthened by the success of the Institute of Economic Affairs and the remarkable revival of both European and American interest in micro-economic analysis popularised by Friedman, Hayek and the Austrian school.

... TO CONSTITUTIONAL CHECKS

The recent emergence of Hayek from obscurity to the elevation of a Companion of Honour is a strong tribute to the power of ideas. Yet in his trilogy *Law, Legislation and Liberty*, Hayek concludes that the damaging pursuit of the 'mirage of social justice' will not finally be checked without far-reaching constitutional reform. Such a remedy, however, itself depends on the eventual triumph of appropriate ideas.

In particular, Hayek has developed elaborate proposals for checking the discretionary power of politicians by a written constitution that would prohibit arbitrary legislation and confine laws to embodying 'general rules of just conduct'.

In the American context, proponents of the Virginian school of 'public choice' have variously called for specific constitutional limits on total spending, taxation and budget deficits, which could be exceeded only by two-thirds or larger majorities. Likewise, British admirers of the Swiss economy have begun to wonder whether the wider use of referenda and the introduction of citizens' initiatives might enable the 'silent majority' to escape from the exactions of marauding minorities that now obstruct reform. By thus concentrating democracy on a single issue at a time, the referendum brings the *table d'hôte* of politics nearer to the *à la carte* of the competitive market.

Yet, in the end, anyone who shares my anxiety about the economic costs and political dangers of over-extended government is obliged to pin his hopes on the power of ideas. The common objective must be to re-establish the classical liberal presumption in favour of liberty and limited government. The common enemy is the appetite of special interests to manipulate the democratic machinery for their own enrichment or security at the expense of exposing others to costs or aggravated insecurity in a relatively declining, unstable and faltering economy.

A PACKAGE DEAL

Even those who believe that nothing short of strict constitutional constraints can save us, are committed to the power of ideas if such novel reforms are to win wide favour. As an Englishman brought up to rejoice in the evolution of our unwritten constitution, I persist in believing with Dicey that the *ideal* entrenchment of limited government would be in the minds of intellectuals and ultimately in the understanding of the common man.

With the help of such piratical examples as Mr Scargill's miners' strike, it should not be so difficult to expose to popular indignation and anger the hidden damage that interest groups impose on the community in higher prices, increased taxes and lost output. As Samuel Brittan has argued, the total costs may be so large that a political entrepreneur might win electoral support by promising to free the present strangulated economy from their grip. Thus special-interest favours are now so widely spread that most sectional groups may stand to gain from general economic disarmament. Hence the strategy suggested by Milton and Rose Friedman in their latest book, *Tyranny of the Status Quo*, which concludes by proposing a 'package deal' whereby:

> 'we' accept cuts in our programme because we recognise that we would gain more from cutting 'their' programmes than we would lose from cuts in 'ours'.

I would boldly claim from the Crossbenches that the present nominally Conservative Government has shown a more radical liberalising intent since 1979 than any previous government this century. One of its earliest reforms was to free long-distance coaches from restrictive licensing. The result promptly proved the benefits of competition in reducing the cost of travel, improving standards of service and widening choice. Once passengers have sampled freedom, they would be unlikely to acquiesce in renewed restriction. This example suggests that where supply is elastic so that the benefits are immediate, government can withdraw producer protection and rely on consumer satisfaction to maintain electoral support.

A contrary example in social policy was the proposed cut last year of £170 million in housing benefits now paid to one in three households at a cost of almost £4000 million. However unjustified on intellectual and even social grounds, the orchestrated 'poverty' lobby were able to force concessions for the simple reason that there was no significant pay-off for individual taxpayers from such paltry savings. Likewise in education and medical care, marginal economies will always be frustrated by the unequal tug-of-war between concentrated losers and dispersed gainers. There is plenty of scope for a radical move towards choice and direct payments in schools, universities, hospitals and GPs, now costing around £30 000 million which is not far short of the total yield from income tax. If any government is to bring the boon of competition to much of this inefficient and choice-denying sector, it will require to stage a massive cut in 'public expenditure'. Such radical reform would have to be sold to the electorate by a package that promised the prospect of simultaneous and equally massive cuts in taxation, particularly on families with low incomes.

For politicians fearful of trying to tame the appetites of voters in an unlimited democracy, I conclude by commending the advice of that master politician and author of the 1944 Education Act, R. A. Butler.

Reflecting on how he had then won support from the snake-pit of warring interests and educational factions – church, secular, trade union, bureaucratic, Labour and Conservative – he explained:

> We decided at the very outset to make reform as comprehensive as possible and if there were any nettles to get a good bunch of them in our arms and not be stung by a little one. That policy has proved extremely successful ... because the more nettles you collect, the more they sting one another and the less they sting you.

The analogy strikes me as apt, since nettles are weeds that inhibit healthy growth, as do restrictions nurtured by special interest groups. The doubt must remain whether, like nettles, weeds in the market will eventually spring up again after being uprooted by determined politicians. Against that possibility, there is no lasting substitute for education in good husbandry, reinforced by the example of such well-managed estates as Switzerland and Hong Kong. Perhaps it is no more than a measure of my belief in the superiority of the case for the market economy. But I hold to my faith in the possibility of democracy saving itself by its own exertion.

10 Economic Obstacles to Democracy

KEITH COWLING

This chapter will examine the compatibility of democracy with the capitalist economic system under which we live. After examining what we mean by democracy and capitalism we will conclude that there are fundamental incompatibilities. We will proceed to consider how democracy is on the retreat as the concentration of economic power tends to grow. Our focus will be on the growth of giant firms, the increase in trans-nationalism in the control of production and markets and the accompanying centripetal tendencies in the control of economic power. Whilst these are general issues, they impinge most immediately on our democracy via the communications sector and therefore some specific developments in this sector will be subjected to particular scrutiny. The question will then be posed as to whether the diminution of democracy is required for economic efficiency. It will be argued that rather than there being a trade-off between these two desirable ends, greater real democracy will contribute to the attainment of superior economic performance, and this could be particularly true in the case of our own country. Institutional changes to secure an extension of democracy within our society will be identified. These will include measures to limit and control existing centres of economic power and initiatives to democratise work and the investment process.

IS DEMOCRACY COMPATIBLE WITH CAPITALISM?

There are some who argue that only under capitalism is democracy feasible. One of the most recent exponents of this view argues that democracy is protected by entrusting the economy with the assignment of income, occupations and authority on the grounds of the intrinsic instability of democracy, see Usher (1981). If we are interested in preserving democracy then we should not lightly tamper with the economy or the outcome of the economic system. For democracy to survive there must be prior agreement among citizens on a set of rules for assignment – a system of equity, and capitalism contains a system of equity sufficient to permit democracy to continue.

The basic problem with this view is that it focusses exclusively on the significance of the independence of the assignment mechanism from the political arena – a degree of independence sufficient to allow democratic government to proceed – but ignores the question of the independence of the political arena from the assignment mechanism (system of equity). In reality the form of political democracy is not fully determined by the system of voting, but also by the distribution of economic power, part of which will be devoted to gaining the consent of the majority. It is also important to emphasise that capitalism existed for extended periods without allowing democracy even to start, and in many places within the capitalist ambit it still does not exist in the limited form we experience in this country. On this point it is interesting to note that Usher argues that the economic conditions for universal franchise have been achieved only in this century. He favours Cromwell's position in the Putney debates during the English Revolution – property qualifications for voting are necessary because property is indispensable for the maintenance of civilised society and the institution of property can be preserved only if the poor are somehow prevented from voting it out of existence. Thus the preservation of democracy, conditional on the preservation of property, implies democracy has a variable meaning since the conditions needed to preserve it imply a diminution in the institution itself as well as in its role. It would appear that the original aim of choosing a form of economic organisation which would secure democracy has been replaced with the aim of securing the form of economic organisation itself, with its existing unequal distribution of power. Such inequality is seen as desirable for reasons of dynamic efficiency: without it accumulation would falter. The old, conservative argument reappears – don't worry about the division of the cake, but notice its size and rate of growth. Whether this is a compelling *economic* argument will be judged later, but what seems to be asserted is the primacy of economic efficiency over democracy. What is desirable is that degree of democracy which is consistent with the prerogative of property, which is required for economic efficiency. All talk of a form of economic organisation consistent with stable democracy is at best secondary.

Despite the variable meaning given to democracy by Usher, the one constant feature is the lack of participation. This echoes the views of much of contemporary political theory and political sociology. Political equality is then simply equated with universal suffrage. Participation is ruled out by 'the facts of political life' – the problems of scale in modern industrial society and the apathy of the citizens. It is also seen to be undesirable because of the instability it would create – the experience of Weimar Germany is cited, as is the then generally observed lack of attachment to democracy of the apathetic masses who would be asked to participate. As Lively (1975) points out, the unspoken assumption is that stability is impossible at a greater level of democracy than is currently observed, and indeed that what is being stabilised is itself desirable. All this is in sharp contrast to those theorists who give a deeper meaning to political equality and require participation by the people in all aspects of society as a precondition of democracy. Rousseau saw economic equality and economic independence as necessary preconditions for political equality, and participation ensured political equality was made effective. The greater the participation of the individual the better able she is to do so. John Stuart Mill also saw participation as providing 'good' government but also better individuals. He also came to see the importance of participation in the workplace but it was G. D. H. Cole who more fully developed the ideas of participatory democracy in a modern industrial society. For democracy to exist a participatory society must exist, not simply for its direct contribution to democracy via participation within that particular sphere of activity, for example the workplace, but also because of the indirect effect on the democratic process in general. Eliminating authoritarianism in one sphere contributes to its elimination elsewhere. This also means that greater democracy within the political arena would be expected to lead to demands for democracy elsewhere. If this is not forthcoming then stable democracy is not possible, assuming congruence is not achieved by less democracy in government! It would suggest however that 'greater participation would enhance rather than detract from the stability of democratic regimes' (Lively, 1975, p. 86). The fact of ignorance, apathy and alienation is not an argument *against* participation, but for it. Extending participation within the work-place is therefore of crucial significance for democracy in its broadest sense, but it is precisely at this point that the incompatibility between democracy and capitalism emerges. Equal participation of all involved in an economic enterprise would undermine the essence of a capitalist firm. It is not the market which is the essence of a capitalist system – a feature which tends to be emphasised by those equating capitalism with freedom and democracy – since it is possible to envisage a non-capitalist market system consisting of independent producers or workers cooperatives. Rather it is the subordination of labour within the production process. Whilst some degree of participation by workers in decision-making within the capitalist enterprise will always be present it can never approach the level of equal participation without transforming social relations within the firm. Again this does not mean that non-capitalist production cannot exist within a capitalist system, rather the point is that non-capitalist production cannot be dominant without transforming such a system.

Thus full democracy implies equal participation for all in all aspects of society and capitalism must deny this within the economic arena. A fundamental antagonism therefore exists between capitalism and democracy, an antagonism which is obscured by the existence of universal suffrage. This does not mean that the winning of universal suffrage was not a significant gain in the march toward a full democracy, nor that further gains cannot be made within the capitalist system. It suggests rather that further gains will be strongly resisted and that ultimately further democratic advance will require a transformation in the system. Some may argue we already have a 'mixed economy', with the public sector assuming an important role, so that the system is already transformed. Without getting into detailed argument it seems clear that capitalist enterprise retains an important (and I would argue dominant) position in the economy and that public enterprise has retained a form of work organisation as authoritarian as that of the capitalist sector, so that the existence of a 'mixed economy' appears not, as yet, to have enhanced the democratic polity.

GROWING ECONOMIC CONCENTRATION – DECLINING DEMOCRACY

Whilst the incompatibility of democracy with the capitalist organisation of production is a feature of any capitalist system, the incompatibility increases as economic power becomes more concentrated. Equal participation within the economic enterprise will always be inconsistent with capitalism but so long as capitalist enterprise remains small-scale its power to subvert the system of political democracy remains circumscribed. Clearly so long as any degree of economic inequality exists then political equality will generally not exist, but the extent of political inequality will be related to the degree of economic inequality. The evolution of capitalism has led to the growth in the concentration of control over economic resources. As a result many people have lost their economic independence and therefore some degree of control over their own lives, others have had some degree of autonomy taken away from them, and centres of economic power have grown up which are capable of subverting the political process. As an index of concentration in the UK consider the share of the hundred largest enterprises in manufacturing net output. In 1909 the top one hundred firms had a 16 per cent share, which rose to 22 per cent in 1949, 32 per cent in 1958, and 42 per cent in 1975 (see Aaronovitch and Smith, 1981). Estimates of the share of the one hundred largest quoted industrial and commercial companies in terms of net assets reveals a figure of 47 per cent in 1948 rising to 64 per cent in 1968 and 80 per cent in 1976. There is every indication that the British economy is increasingly dominated by a relatively few firms, and indeed the measures of concentration used above will tend to understate the true position because no account is taken of the interrelationships between firms of a minority or informal kind, such as common shareholders, interlocking directorates or joint ventures.

But growth in sheer size is not the only threat to democratic control; there are also parallel changes in the organisation of big business which will tend to undermine democracy. Two tendencies which stand out in this regard are transnationalism and centripetal developments. At one and the same time the dominant centres of economic power, the major corporations, are internationalising production and drawing the control of the use of an ever increasing share of the world's economic resources into the ambit of the key cities of the world. These twin developments pose problems for the democratic control of work and the strategy of the firm, for democratic control within the evolution of the city or region and ultimately undermine the autonomy of the nation state itself.

Take transnationalism first. Production and markets are increasingly controlled by giant corporations with a transnational base. This is not simply a matter of the ownership of production facilities in many different countries, although this is an extremely important development with most of the world's trade being conducted between the affiliates of the same corporation, but also involves links across countries which are dominated by the giant corporations without a significant degree of ownership. This would include various forms of franchising, sub-contracting and joint venture arrangements. Given such emerging international control of production and markets, and given the progressive reductions in national and international controls over trade and capital flows, the leverage of the giant corporations over the individual nation state has been considerably increased. Democratic national decisions to control the activities of the major corporations, or to tax them, will be increasingly circumvented by the appropriate international reallocation of production and trade flows, accompanied by appropriate transfer pricing policies. At the same time the increased international competition for investment and jobs created by the existence of international firms, which can flexibly reallocate production and investment, and accentuated in the current world economic crisis, will force nation states to reduce corporate taxation and the regulation of production, increase the subsidisation of investment and employment and act to restrain, by government action, the growth of wage costs. Thus, while we might expect the advent of universal suffrage to lead to demands for the redistribution of income, wealth and power in favour of the majority, the existence of giant transnational centres of economic power will undermine such democratic demands. Indeed we can see the growth of transnationalism as partly a response to the problems posed for the giant corporations by the advent of greater political democracy, and the result will not only be the attenuation of the significance of such political institutions, but also a tendency to undermine the growth in the institutions themselves. The provision of investment and jobs is being made conditional on the suppression of progressive forces which would allow the growth of economic and political self-determination. This is most vividly seen in Latin America but it is a general tendency.

The other characteristic of central importance for democratic control which arises with the growth of giant corporations are the underlying centripetal tendencies inside such organisations. Within the advanced industrial countries the giant firm has emerged largely as a result of merger activity. Large numbers of small firms have, over sometimes extended periods of time, become agglomerated into large multi-plant firms. As an example of this process at work, the number of plants controlled by the hundred largest manufacturing enterprises in the UK rose from an average of twenty-seven in 1958 to an average of seventy-two in 1972, and this was largely the result of the acquisition of other firms by the giants. This sort of transformation of the industrial structure of this country has, in many cases, led to the loss of a degree of local and regional autonomy, and in some cases where the acquirer is a foreign based corporation, a loss of national autonomy. This is not to say the system of relatively small firms, with a local base, which characterised the earlier industrial structure of this country represented a thriving democracy in microcosm; but there was nevertheless an element of local control which disappeared following merger. Higher-level decision-making and associated higher level occupations have been pulled to the centre and the periphery has developed all the characteristics of a branch plant economy. Strategic decisions with major implications for many local and regional (and even national) communities are being made elsewhere. For an increasing proportion of people control over their lives is being eroded by such centralising economic forces.

But not only is local autonomy being reduced. The same centralising forces imply a siphoning-off of resources to the centre which reduces the capacity of the periphery to sustain its own economic, political and cultural development on which future self-determination is based. For a largely autonomous local or regional economy, not only will the community receive the wage share of the income generated but most of the profit share as well. As the economic base of the area is taken-over by outside interests so the profit share is extracted for use at the centre and lost to the local community. Now of course it was always the case that only a small fraction of the community had a direct claim on the profit share, and it is also the case that at least part of the profit share after takeover will be returned for reinvestment. Nevertheless it was probably generally true that the philanthropy of the local rich made a contribution to the cultural development of the local community which has been lost in the centralising process. Generally the growth of economic dependency has stunted the broader development of a local, regional or national community and therefore imperilled its future hopes of self-determination.

Thus democratic control suffers in two respects: control over higher-level decisions is being lost, as is control over the resources required for community self-determination. The almost inevitable outcome is the outmigration of the educated, leading to further decline in the cultural development of the community. Centripetal economic tendencies become centripetal political and cultural tendencies and the community enters a vicious circle of relative decline. Thus whole communities lose effective control over their own lives – the essence of true democracy. It is also the case that such communities cannot easily break out of these processes of cumulative causation by supply-side adjustments, such as investing in education – which might be a typical, democratic response, so long as the demand-side remains outside their control. If such supply adjustments are made the most likely outcome would be a speeding-up of the rate of outmigration and thus an increase in the rate of relative decline. Increasing educational investment would only contribute to the economic and cultural resurgence of the community if parallel action were taken to secure control of production, employment and investment.

CONCENTRATION OF POWER IN COMMUNICATIONS

Whilst the increasing concentration of economic power is of general concern for democracy, perhaps the most direct and most pervading influence on the effective functioning and growth of a democracy will be felt in the case of the communications sector. Despite a communications revolution, ownership and control is highly concentrated and diversity is more apparent than real. The sector is characterised by a highly concentrated structure *within* each form of communication – press, television, sound broadcasting, cinema, books; but also interlocking ownership and control patterns *across* forms of communication – national and local newspapers; newspapers and television; newspapers and local radio; newspapers and books; and vertical links *between* production and distribution, as in the cinema. As Raymond Williams (1966) has commented:

> the extension of communications has been part of the extension of democracy. Yet, in this century, while the public has extended, ownership and control of the means of communication have narrowed. ... In the modern trend towards limited ownership, the cultural conditions of democracy are in fact being denied: sometimes ironically in the name of freedom.

Four groups control *both* the national popular daily and Sunday newspapers, and one of them also controls the only surviving London evening newspaper. These same groups are also active in the provinces. To take Associated Newspapers as an example, the Royal Commission on the Press (1977) reported that in 1976 in addition to its national and London titles it also owned a provincial morning newspaper, thirteen provincial evenings, and thirty-three provincial weeklies or biweeklies, 43 per cent of this latter group of newspapers having been acquired over the period 1962–76. Continuing with the same example, the Commission also revealed that Associated Newspapers' interests in communications at that time spread beyond the written word into television and radio. It had substantial shareholdings in Southern TV, and small holdings in HTV and Westward, together with substantial holdings in three local radio stations (London Broadcasting, Swansea and Plymouth) and a smaller holding in Greater Manchester. This is a fairly typical pattern. The proprietors of the national dailies tend also to have a strong provincial press presence coupled with a major interest in regional television and local radio. There also appears to be a strong geographical correlation between their press and broadcasting interests.

There is no denying the fact that the ownership and control of the press has been highly concentrated for some considerable time, but changes over the post-war period have contributed to a further narrowing of choice and diversity. Over the period 1948–76 the Royal Commission reported a loss of two national dailies, three national Sundays, one London evening, eight provincial mornings and two hundred and twenty-eight provincial weeklies. Coupled with this was the large scale acquisition of weeklies by the dominant national and provincial groups – the increase in weeklies (in terms of circulation) controlled by these groups over the period 1962–76 varied between 40 per cent and 100 per cent. Lastly with the advent of independent television and radio the possibility of real diversity in news coverage and comment was eroded by the acquisition of major shareholdings by the existing, dominant newspaper interests.

How has this concentration of ownership affected the democratic process? Hirsch and Gordon (1975) have argued that the press is fundamentally unrepresentative because the pursuit of profit implies that the interests and views of those with high spending power will command excessive attention since advertising revenue will be dictated by the spending power of the audience rather than its size. The so-called quality newspapers will play a leading role: they provide an informed but restricted discussion of public issues and ensure that their affluent readers get an especially powerful voice through the press. The views and coverage of public affairs of the quality newspapers gets reflected in broadcasting and in the popular press leading to a general conformity in both viewpoint and coverage. Hirsch and Gordon provide interesting examples of conformity – on the Common Market there was no committed anti-market quality newspaper; there was a press consensus about industrial relations legislation with legal teeth in the early seventies; there was a common neglect of distributional issues in the fifties and sixties; there was a common concern that the government should not drive too hard a bargain over concessions for the development of North Sea oil. More generally at the crucial divide in British politics – between the right and left in the Labour Party – the mainstream newspapers are all on the same side.

It is interesting to note that the quality press, which, according to Hirsch and Gordon, play this pivotal role in our democracy, has a significant working class readership *despite* its bias in favour of other social groups. It is also perhaps significant that when the editors of the quality papers were asked about their readership they underestimated manual workers by an average of twenty percentage points. The qualities are not interested in a working class audience because that is not what their advertisers are looking for. As a result there is little informed discussion reflecting the interests and viewpoint of this class. The press is polarised between so-called 'popular' and so-called 'quality' newspapers and given the targeting demands of advertisers neither type of newspaper caters for minorities without significant spending power.

This would seem a plausible if incomplete story. First the proprietors, editors and senior journalists are unlikely to be passive in this process. However this is likely to strengthen the conclusions already arrived at. It is likely that the view of the world held by the affluent reader will be similar to those who control and man the senior positions within the newspapers. Second, the polarisation into 'quality' and 'popular' groups, and the views and coverage they offer, are likely to 'create and reinforce the situation they apparently describe' (Williams, 1966). Many of the characteristics of the population we observe are determined within the system of communications we experience. When it is said we get the culture we deserve, it is surely correct to say, as Raymond Williams does, that this implies a confusion between tastes and values and *potential* tastes and values. With concentrated ownership throughout the communications sector, and with formidable barriers to entry, significant minorities can be safely ignored and minority views can be excluded from any sort of adequate representation in the mainstream output of the industry. As a result it is almost inevitable that the influence of such minorities, or such views, will be effectively curtailed. Whilst individuals and families within specific social groups may initially be highly variable in terms of values and tastes, extended exposure to a conforming media will tend to move them to conformity.

GREATER DEMOCRACY MEANS BETTER ECONOMIC PERFORMANCE

In considering the question of economic obstacles to democracy the orthodox view would be that there is some trade-off between democracy and economic efficiency – both are desirable but to get more of the one we have to give up some of the other. I believe this view to be incorrect, and therefore I do not see that creating the required conditions for better economic performance need get in the way of greater democracy – in fact just the reverse.

Let us examine the origins of the present deep slump of the British economy. Three interacting tendencies have been at work: the general movement of the world economy into slump; the growing relative weakness of the British economy and the move by successive British governments away from Keynesian demand management. Putting the first tendency to one side, it can be argued that the other two tendencies have arisen because of an inadequate degree of democratic control within the economic system.

The British economy has had a long-term tendency to generate a significantly lower rate of productivity growth compared with rivals. The underlying causes are a matter of considerable controversy but I would suggest that two, partially complementary, explanations warrant some attention. One of the significant features of the British economy is the relatively high degree of internationalisation of British capital, both industrial and financial. These strong international links and commitments imply that money capital can be easily shifted abroad with a consequent retarding effect on investment in Britain. This could easily trigger off a cumulative process of relative decline. In contrast, the continental European countries and Japan exploited foreign markets from a domestic production base, and entered a cumulative process of relative expansion. But what is it about the British economy that leads British capital to such a peculiarly international orientation? The other explanation of relative decline may offer a partial explanation. This view stresses the peculiar strength and militancy of British labour at the point of production which has retarded innovation and productivity growth. The international orientation of

British capital could then be seen as a response – although the converse argument is also made, that the lack of growth of the British economy, due for example to its international orientation, has forced workers and their unions into a defensive posture which has retarded the growth process even further. If Britain's relative economic decline is at least partially explicable in terms of the particular strength of labour's workplace organisation, then the extension of democratic control offers the prospect of a transformation of Britain's economic prospects. A defensive posture would be transformed into positive participation if it were clear that those who were participating had effective, democratic control over both operating and strategic decisions.

Of course there is another way, and that way is the major project of the present government. However, as well as being basically undemocratic in terms of smashing the defensive strength of the organisations of working people, it is also extremely costly in social terms. This brings us to the third tendency underlying the present slump of the British economy: the progressive movement away from Keynesian demand management we have witnessed since the mid-seventies. A commitment to full employment will have a fundamental impact on the balance of power between capital and labour and will eventually lead, via rising confidence and militancy, to rising wage demands and ultimately a wage-price spiral, which the government will sooner or later seek to clamp down. Incomes policies have been tried and abandoned and eventually monetarism was wheeled-out as a replacement for the old, 'discredited' policies. Clearly the Thatcher government has been acting in a manner aimed at securing labour discipline and, at least until very recently, such policies have undoubtedly met with substantial success. However they have been gained at enormous cost and their long-term benefits now look dubious.

Is there a better way? The history of incomes policy in the sixties and seventies, when it had any impact at all, was one of reducing the growth in real wage. As Burkitt (1982) points out, the state was essentially nationalising part of the product which it then handed over to capitalists. Workers were, in effect, compelled to restrict consumption in order to facilitate investment, yet they possessed no rights in the ensuing accumulation of capital. Not surprisingly they eventually baulked at this and the system of wage control broke down. At the same time it is clear that wage militancy by itself cannot secure a permanent redistribution of income between capital and labour. Thus labour has a strong interest in a prices and incomes policy, but a necessary precondition is the increasing socialisation of capital. This implies not simply an extension of the communal ownership of capital but also an extension of economic democracy, that is worker involvement and representation in all areas and all levels of decision-making within the enterprise. Only in such circumstances is the abandonment of free collective bargaining likely to be a stable solution.

But it will be argued that giving the workers more say in the organisation and operation of industry will mean that industry will suffer in terms of loss of efficiency and loss of dynamism. 'It is all very well talking about increased economic democracy, but that is just so much ivory-towered nonsense.' Not so. All the evidence points to the real gains which can be obtained by democratising the place of work. A survey in 1970 of the existing empirical research on participation concluded that not only did it have a favourable effect on the development of the individual but that it did not harm the efficiency of the enterprises – indeed it may have increased it (Pateman, 1970). A more recent survey went further and concluded that there is 'overwhelming evidence that increased participation... raises productivity' (Hodgson, 1984). In the case of worker cooperatives, the empirical evidence reveals that participation increases worker self-discipline; fewer resources are devoted to supervision compared with capitalist firms; and absenteeism drops significantly following the introduction of worker control, with absenteeism in the Mondragon cooperatives only half that of capitalist firms in the region (Stewart, 1983). Even the macroeconomic technicians are now coming round to the view that participation is a necessary condition for any sustained recovery (see Huhne, 1984).

NEW INSTITUTIONS TO PROMOTE DEMOCRACY AND ECONOMIC EFFICIENCY

Given the degree to which our democracy is limited by the lack of economic democracy and the growing concentration of economic power, the significant extension of democracy, and thereby economic efficiency, can only proceed by the democratisation of work and investment decisions, and by increasing the degree of democratic control over the monopolisation of the economy and over the transnational corporations. Such an extension of democracy will also require an opening-up of the communications sector to a broader range of ideas and viewpoints. We will briefly identify institutional arrangements which may contribute to this process.

Economic democracy and economic efficiency requires the control and management of economic enterprises by those working in them. Plans and structures are then required to mesh-in such self-management with more general interests, such as those of the local community and the consumers of the product, in order to sustain the conditions for a true democracy and to avoid the reproduction of a system of economic and political inequality. Such an arrangement should be sharply distinguished from the decentralisation of power which assumes that the authentic source of power lies at the centre (see Williams, 1982). Power would spring from the base, from direct social relations into all necessary indirect and extended relations. A complex of inter-locking democratic institutions would have to be built complementing the existing form of political representative democracy. They could come together at the apex with a second chamber based on the economic edifice interacting with the existing House of Commons, but local and regional assemblies would also be possible (see Williams, 1982).

Whilst markets would have an important role in such a system, planning would be dominant and its strong democratic base would ensure that it would not easily degenerate into an excessively centralised bureaucratic structure. There remains the question of where to draw the boundary between local autonomy and the collective interest. I would be inclined to keep price and wage control at the national level, leaving production and investment decisions to be worked out in the complex interactions within and between enterprises and industries with some form of indicative planning institutions providing coordination at the aggregate level. Employment decisions and the organisation of work would be determined in the local community with the various enterprises being represented on local employment boards whose remit would be to find work for everyone interested in work.

How might we begin on the path to economic democracy? A useful start would be legislation requiring participation within the enterprise. The Vredeling directive, vehemently opposed by British business, would be a modest move in the right direction. But full participation would not be realised before workers got some direct and substantial economic leverage. This could be provided via pension fund equity holdings by which means workers' savings could be used to secure an increase in worker participation. A government sympathetic to increased participation could directly contribute to the same end by extending its own equity holdings in private industry and by initiating new public ventures with fully participative structures. The existing nationalised industries would be opened-up and operated with a judicious mixture of central planning and workers' control.

But we would still be left with a system within which economic power would be spread very unevenly for many years to come and with an inbuilt tendency for such power to become more concentrated. As well as a postivie strategy to secure an extension of economic democracy we would also need a negative strategy to control existing concentrations of economic power and prevent their strengthening. This would necessarily include a rigorous anti-merger policy coupled with divestiture in cases where major centres of power can be broken up without significant efficiency loss (see Cowling, 1982). However there will be cases where divestiture is not desirable, in which case we would need to consider methods of control. Despite the existence of institutions like the Monopolies Commission there would seem to be compelling arguments for an additional institutional framework for the regulation of major centres of economic power. First, society needs institutions to keep such organisations under continuous observation and control, and the present system does not allow this. There is no way at the moment in which the public regulatory system can systematically accumulate experience concerning the multifarious activities of the major corporations. Without continuous observation and access to internal information society will never be able to effectively control the behaviour of such companies. Second, we need to consider the control of the corporation as a whole, whereas existing institutions look merely at particular activities. Lastly, we need to bring more of the evidence and discussion regarding the activities of the major corporations into the public arena given the asymmetry in the representation of conflicting interests within Whitehall.

The appropriate response would seem to be parliamentary committees allocated to each major sector of the economy. Such committees would provide continuous surveillance of the major private centres of economic power and would allow for the growth of experience and expertise in the affairs of such corporations by both parliamentarians and their staff. Most of their activities could and should be open and public and they would provide an effective countervailing power to the pressures put on government departments. They would of course be subject to pressures themselves, but operating in the public eye and with parliamentary responsibilities may provide at least a partially effective antidote.

However, policies to control private centres of economic power could still be undermined from within Whitehall. Whitehall is an arena of conflict between different groups, but certain groups have inbuilt advantages which guarantee unequal access and influence. The notion of 'sponsoring department' is a case in point. It is one of the specific functions of government departments such as Industry, Agriculture and Transport, to represent the interests of their associated firms and industries within the government apparatus. It would seem important to challenge this institution. 'Industry's' case should be made openly so that everyone can see clearly where the view of vested interests is being put. If the bureaucracy is to act for specific vested interests then advocacy must be seen to be balanced and equitable. Patently this is not now the case. Although 'industry' is in close contact with its 'sponsors' the same cannot be said for consumers. Some might argue that the Office of Fair Trading takes on the role of consumers' advocate, but this was not the view taken by the former Director (Mr Methven) who made it quite clear that he regarded himself as a referee, trying to balance out the interests of 'industry' and the consumer. Not only does this result in a basic asymmetry, it would also seem an inappropriate stance for such a department. But irrespective of this, there would remain a basic asymmetry given the fact that final consumers – individual households – are obviously not organised (as consumers) or represented in as efficient a manner, as is 'industry'. This becomes more and more the case as industry becomes more concentrated. The bigger firms become, the more dominant they are within individual industries, the more incentive they have to represent 'industry's' view, in aggregate or as a specific industry. The benefits from lobbying activities accrue more completely, and more directly, to the firm in question the bigger or more dominant is that particular firm. Given this, it becomes more and more crucial to develop new methods of democratic control of the operations of the state as concentration increases.

A piece in the *Guardian* of 21 July 1984 gives the flavour of the problem (Erlichman, 1984). The article concerns the Public Accounts Committees' criticism of the failure of the government to control the profits of the drug companies. It comments on the government's apparent unwillingness or inability to restrict profits which are deemed excessive and complains of the 'disgraceful secrecy which shrouds the drug companies' profit negotiations with ministers and Whitehall civil servants'. It reveals that 'By design, the Government has ensured that no member of the public – or even the Public Accounts Committee – can scrutinise the real profit returns of the drug companies ...', also that the new president of the Association of the British Pharmaceutical Industry will be the DHSS senior civil servant in charge of the control of the safety and promotion of drugs. Could things be cosier?

This specific example provides a nice lead-in to the issues posed by the transnationals, since the problems posed by the transfer pricing of the transnational firms looms large in the control of drug industry profits. Democratic control over the transnationals is an objective not easily realised. International banking is a particularly crucial and difficult sector. The phenomenal growth of the Eurocurrency market, which recorded a 3353 per cent increase between 1965 and 1981 – ending up with 1.35 *trillion* US dollars of expatriate currencies, 'dramatically altered the balance of power ... between the international commercial banking system and the national monetary authorities and their central banks. Like multinational corporations in their field, international commercial banks emerged as a main focus of financial power, largely independent of the control of national monetary authorities', Bhaduri and Steindl (1983). However it is also true that such banks will be driven to seek the assistance of the governments of their home bases in the current climate of looming large-scale defaulting. Whilst an international approach to the regulation of the transnationals in general is obviously desirable it is important not to be pessimistic about what can be achieved at the national level. Although banking is a peculiarly difficult case, the nation state obviously has substantial leverage, if it chooses to use it. Clearly there are enormous political difficulties, but a determination to intervene decisively in a crucial sector would provide a salutary lesson for the transnationals in general. However, as well as acting independently, the British government should be pressured to reverse its present stance regarding the international control of the transnationals. Whether Labour or Conservative, the British government has consistently voted within the UN against regulating the transnationals (Cable, 1980). It is clear that a voluntary code of conduct is insufficient. As Fine (1983) has argued, whilst such a code may appear under the guise of international control *over* the transnationals, it is better seen as a code of conduct *amongst* the transnationals themselves. Perhaps the most receptive arena within which to campaign for effective controls would be within Europe, and specifically within the EEC. The general concern with deindustrialisation, and the general disillusionment with the giant firms' role, could be used to promote policies for effectively regulating their production and investment strategies.

Lastly, communications. Raymond Williams (1966) has argued that an educated and participatory democracy can only be achieved with a communications revolution. Women and men have to grow in capacity and power to direct their own lives which requires, among other things, an extension of the expression and exchange of experience which the system of communications provides. He identifies four main types of system of communication: authoritarian, paternal, commercial and democratic. Within the commercial system, minority control is achieved as a matter of practice, rather than as a matter of power for the authoritarian and principle for the paternalist – 'anything can be said, provided that you can afford to say it and that you say it profitably'. The democratic system we have not yet experienced – but he makes some valuable suggestions. In the case of broadcasting and television he argues for the ending of the commercial structure with the close links to the commercial press. He advocates a new form of organisation outside the BBC, with four or five regionally-based independent public corporations. In the case of the press he wants to free local newspapers from remote control by large companies and wants to set up Newspaper Trusts to finance working journalists to produce new local and national newspapers. For the cinema he proposes public production facilities available for use by professional film-makers and the opening up of the cinema circuits for their use. For books he suggests public funding of a chain of new bookshops and as an alternative to advertising he advocates the funding of Citizens Advice Bureaux to provide information on products and services. The general thrust seems right although one can argue with the detail. He is seeking to open up the system to new, small-scale entrants and at the same time reduce the power of the existing centres of concentration. Interestingly he also argues that all that is required is some suitable public credit arrangements – these activities can generally be relied on to pay for themselves. If this is more or less true, and we recognise the enormous significance of the system of communications in the development of our democracy, then action of the sort he proposes is surely long overdue. We could then replace the present expansion of the system with 'real growth', offering real choice and variety and moving away from minority control to broad involvement.

REFERENCES

Aaronovitch, S. and Smith, R. *The Political Economy of British Capitalisation* (London: McGraw-Hill, 1981).

Bhaduri, A., and Steindl, J. 'The Rise of Monetarism as a Social Doctrine', *Thames Papers in Political Economy*, Autumn, 1983.

Burkitt, B. 'Collective Bargaining, Inflation and Incomes Policy', in D. Currie and M. Sawyer (eds) *Socialist Economic Review* (London: Merlin, 1982).

Cable, V. *British Interests and Third World Development* (London: Overseas Development Institute, 1980).

Cowling, K. 'Monopolies and Merger Policy: A New Perspective', *Socialist Economic Review* (London: Merlin, 1982).

Erlichman, J. 'If only the Watchdog had a Bite, a Chunk might be taken out of Drug Profits', *Guardian*, 21 July 1984.

Fine, B. 'Multinational Corporations, the British Economy and the AES', *Economic Bulletin*, no. 10 Spring/Summer, 1983.

Hirsch F. and Gordon, D. *Newspaper Money* (London: Hutchinson, 1975).

Hodgson, G. *The Democratic Economy* (Harmondsworth: Penguin, 1984).

Huhne, C. 'Thatcherism ... Besieged on all Possible Fronts', *Guardian*, 12 July 1984.

Lively, J. *Democracy* (Oxford: Basil Blackwell, 1975).

Pateman, C. *Participation and Democratic Theory* (Cambridge University Press, 1970).

Royal Commission on the Press: Final Report (London: HMSO, 1977).

Stewart, G. 'Workers Cooperatives and the Alternative Economic Strategy', *Socialist Economic Review* (London: Merlin, 1983).

Usher, D. *The Economic Prerequisites to Democracy* (Oxford: Basil Blackwell, 1981).

Williams, R. *Communications* (London: Chatto and Windus, 1966).

Williams, R. 'Democracy and Parliament', *Marxism Today*, June, 1982).

Index

accountability, public sector 196–7
Advance Corporation Tax 44, 45
agenda-setting, public sector 193, 193–5
aid, Third World 118
Alliance 123, 124
altruism 81
   voting behaviour 162
Anderson, Sir John 221
asset sequestration, trade unions 146, 148
Associated Newspapers 242–3
Association of the British Pharmaceutical Industry 250
AUEW 213
authority 3–8
autocracy 1

ballots, strikes 136
Bank of England 34
Barnett, Joel 196
beverage crops, Third World 94–5
Beveridge, Sir William 221
Bevin, Ernest 115
BL 212–13
Botswana, Tribal Grazing Lands Programme 77
Bow Group 115
British Leyland 212–13
British Medical Association 120
British Steel Corporation 211–12
British Telecom 145
broadcasting, regulation 252
budgets, maximisation 176–80
bureaucracy xi
   as agent of social control 171–2
   budget maximisation 176–80
   defined 169–70
   economic analysis 175–84
   emergence 170–1
   relationship with legislature 177–80
bureaucrats 132, 133
Butler, R. A. 115, 209, 221, 233
Butler, R. A. B. 209
Butskellism 33, 122, 221

Callaghan, James 27, 42, 116, 137
capital, internationalisation 245–6
capital expenditure, government 38–40
capital gains, taxation 44
capitalism, compatibility with democracy 235–8
CBI 210
centralisation
   economic power 240–2
   efficiency gains 187
   local authority control 188
Centre for Socio-Legal Studies 127
charges, water management 85–6
Child Poverty Action Group 121
Churchill, Winston 220
Citizens Advice Bureaux 252
Civil Service 33, 34
class, political parties 116
class conflict 31
closed shops 136
coach services, abolition of licensing 233
coal strike 1984 140, 147–8, 232
Coase's Outcome 49–54, 58, 59
   population decisions and 91–4
   tragedy of the commons and 75–83
   urban migration 88–91
   water management 85–8
Coase's Theorem x, 52, 54–5
collective bargaining 206–7
collusion, competition and 15
common law 152, 153
   compensation in 154
   trade union immunities 135–6
Common Market 114
communications
   concentration of power 242–5
   regulation 251–2
company taxation 44–5
compensation xi, 71–2, 153–6
   rules of 52
competition 1–3
   market place 225–6
   stability of 14–16

Index

competition for authority ix, 3–7
  Labour Party 115
  working 7–14
competition in transactions ix, 3–7
Confederation of British Industry 210
consensus
  Keynesian 123
  political 33, 122, 221
Conservative Party 27, 113–14, 115, 116, 121, 123–4
Conservative Political Centre 115
constitutional checks, government spending 231–2
constitutional rules 134
consumption, public services 182–3, 188, 222
Contributor's Dilemma 95–8
cooperative institutions, water management 85
Corporation Tax 44, 44–5
corporations, transnational 239–40, 251
costs, public services 224
Cripps, Sir Stafford 115

decision-making
  collective 4–5
  discretionary 190
  free market 185
  public expenditure 181–2
  within bureaucracies 173–4
  within parties 11–12
  workers' involvement with 207
defence expenditure 37–8
demand, for public services 180–1
demand management 220
democracy
  capitalism and 235–8
  competition for authority and 9–10
  economic model 113, 121
  economic performance and 245–7
  elite theory of 186, 193
  in LDCs 53, 82, 98–101
  new institutions for 247–52
  political competition and 1
  representativeness 187
  X-efficiency and 190–7
Democratic Party 23, 24, 114
Denning, Lord 130
Department of Economic Affairs 111
Department of Employment 29, 34
developmental change, LDCs 50
Dimbleby and Sons Ltd v. *National Union of Journalists* 146–7
disabled, compensation 157

Disablement Income Group 121
distributive justice 130
Donaldson, Sir John 146
drug companies 250–1
Du Cann, Edward 196
dwellings, investment 38, 40

economic analysis, of politics 227–8
economic competition ix, 1
economic growth 110–11
economic model
  of democracy 113, 121
  of judicial law-making 158–60
  of legislation 156–8
economic performance
  and political popularity 22–7
  democracy and 245–7
  new institutions for 247–52
  voters' perceptions of 25–6
economic policies
  British 32–46
  effects on electoral popularity ix–x
  underlying principles 31–2
economic power
  concentration 238–42
  control 249–51
  distribution 236
economic success, changing criteria 28
economics
  analysis of bureaucracy 175–84
  law and xi, 128–35
economies of scale, competition and 14–15
economy, mixed 219–22
Eden, Anthony 27
Edwardes, Michael 212, 213
EEC 120
EEC Referendum 118
efficiency, judicial process 163
egalitarianism 81
electoral cycles, of popularity 24–5
electorate, economic policy and ix–x, 21–2
elites 187
  theory of democracy 186, 193
employees
  attitudes to participation 214–15
  see also workers
employment, full 246
Employment Act (1980) 137, 145
Employment Act (1982) 137, 145
enclosure laws, England 77
equity 52–3

Index

exploitation 1–2
  competition for authority and 5, 16
Express Newspapers Ltd v. *McShane and Another* 143–5

family planning, LDCs 91–4
free market, decision-making 185
free riding, public goods provision 97–8

Gaitskell, Hugh 113, 115, 119
game theory 130
GDP, government expenditure and 36–7
General Household Survey 29
Giant's Tank, Mannar 83
government 51
  accountability to Parliament 197
  attitudes to trade unions 209–11
  big 185
  expenditure 35–41, 228, 231–2
  increased role 220–1
  limits to xii, 229–30
  popularity 27–31
  revenues 42–6
  true costs 228
grazing, privatisation 75, 77–8
grazing land, increase in 75, 76
gross domestic product *see* GDP
groundwater systems 86–7
growth *see* economic growth
Guild Socialism 205

Hart, Gary 120
'head-enders', irrigation 51
Heath, Edward 21, 36–7, 42, 120
herd ownership, common 75, 77
herd sizes, reduction 75, 76, 78–83
hierarchies, Coase's Outcome and 81–2
Home, Lord 27
House of Commons, composition 117
house purchase, subsidies 121
housing, public investment 38, 40
housing benefits, cuts 233
HTV 243
Humphrey, Hubert 114

ideology 16
  political parties 113–14
  politicians and 10–11
ILP 115
IMF 37
incomes policy 246–7
Independent Labour Party 115
indirect taxation 45–6

industrial action
  secondary 137, 146–7
  see also picketing; strikes
industrial democracy 204–5
  joint regulation 207–8
  public sector 211
industrial relations, pluralist view 208–9
Industrial Relations Act (1971) 136, 143
inefficiency 1–2
  competition for authority and 5, 16
inflation 221
  differential impact 30
Institute of Economic Affairs 231
interest groups 229–30
International Monetary Fund 37
investment
  British 245
  public 38–40
irrigation 51, 83–8
  physical structures 86
  rotational 86
isolation paradox 91–2

joint regulation 207–8
Joseph, Sir Keith 211
judicial law-making xi
  economic theories of 158–60
  efficiency 163
  model of 152

Kandyan kings 51, 83
Keynes, J. M. 221
Keynesian consensus 123

labour, militancy 245–6
labour laws
  UK 135–8
  USA 136
Labour Party 27, 111, 114, 115–16, 121, 123–4
  link with trade unions 116, 142
Lansbury, George 115
law
  economics and xi
  fair applications of 52–3
law and economics 128–31
LDCs
  and Coase's Theorem 56–7
  democracy 98–101
  non-cooperative outcomes 50–1
leadership, trade unions 139–41
legal immunities, trade unions xi, 135–6, 141–3

legislation xi
  anti-monopoly 189
  compensation and 155
  economic theories of 156–62
  public interest model 152–3
  trade unions 135–8
legislature, relationship with bureaucracy 177–80
legitimacy, of competition 15–16
less-developed countries *see* LDCs
liability 79
liberty, erosion 185
living standards, higher 112
local authorities, centralised control 188

MacGregor, Ian 212, 213
Macmillan, Harold 21, 27, 111, 112, 120
management
  by confrontation 213
  decisions 206–7
  discretionary behaviour 190
managers, attitudes to participation 214–15
market forces 121–2, 185–6
markets, competitive 225–6
Marshall Plan 111
Members of Parliament 116–17
Mercury Communications Ltd v. *Stanley and Another* 145–6
mergers 240
metering, water management 85–6
migration, to towns 88–91
militancy, labour force 245–6
Militant Tendency 115
military expenditure 37–8
MIND 121
minimax criterion, game theory 130
MINIS 184
minorities, oppression 13–14
mixed economy 219–22
Mondale, Walter 120
monetarist experiment 33
monopolies 1
  bilateral 178
  legislation 189
  private sector 191–2
Monopolies Commission 249
mortgages, tax concessions 121
motivation, politicians 10–11
MPs 116–17
multinationals 239–40
  regulation 251

National Coal Board 213
National Dock Labour Board 207
National Farmers' Union 120
National Graphical Association 146
National Insurance benefits 40–1
National Plan 1965 111
National Union of Journalists 143–4, 146–7
National Union of Manufacturers 120
National Union of Mineworkers 147–8
newspaper trusts 252
newspapers
  concentration of power 242–5
  regulation 251–2
Nixon, Richard 115

Office of Fair Trading 250
oil crisis, 1973 120
oligarchy 186–7
oligopoly, competition for authority and 8
One Nation group 115
organisations xii
  collective decisions in 4–5
Owen, David 230

Parliament, accountability to 197
Parliament Act (1911) 137
participation xii, 100–1, 186, 187, 237–8
  industrial 214–16
  workers 248–9
parties
  decision-making within 11–12
  vote-maximising 10
party activists 11–12, 114–15
pay policy 119
personal taxation 42–4
picketing 137
  secondary 147–8
Plowde, Edwin 110
Pneumoconiosis (Workers Compensation) Act (1979) 157
political competition ix, 1
political consensus 33, 122
political decisions, short-term 118
political parties x–xi, 113–16
political popularity, and economic performance 22–7
politicians, motivation 10–11
politics
  economic analysis 227–8
  market forces in 121–2
'population-contract-isolation-paradox' 92–3

population decisions, LDCs 91–4
population growth
  LDCs 50, 57
  tragedy of the commons and, 71–2, 80–1
position issues, politics 23
positive economics 129
press
  concentration of power 242–5
  regulation 251–2
Press Association 143–4
pressure groups 116, 120–1
Price Waterhouse 148
pricing, water management 85–6
principal–agent relationship 195–6
Prior, James 208
prior rights, tragedy of the commons and 72
Prisoners' Dilemma x, 49–54
  answers 62–70
  beverage crops 94–5
  Contributor's Dilemma 95–8
  explained 58–62
  rent-seeking 149–50
  tragedy of the commons and 80–1
private bureaucracies 170
private sector monopolies 189
privatisation xi, 185, 188–9, 191–2
profits, retained 44
Programme Analysis and Review 176
Programme Planning and Budgeting Systems 176
property, qualifications for voting 236
Proportional Representation 122–3
Public Accounts Committee 250
public choice 4, 128, 131–4, 173, 227, 232
public expenditure 181–3
Public Expenditure Survey Committee 177, 181–2
public goods 95–8
public interest, model of legislation 152–3
public investment 38–40
public sector
  accountability 196–7
  efficiencies 192–3
  housing 38, 40
  industrial democracy 211
public services
  consumption 182–3, 188, 222
  costs 224
  demand for 180–1
pyramiding 12–13, 16

Rayner scrutinies 192
Referendum, EEC membership 118
rent-seeking xi, 132–4, 138, 149–50
representative democracy 186, 187
Republican Party 23, 24, 115
resource allocation 54–5
revenues, government 42–6
rights 130
risk aversion
  LDCs 50, 56
  Rawlsian original position 130
  tragedy of the commons and 78–9
  water management 88
Road Haulage Association 121
Road Lobby 120
Roads Campaign Council 121
Robinson, Derek 213
rotational irrigation 86
Royal Commission on Civil Liability and Compensation for Personal Injury 157
Royal Commission on Taxation of Profits and Incomes 44
Royal Commission on the Press 242–3
rural unemployment 89–90
rural–urban migration 88–91

Salter, Sir Arthur 221
Scargill, Arthur 232
secondary industrial action 137, 146–7
secondary picketing 147–8
secondary strikes 143–4
Shelter 121
side payments 51–2, 53, 71–2
  changing prisoners' dilemma structure 81
social benefits, non-market entitlement 226
social control, bureaucracy as 171–2
social cost 127
Social Democratic Party 230
social policies, choice between 8–10
social security benefits 40–1
social services, increased spending 221
Southern Television 243
special interest groups
  rent-seeking 132–4
Sri Lanka 51, 94
  water use 83–5
status polarisation, voting behaviour 23–4
sterling crises 221
Stockport Messenger Group v. *National Graphical Association* 146

strikes
  ballots 136
  secondary 143–4
suffrage, universal 236, 237

Taft Hartley Act (1947) 136
'tail-enders', irrigation 51
tax concessions, house purchase 121
taxation
  changing prisoners' dilemma structure 81
  policy 42–6
TBF (Printers) Ltd 147
TBF Ltd 146–7
tea, LDCs 94–5
technology, bureaucracy and 171
television, regulation 252
Thatcher, Margaret 28, 33, 37, 42, 119, 123, 124, 125
Third World 118
time preference, tragedy of the commons and 72
townward migration 88–91
Trade Union and Labour Relations Act (1974) 136
trade unions 229
  asset sequestration 146, 148
  government attitudes to 209–11
  legal cases 143–8
  legal immunities xi, 141–3
  legislation 135–8
  link with Labour Party 116, 142
  nature of 138–41
Trades Disputes Act (1906) 135, 138
Trades Union Congress 209–10
tragedy of the commons 52, 61
  conditions for 70–5
  prevention and cure 75–83
transition of trust 51, 56
  tragedy of the commons and 73
transnationals 239–40
  regulation 251
Treasury 33, 34–5, 181
Tribal Grazing Lands Programme, Botswana 77

tubewells 86–7
TUC 209–10

unemployment
  differential impact 28–30
  government popularity and 24–5
  LDCs 89–90
universal suffrage 236, 237
urban unemployment, LDCs 89–90
utility incomes, voting preferences and 22–3

valence issues, politics 23
VAT 45–6
vel vidane 84
vote-maximising 11–12
vote-satisficing 12
voters
  as consumers 117–19
  perception of politics x–xi, 112–13
  perceptions of economic performance 25–6
  understanding of issues 119–20
voting
  altruism and 162
  property qualifications 236
  theory of 22–4
voting intentions, economic performance 26
Vredeling directive 248

wage restraint 119
warabandi 86
water 51, 83–8
welfare state, criticism of 185
Westward Television 243
Wilson, Harold 20, 27, 36, 37, 42, 111, 112, 114, 120
Winter of Discontent 116, 137
workers
  involvement with decision-making 207
  participation 238, 248–9
workers' control 205–6

X-efficiency 190–7